EBURY PRESS
THE ORIGIN STORY OF INDIA'S STATES

Venkataraghavan Subha Srinivasan is a writer, actor and strategy consultant from Bengaluru, India. This is his first non-fiction book.

The
ORIGIN STORY
of
INDIA'S
STATES

VENKATARAGHAVAN
SUBHA SRINIVASAN

EBURY
PRESS

An imprint of Penguin Random House

EBURY PRESS

USA | Canada | UK | Ireland | Australia
New Zealand | India | South Africa | China

Ebury Press is part of the Penguin Random House group of companies
whose addresses can be found at global.penguinrandomhouse.com

Published by Penguin Random House India Pvt. Ltd
4th Floor, Capital Tower 1, MG Road,
Gurugram 122 002, Haryana, India

First published in Ebury Press by Penguin Random House India 2021

Copyright © Venkataraghavan Subha Srinivasan 2021

ISBN 9780143451495

Typeset in Adobe Garamond Pro by Manipal Technologies Limited, Manipal
Printed at Replika Press Pvt. Ltd, India

www.penguin.co.in

To every person who researched and wrote about the states of India before me, thank you. Your work makes mine possible.

'The Federation is a Union because it is indestructible'
—Dr Bhimrao Ramji Ambedkar,
Constituent Assembly Speech, 4 November 1948

'What has already been achieved is nothing short of a revolution'
—White Paper on Indian States, Ministry of States,
Government of India, 1950

CONTENTS

Introduction   xiii

States

Andhra Pradesh   1

Arunachal Pradesh   9

Assam   15

Bihar   27

Chhattisgarh   33

Goa   37

Gujarat   50

Haryana   58

Himachal Pradesh   66

Jharkhand   75

Karnataka   82

Kerala   90

Madhya Pradesh   94

Maharashtra   105

Manipur   112

Meghalaya   118

Mizoram   127

Nagaland   138

Odisha   145

Punjab   149

Rajasthan   161

Sikkim   167

Tamil Nadu   178

Telangana   182

Tripura   192

Uttar Pradesh   196

Uttarakhand   205

West Bengal   210

Union Territories

Andaman and Nicobar Islands   215

Chandigarh   217

Dadra and Nagar Haveli and Daman and Diu   221

Delhi   230

Jammu and Kashmir   235

Ladakh   249

Lakshadweep   258

Puducherry   261

Bibliography   267

Government of India Documents   275

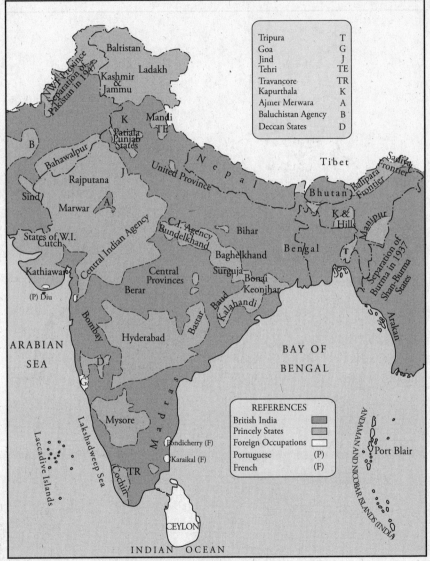

Tripura	T
Goa	G
Jind	J
Tehri	TE
Travancore	TR
Kapurthala	K
Ajmer Merwara	A
Baluchistan Agency	B
Deccan States	D

NWF Province
Separation of
Pakistan in 1947

Baltistan

Ladakh

Kashmir
&
Jammu

Mandi
TE

K

Patiala
Punjab
States

B

Bahawalpur

Rajputana

J

United Province

Nepal

Tibet

Sadiya
Frontier

Bhutan

Balipara
Frontier

Sind

Marwar

A

Bihar

K &
J
Hills

Manipur

States of W.I.
Cutch

Central Indian Agency

Cd. Agency
Bundelkhand

Bengal

T

Separation of
Burma in 1937
Shan-Burma
States

Kathiawar

Baghelkhand

Surguja

Bonai
Keonjhar

(P) Diu

Central
Provinces

Band
Kalahandi

Arakan

Berar

Bastar

Bombay

Hyderabad

ARABIAN
SEA

D

BAY OF
BENGAL

G

Madras

Mysore

ANDAMAN AND NICOBAR ISLANDS (INDIA)

Port Blair

Lakshadweep Sea

Pondicherry (F)

Karaikal (F)

REFERENCES

British India
Princely States
Foreign Occupations
Portuguese   (P)
French   (F)

Laccadive Islands

TR

Cochin

CEYLON

INDIAN OCEAN

Credit: TTK Maps

India at the time of Independence, 1947

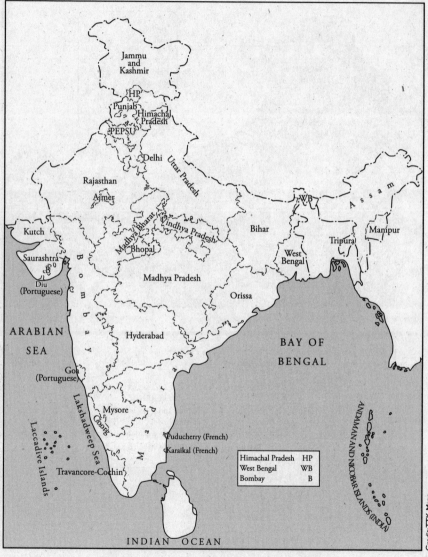

India after adopting the Constitution, 1950

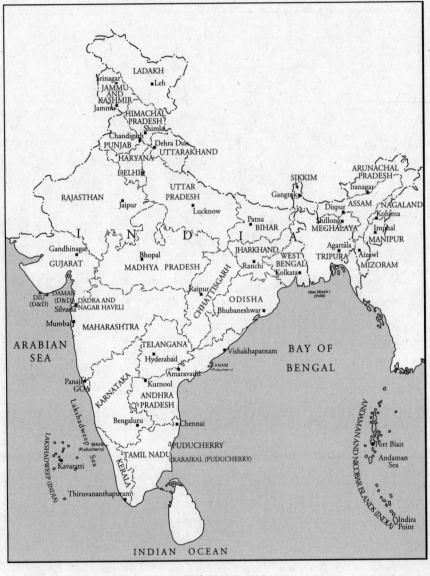

India, 2021

INTRODUCTION

I love looking at maps of India. Road maps allow me to dream about great cross-country adventures. Topographic maps highlight the textures of the land through the mountains' wrinkles and the rivers' meanderings. Satellite maps trace the coastline's undulations that give the country its distinctive shape. Maps show me the beauty of India.

When I was a child at school, my absolute favourite map of India was the political map that clearly demarcated its states. India's states fascinated me with their various shapes and sizes. My favourite activity was colouring in the states neatly and meticulously with sketch pens.

The stories of the states of India are also the story of India. The states of India are all-encompassing—they cover every inch of land and hold every single person that makes up India. Every person in India belongs to a state, lives and works in a state, has family and childhood memories in a state. States give every Indian a home and an identity. Every time a new state is created or an old one altered, India and Indians are remade, recreated, reborn. Every single Indian deserves to know the story of their state, their home, their identity.

That's how this book was born. We know the origin story of India, but what are the origin stories of each of its states?

*

15 August 1947.

It is tempting to view this date as the singular date on which India was formed. However, India was not formed all at once. There was no process of formation that was completed on 15 August 1947. In fact, if anything, this was the date when the first process of the formation of India *began*.

On 15 August 1947, not only did the British Crown partition India on both its western and eastern sides, they also left behind an internal mess that threatened to destroy the country from within. For starters, the outgoing British administration handed over only about 60 per cent of the country's land to the new Indian government. The remaining 40 per cent of the country belonged to the rulers of 565 princely states. The British Empire had administered India with two systems running in parallel—a direct system in its provinces and a separate indirect system across the princely states. When British Paramountcy lapsed on 15 August 1947, only the administration of the provinces transferred to the new Indian government. The ruler of every princely state was offered three options: join India, join Pakistan, or remain independent.

This was a massive problem for the new Indian administrators. Each of these rulers scattered across the land had to be convinced individually and collectively to merge with the new Union of India. The States Ministry—headed by Sardar Vallabhbhai Patel and executed phenomenally by V.P. Menon—visited every ruler and secured their signature on a Standstill Agreement and an Instrument of Accession in record time. They reimagined the landscape of the country, merging and integrating princely states with each other and with neighbouring provinces to create a complete coalesced whole. It was the first time India had been successfully integrated as one nation. At the same time, they recognized that these internal mergers were fluid and allowed for future reimaginings.

On 26 January 1950, India adopted its Constitution and became a 'Union of States' with twenty-eight states. The Constitution mentioned each state by name as an integral part of this Union, and classified them into four categories based on administrative set-up.

The Constitution of India is an incredibly flexible document, but it is equally firm as well. New states may be admitted and established in the Union, but no state has the power to secede or leave the Union. For this reason, the chief architect of the Indian Constitution, Dr Bhimrao Ramji Ambedkar, described the Union of India as 'indestructible'[1].

The states themselves, however, were entirely destructible. A state could be split into multiple new states. Or multiple states could be merged to form a new state. Or portions of multiple states could be merged to form a new state. The areas of states could be increased or decreased. State boundaries could be redrawn. States could be renamed.[2] Every state in India has been altered in the above manner, many of them more than once.

After the initial amalgamation of the country in 1947–49, the next large-scale reorganization came in 1956 with the States Reorganisation Act. This was triggered by the agitation for and the creation of Andhra State in 1953. The States Reorganisation Commission considered the future of all the states of India with a balanced approach 'in the interest of our national unity'[3]. The Commission recommended doing away with the four-part classification of states and introducing a new category called Union

---

[1]   Dr B.R. Ambedkar, Constituent Assembly Speech, 4 November 1948.

[2]   'Article 3,' The Constitution of India, 1949.

[3]   Report of the States Reorganisation Commission, 1955, p. 45.

Territories. The reorganization resulted in fourteen states and six union territories.

Starting from the 1960s, states began to be reorganized on an individual or cluster basis. Gujarat and Maharashtra separated in 1960. India integrated Portuguese territories in 1961 and French territories in 1963 as union territories. Nagaland was created in 1963. In 1966, in one move, the states of Punjab and Haryana were created in the north along with the union territories of Chandigarh and Himachal Pradesh (which later gained statehood in 1971). In 1972, the North-east and Assam were reorganized, which brought into existence the states of Manipur, Meghalaya and Tripura as well as the union territories of Arunachal Pradesh and Mizoram. In 1975, India's international borders expanded to include Sikkim. 1987 saw the transformation of the union territories of Arunachal Pradesh, Mizoram and Goa into states. In 2000, three states in central and north India split into six—Uttar Pradesh and Uttarakhand, Madhya Pradesh and Chhattisgarh, and Bihar and Jharkhand. In 2014, Andhra Pradesh and Telangana separated. In 2019, the union territories of Jammu and Kashmir and Ladakh were created in place of the erstwhile state.

*

The states of India are alive and fluid. They meet and dance and meld and flow with their neighbours. The stories of the states are the stories of its people and their homes. These stories are dramatic and emotional, filled with struggle and hope and despair and joy.

Researching and writing this book was a profoundly moving and emotional experience for me. I discovered India through numerous published writings by multiple people, including researchers, academicians and government officials, who studied and wrote on matters related to individual states. Through their works, I met historical figures and witnessed key events from across seventy-five years. I owe them my eternal gratitude and respect. This was the journey of a lifetime in a year when we all had to stay at home. And it allowed me to indulge in my childhood joy of colouring in the states map of India all over again.

ANDHRA PRADESH

> **Did You Know?**
>
> *Andhra Pradesh is the only state to have three functioning capitals—Amaravati (the Legislative Capital), Visakhapatnam (the Executive Capital), and Kurnool (the Judicial Capital).*

I: Andhra State

In 1947, present-day Andhra Pradesh formed the northern part of Madras Province, which was British India's largest administrative subdivision in south India. Madras Province (Madras State from 1950) was so large that it contained within its boundaries all the major language groups of south India.

Linguistically, the northern districts were Telugu-dominant and the southern districts were Tamil-dominant while the city of Madras lay almost on the linguistic border. This was a curious situation, for Telugu was the second-largest language spoken in independent India. According to the 1951 census, which combined Hindi, Urdu and Punjabi into the single-largest language, Telugu was spoken by 9.24 per cent of the Indian population while Tamil was fourth, after

Marathi, spoken by 7.43 per cent of the population.[1] Rarely does it transpire that a majority faction has to petition for its own space.

The demand for a separate Andhra Province was articulated first in 1913 with the creation of the Andhra Mahajana Sabha.[2] However, tensions soon cropped up between the two regions within Andhra. Rayalaseema feared that they were unequally placed in relation to Coastal Andhra and that integration would result in greater advantages to Coastal Andhra. These fears were allayed when leaders from the two regions came to an agreement in November 1937 to ensure equitable development and representation in both regions. This was known as the Sri Bagh Pact,[3] which also provided for separation of the high court and the capital city.[4]

Pre-Independence, the Indian National Congress (INC) had supported the formation of linguistic provinces. In 1927, the INC had opined that Andhra, Utkal, Sind and Karnataka could be constituted into separate provinces on the basis of the people speaking the same language and following the same tradition and culture.[5] At its Calcutta session in 1937 and in its 1938 Wardha resolution, the INC had recommended the formation of Andhra and Karnataka and assured to undertake it as soon as they had the power to do so.[6]

However, after witnessing Partition, the Centre wasn't keen to immediately create linguistic provinces. The Linguistic Provinces Commission—popularly known as the Dhar Commission after its chairman S.K. Dhar—was set up in 1948 to explore the feasibility

---

[1]   Government of India, Census of India, 1951.

[2]   K. Seshadri, 'The Telangana Agitation and the Politics of Andhra Pradesh,' *The Indian Journal of Political Science,* 31(1) (Jan–Mar 1970), p. 61.

[3]   G. Samba Siva Reddy, 'Making of Micro-Regional Identities in the Colonial Context: Studying the Rayalaseema Maha Sabha, 1934–1956,' *Proceedings of the Indian History Congress,* 67 (2006–07): p. 504.

[4]   Seshadri, 'The Politics of Andhra Pradesh,' p. 61.

[5]   Report of the States Reorganisation Commission, 1955, p. 13.

[6]   Ibid., p. 14.

of reorganizing states linguistically. It recommended postponing the matter for a few years.[7] The following year, a JVP Committee—named after its members Prime Minister Jawaharlal Nehru, head of the States Ministry Sardar Vallabhbhai Patel, and Congress president Pattabhi Sittaramaya—was set up to study the issue. It cautioned against the 'disintegrative effects of reorganisation'[8]. Prime Minister Nehru further stated that the consolidation of India was paramount at the moment and 'this would obviously be the wrong time'[9] to create linguistic provinces.

Potti Sriramulu, a fifty-one-year-old former sanitary engineer and railway-man, changed the course of events. Seeing much talk but little discernible progress on Andhra, Sriramulu began a fast-unto-death in Madras on 19 October 1952.[10] His fast fast-tracked the demand for statehood by the Telugu population, adding a sense of emotional urgency to the demand.

Both language groups claimed the city of Madras as their own, believing they had a more significant demographic and economic presence in the city. The Tamils, however, held the advantage. In November 1949, the Congress Working Committee had said that Andhra State could only be formed without Madras. In December 1952, Nehru repeated this in a letter to Madras State Chief Minister C. Rajagopalachari.[11]

Sriramulu died on 15 December 1952 after fifty-eight days of fasting. His death blew the lid off the anger and resentment simmering

---

[7] Asha Sarangi and Sudha Pai, 'Introduction: Contextualising Reorganisation,' in *Interrogating Reorganisation of States: Culture, Identity and Politics in India,* ed. Asha Sarangi (India: Routledge, 2020), p. 7.
[8] Ibid.
[9] Ramachandra Guha, 'Redrawing the Map—III,' *India After Gandhi: The History of the World's Largest Democracy* (United Kingdom: Macmillan, 2017).
[10] Ibid.
[11] Gautam Pingle, 'The Historical Context of Andhra and Telangana, 1949–56,' *Economic and Political Weekly,* 45(8) (February 20–26, 2010), p. 58.

in the pro-Andhra camp. In the Andhra region, government offices, public transportation and public property were attacked and damaged. Sriramulu's death had shifted the terms of discussion of Andhra statehood irrevocably from the rational to the emotional. Nehru had wanted to settle the issue with 'facts, not fasts'[12] but the narrative and the decision had both been wrested from him. Two days after Sriramulu's death, on 17 December 1952, Nehru announced that Andhra State would indeed become a reality.[13]

On 1 October 1953, the new Andhra State was inaugurated as a Part A state[14] with its capital city at Kurnool. Tanguturi Prakasam of the INC was appointed as the first chief minister.

*

II: Andhra Pradesh

The effect of Andhra's birth was seismic. Less than three months after the state came into being, in December 1953, the Union government constituted a States Reorganisation Commission (SRC) to look into the matter of redrawing state boundaries across the country. Less than two years later, in September 1955, the SRC submitted its report. Based on this, the States Reorganisation Act was enacted the following year. It remains the single most extensive change in state boundaries since India's independence.

Rayalaseema and Coastal Andhra (which formed Andhra State) were not the only Telugu-dominant regions of India. Telugu was also dominant in the adjoining Telangana region, which formed the southern and south-eastern districts of the

---

[12]   Guha, 'Redrawing the Map—III', *India After Gandhi*.
[13]   Ibid.
[14]   Note: In 1950, the Constitution of India specified four classifications of States. Part A states were former provinces and had an elected governor and state legislature.

neighbouring Hyderabad State. Hence, a demand for the creation of Vishalandhra, which would integrate Andhra State and Telangana, was presented before the SRC.

The SRC noted the impressive arguments for Vishalandhra by detailing a number of mutual benefits in case of a merger, including developmental and economic ones. The SRC also noted the arguments against a merger, which largely rested on Telangana's fears and apprehensions of losing its independent rights over the Rivers Krishna and Godavari and of being unequally placed in comparison with Andhra State. Further, it was argued that Telangana could be a stable and viable state by itself, while Andhra State was still transitioning from its separation from Madras State. Hence, the SRC advocated a wait-and-watch approach for integration. It suggested first spinning Telangana off as a separate state for about five years until 1961, at which point the Telangana legislature would have the provision to voluntarily vote themselves into Andhra State by a two-thirds majority.

However, in February 1956, Telangana and Andhra leaders reached a 'Gentlemen's Agreement' which promised equitable development and representation in Telangana, including the establishment of a regional council.[15] As a result, when the States Reorganisation Act was passed later that year, the government merged Andhra State and Telangana into a single state called Andhra Pradesh. The new state came into being on 1 November 1956. Neelam Sanjiva Reddy of the INC became the chief minister. Kurnool lost its capital city status and Hyderabad became the new capital city.

*

---

[15] Rama S. Melkote, E. Revathi, K. Lalitha, K. Sajaya, and A. Suneetha, 'The Movement for Telangana: Myth and Reality,' *Economic and Political Weekly*, 45(2) (Jan. 9–15, 2010), p. 9.

III: Andhra Pradesh and Telangana

One would have thought this would mark the end to Andhra Pradesh's cycle of birth and rebirth. However, the story would soon come full circle and culminate in a second rebirth with similar elements to the first birth—a fast-unto-death, a separation, and the loss of a capital city.

The Telangana region had 'Mulki Rules'—domicile rules instituted in 1919 by the last Nizam of Hyderabad State, Mir Osman Ali Khan. The Mulki Rules were meant to protect the locals (Mulkis) in government job appointments. In order to be considered a Mulki, essentially, one had to have been born in Hyderabad State or lived there for at least fifteen years.[16] Eligible outsiders had to apply for the grant of a Mulki Certificate. The first Mulki agitation had occurred in Hyderabad State in September 1952, four years after it had acceded to the Union of India, over the large-scale recruitment of non-locals in the newly-formed Hyderabad state government.[17] In January 1969, students from a number of colleges held demonstrations and burnt effigies of ministers to protest against the violations of the safeguards in the Gentlemen's Agreement.[18] Political leaders of Andhra Pradesh responded swiftly and unanimously, resolving to transfer out 'all non-Telangana employees holding posts reserved for Telangana domiciles'[19] and to develop Telangana over the next five years.[20] But the protests soon became violent, resulting in damaged public

---

[16] Gopal Rao Ekbote, 'Judgement—P. Lakshmana Rao vs State of Andhra Pradesh and Ors. on 9 December, 1970,' Andhra High Court.

[17] 'Dated September 6, 1952: Hyderabad Incidents,' This Day That Age, *The Hindu*, 6 September 2002.

[18] 'College Students in Telangana Agitation,' *Indian Express*, 16 January 1969, p. 8.

[19] 'Accord Reached on Telangana Demands,' *Indian Express*, 20 January 1969, p. 1.

[20] Ibid.

property, police firing and injuries.[21] The chief minister of Andhra Pradesh, Kasu Brahmananda Reddy, assured both camps that the Mulki Rules would remain in force for another five years with no extensions beyond that.[22]

In late 1972, the Supreme Court upheld the Mulki Rules and Parliament passed the Mulki Rules Act in December 1972. This kick-started a counter 'Jai Andhra' movement in the Rayalaseema and Coastal Andhra districts that advocated the formation of an Andhra State separate from Telangana. Ministers resigned from Chief Minister P.V. Narasimha Rao's government and Andhra Pradesh was placed under President's rule in January 1973.

Tempers cooled on both sides after the Union government headed by Prime Minister Indira Gandhi released a six-point formula in September 1973, which also became the thirty-second amendment to the Constitution of India. This formula divided the state into six zones. 85 per cent of lower-level government jobs and seats in government colleges and universities were reserved for the local people from that particular zone, while the remaining 15 per cent of non-local jobs and seats were open to people from the remaining five zones.[23] Through this zoning approach, the six-point formula rendered the continuance of the Mulki Rules unnecessary and the Mulki Rules (Repeal) Act was passed in December 1973.

The Telangana movement came back into focus in April 2001. Kalvakuntla Chandrashekar Rao (KCR) of the ruling Telugu Desam Party (TDP) resigned from the party to establish his own party, the Telangana Rashtra Samithi (TRS), with the single-point agenda of Telangana.

---

[21] 'Telangana Agitators Fired on: 17 Hurt,' *Indian Express,* 25 January 1969, p. 1.
[22] 'Transfers Challenged in Court by Andhra Employees,' *Indian Express,* 25 January 1969, p. 1.
[23] R.J. Rajendra Prasad, 'Bitter Memories,' *Frontline,* Vol. 18 Issue 12 (June 9–22, 2001).

While KCR's individual political fortunes rose—even earning him a Union cabinet role—the TRS performed poorly in the 2009 Assembly elections in Andhra Pradesh, including in the Telangana region. The incumbent chief minister, Y.S. Rajasekhara Reddy (YSR) of the INC, was re-elected. The Telangana sentiment appeared to have faded; the vote seemed to be against bifurcation.

On 2 September 2009, the situation changed dramatically. Chief Minister YSR's helicopter went missing in the remote Nallamala Forest. The wreckage and the bodies were discovered a day later. In the resulting political turmoil, KCR seized his opportunity.

On 29 November 2009, KCR started a fast-unto-death demanding Telangana State, which quickly gathered popular support. A mere ten days later, on 9 December, the Union Home Minister, P. Chidambaram, of the Congress-led coalition government at the Centre, announced that Telangana would become a reality.

The actual bifurcation of Andhra Pradesh and Telangana came four-and-a-half years later on 2 June 2014, with KCR as the first chief minister. The city of Hyderabad was to be the permanent capital of Telangana. Andhra Pradesh had lost another capital city, even though both states were allowed to use Hyderabad as a joint capital for a period of ten years.

Andhra Pradesh responded in July 2020 by creating not one or two, but three new capital cities. It built an entirely new city called Amaravati as the Legislative Capital. The largest city in Andhra Pradesh, Visakhapatnam, became the Executive Capital. Kurnool, the first capital of Andhra State from 1953–56, became the Judicial Capital.[24] However, following protests and a high court stay, the assembly passed a bill in November 2021 to repeal this Act.

* *

---

[24] The Andhra Pradesh Decentralisation and Inclusive Development of All Regions Act, 2020.

ARUNACHAL PRADESH

> **Did You Know?**
>
> *Until 1972, Arunachal Pradesh was known first as North East Frontier Tract (NEFT) and then as North-East Frontier Agency (NEFA).*

1947–54: North East Frontier Tract (NEFT)

In 1947, the present state of Arunachal Pradesh constituted the North East Frontier Tract (NEFT) of Assam. The entire region had been labelled as an 'excluded area' by the British, placed directly under the care of the Governor of Assam.[1] In 1945, the British Governor passed a regulation to officially recognize the traditional tribal village councils as the authorities to self-govern and administer justice in NEFT.[2] After Independence, the government of Assam took over

---

[1] Manju Singh, 'Arunachal Pradesh: Wonderland with Explosive Frontier,' *The Indian Journal of Political Science,* 72(1) (Jan.–Mar. 2011), p. 210.
[2] Pratap Chandra Swain, *Panchayati Raj: The Grassroots Dynamics in Arunachal Pradesh* (India: APH Publishing Corporation, 2008), pp. 45–46.

the administration of NEFT. The Governor, Sir Muhammad Saleh Akbar Hydari, would now act on the advice of Chief Minister Gopinath Bordoloi of the Indian National Congress (INC).[3]

Internationally, NEFT shared three borders—with Bhutan, Myanmar (partially undefined), and the Tibet Autonomous Region of China (now known as the McMahon Line). Internally, the region constituted numerous frontier tracts, which were further split into administrative units. The western Balipara Frontier Tract contained two administrative units, Sela and Subansiri. The northern Sadiya Frontier Tract was split into two districts in 1948, Abor Hills and Mishmi Hills. To its south lay the Lakhimpur Frontier Tract and furthest east lay the Tirap Frontier Tract.

The constituent assembly of India set up a subcommittee—headed by Gopinath Bordoloi, the Premier of Assam—to study the 'excluded and partially excluded areas' that were outside of direct purview by the British. The Bordoloi Committee recommended merging the Lakhimpur Frontier Tract and parts of the Tirap Frontier Tract with the regularly administered areas of Assam. The reasoning was that these areas were not different in any way from the surrounding plains and possessed none of the characteristics of the hill areas. Accordingly, these as well as other areas from the Balipara and Sadiya Frontier Tracts were transferred to the Assam plains and removed from the Sixth Schedule of the Indian Constitution. This brought the boundaries of the tracts 'almost to the foot of the hills'[4].

When India adopted its Constitution on 26 January 1950, NEFT became 'a separate politico-administrative entity'[5] although it was constitutionally still a part of Assam. Its administration was

---

[3]   Singh, 'Arunachal Pradesh,' p. 210.
[4]   S.K. Chaube, *Hill Politics in Northeast India,* (India: Orient Blackswan, 2012), p. 183.
[5]   Swain, *Panchayati Raj,* p. 46.

brought directly under the President of India with the Governor of
Assam acting as his agent.

*

1954–71: NEFA and Democratic Decentralization

After Assam blocked a plan in 1953 to appoint a special commissioner
to administer the area, a full-scale administration was inaugurated
in 1954 with the North-East Frontier Areas (Administration)
Regulation.[6] NEFT was renamed as North-East Frontier Agency
(NEFA). It comprised the administrative units—called 'frontier
divisions'—of the Balipara and Tirap Frontier Tracts, the Abor and
Mishmi Hills Districts, and the Naga Tribal Area. The westernmost
Balipara Frontier Tract was then split into two divisions—Kameng
and Subansiri. Going east from there, Abor Hills District was
renamed as Siang and Mishmi Hills District as Lohit. Going south
from there, Tirap retained its name while the Naga Tribal Area was
renamed as Tuensang. A deputy commissioner was in charge of each
division. To give impetus to developmental activities, the Indian
Frontier Administrative Service (IFAS) was created in 1956.

Meanwhile, in the Naga Hills District further south, Dr Imkongliba
Ao of the Naga National Council (NNC) chaired a Naga People's
Convention at Kohima in August 1957. Advocating negotiation over
the violence that had dominated proceedings for the past few years, the
convention formally gave up the demand for Naga independence and
instead asked for 'a single administrative unit comprising the Naga Hills
district of Assam and Tuensang Frontier Division of NEFA'.[7] Prime
Minister Jawaharlal Nehru accepted this demand.

---

[6]   Chaube, *Hill Politics*, p. 184.
[7]   B.B. Kumar, *Reorganization of North-East India: Facts and Documents*
(India: Concept, 2017), p. 29.

On 1 December 1957, the Naga Hills–Tuensang Area came into being as a new administrative unit in the state of Assam but under the direct control of the ministry of external affairs.[8] The unit was also simultaneously separate from Assam as it was governed by the Governor of Assam acting on behalf of the President of India.[9]

Although NEFA was under the ministry of external affairs due to its strategic borderland location, the policy was to strengthen and work with the traditional village councils. However, this changed with the Chinese aggression in this region in 1962.

In May 1964, the Governor of Assam, Vishnu Sahay, constituted a four-member committee to explore the feasibility of democratic decentralization in NEFA. This committee's chairman was Daying Ering, a member of Parliament (MP) nominated from NEFA and also the parliamentary secretary in the ministry of external affairs. The committee submitted its report containing certain landmark recommendations in January 1965.[10]

The most crucial recommendation of the Ering Committee was the establishment of four tiers of representative bodies in NEFA, modelled along the lines of the Panchayati Raj style of democratic decentralization recommended for the rest of India by the Balwant Rai Mehta Committee in 1957. The four tiers, which were organically linked with each other, were:[11]

- Village: The existing tribal councils would continue to function as per the tribal customary laws and would be renamed 'Gram Panchayats'.

---

[8]   The Naga Hills–Tuensang Area Act, 1957.
[9]   Chandrika Singh, 'Nagaland: From a District to a State: Culmination of Democratic Political Process,' *The Indian Journal of Political Science*, 41(4) (Dec. 1980), pp. 822–23.
[10] Swain, *Panchayati Raj*, pp. 47–49.
[11] Ibid.

- Circle: Called 'Anchal Samiti' and headed by a sub-divisional officer, these would undertake developmental activities.
- District: Called 'Zilla Parishad' and headed by the district's deputy commissioner, these would be advisory bodies to the district administration.
- Territory: Called 'Agency Council', this would comprise NEFA MPs as members and be presided over by the Governor of Assam. This would take care of the budget and five-year plans for NEFA, and advise the Governor on the administration and development of NEFA.

In 1967, Parliament passed the North-East Frontier Agency Panchayati Raj Regulation, incorporating most of the Ering Committee recommendations. NEFA was also moved under the care of the ministry of home affairs. The regulation came into effect on 2 October 1968.

In effect, the regulation helped integrate the isolated NEFA better with the rest of the country by introducing an integrated political system. It also contained 'the nucleus of a separate state'[12], as the constitution of the Agency Council gave NEFA a territorial identity and a people's forum for the first time.[13]

*

---

[12] Swain, *Panchayati Raj*, p. 49.

[13] Aruna Gyati, 'Panchayat Raj Institutions in Arunachal Pradesh: A Historical Perspective,' *The Indian Journal of Political Science,* 72(4) (Oct.–Dec. 2011), pp. 1019–30.

1971: The Birth of Arunachal Pradesh

NEFA's territorial identity was further strengthened on 30 December 1971 when Parliament passed the North-Eastern Areas (Reorganisation) Act. This Act reorganized Assam and created three new states—Meghalaya, Manipur and Tripura—and two new union territories—Mizoram and Arunachal Pradesh. On 21 January 1972, NEFA, formerly NEFT, began its new identity as the union territory of Arunachal Pradesh.[14]

The agency council was converted to a pradesh council, which itself was converted in 1975 to the legislative assembly of Arunachal Pradesh. This enabled Prem Khandu Thungan of the Janata Party to take office as the first chief minister of Arunachal Pradesh in August 1975.

On 24 December 1986, Parliament passed the State of Arunachal Pradesh Act. The Act came into effect on 20 February 1987. Arunachal Pradesh was reconstituted from a union territory to a state. The incumbent chief minister, Gegong Apang of the INC, continued in office.[15]

* *

---

[14] Government of India. The North-Eastern Areas (Reorganisation) Act, 1971.
[15] Government of India. The State of Arunachal Pradesh Act, 1986.

ASSAM

> **Did You Know?**
>
> *Five of the eight states in the North-east were once a part of Assam.*

In 1947, Assam occupied a large part of what is today referred to as North-east India. Assam was affected by Partition, losing the region of Sylhet to East Pakistan (today's Bangladesh). Over the next twenty-four years, Assam would be reorganized multiple times, eventually resulting in four additional states.

*

Autonomous Districts within Assam

A large part of the outer hilly reaches of Assam had been demarcated as 'excluded and partially excluded areas' by the British, removing them from direct purview. In addition, they had isolated the inhabitants of these areas through the Inner Line Regulation, which required outsiders to acquire permits to enter. As India approached

Independence, the constituent assembly set up a subcommittee to report and recommend on these areas. The Committee—headed by Gopinath Bordoloi, the Premier of Assam, and hence referred to as the Bordoloi Committee—submitted its report in July 1947 after touring all the hill districts of Assam. Its suggestions included a federation to bridge the gap between the states—which enjoyed certain rights—and the British portions, where there was no statutory local body for local self-government.[1]

The Bordoloi Committee report led to the inclusion of the Sixth Schedule in the Indian Constitution in 1949, which created autonomous districts around Assam, each with its own district council that would have the power to legislate on the usage of land, management of forests, establishment of town councils and inheritance of property, among others. Importantly, without the assent of the district councils, no act of the state legislature could apply to the autonomous districts. In Assam's south-eastern border region, two autonomous districts were created—Garo Hills District and United Khasi–Jaintia Hills District. In the middle of Assam, two more autonomous districts were created—North Cachar Hills District and Mikir Hills District. In Assam's deep south, Lushai Hills District (later renamed Mizo District) was created.

The north-eastern extremities of Assam that bordered Bhutan, Myanmar and Tibet were known as the North East Frontier Tract (NEFT). The region constituted numerous frontier tracts, which were further split into administrative units. The Bordoloi Committee felt that certain areas from the various frontier tracts were more like the plains they abutted and less like the hill areas they belonged to. Hence, in its report, the committee recommended merging certain areas from the various frontier tracts with the plains of Assam, thereby ending the boundaries of the frontier tracts almost at the foot of the hills.[2] When India

---

[1]   S.K. Chaube, *Hill Politics in Northeast India,* (India: Orient Blackswan, 2012), pp. 81–84.
[2]   Chaube, *Hill Politics*, p. 183.

adopted its Constitution on 26 January 1950, NEFT became 'a separate politico-administrative entity'[3] although it was constitutionally still a part of Assam. Its administration was brought directly under the President of India with the Governor of Assam acting as his agent.

On Assam's eastern edge, Naga Hills District was created. However, the Naga National Council (NNC), a local political organization, sought self-determination for the Nagas based on ethnic, social and religious distinctiveness. In 1951, it conducted a plebiscite (a public opinion poll) and 'claimed that 99.9 per cent of Nagas had voted in favour of independence'.[4] When India's first general elections rolled around in 1952, the Nagas completely boycotted it and began a non-cooperation movement. As a result, the Naga Hills District Council could not be formed and the area had to be administered directly by the Assam government.

In 1954, NEFT was renamed as North-East Frontier Agency (NEFA) and a full-scale administration was inaugurated with the North-East Frontier Areas (Administration) Regulation.[5] The administrative units were called 'frontier divisions'. To give impetus to developmental activities, the Indian Frontier Administrative Service (IFAS) was created two years later.

*

The SRC Report and the Response

Responding to multiple calls from across the country to redraw state boundaries, the Union government set up the States Reorganisation Commission (SRC) in December 1953 and invited written

---

[3] Pratap Chandra Swain, *Panchayati Raj: The Grassroots Dynamics in Arunachal Pradesh* (India: APH Publishing Corporation, 2008), p. 46.
[4] Makepeace Sitlhou, 'Accord', *Fifty-Two* (27 Nov. 2020), https://fiftytwo.in/story/accord/
[5] Chaube, *Hill Politics*, p. 184.

memoranda from the public. Delegates from the autonomous districts—Garo Hills, United Khasi–Jaintia Hills, North Cachar Hills, Mikir Hills and Mizo Hills—convened an Assam Hills Tribal Leaders' Conference at Tura in October 1954. The hill leaders called for a separate state for the autonomous districts of Assam as well as an amendment of the Sixth Schedule as it conferred no real autonomy.[6] The NNC did not join this demand for unification as it continued to seek 'independence from Assam and India'.[7]

In its report released in late 1955, the SRC dismissed the claims both for a separate hill state and a separate Nagaland. It viewed the demand of a hill state as 'partly a hang-over'[8] from the British isolationist policy of Inner Line Regulation and that continuing such a complete segregation would further accentuate these distinctions and hamper their development. As a result of the internal differences among the hill leaders, the SRC found the demand for a hill state to be confined virtually to the Garo and Khasi and Jaintia Hills and too expensive to create and maintain.[9] For the Naga Hills, it cited the past violence as well as the recent relative peace and recommended no change to the area's status.[10] Finally, it refused to entertain any amendment to the Sixth Schedule and instead proposed constituting a separate body to study its working.[11]

The hill leaders responded by creating the Eastern India Tribal Union (EITU). However, some leaders refused to merge their parties with the EITU as it was heavily backed by the siems (Khasi chiefs), thereby confining it to the Khasi–Jaintia Hills.

Meanwhile, violence escalated in the Naga Hills District. After failing to quell it, the government eventually passed the Assam

---

[6]   Chaube, *Hill Politics*, p. 119.
[7]   Report of the States Reorganisation Commission, 1955, p. 184.
[8]   Ibid., 186.
[9]   Ibid., 188.
[10] Ibid., 193.
[11] Ibid., 189.

Disturbed Areas Act. The NNC split into two 'irreconcilable'[12] camps—the extremists led by Zapu Phizo pursuing Naga independence, and the moderates led by T. Sakhrie trying to find a Naga future within the Indian Constitution. In January 1956, Sakhrie was killed, allegedly by Phizo's extremist faction, to try and disrupt peaceful negotiations.[13]

In March 1956, Phizo founded the Federal Government of Nagaland with a national flag and a constitution that declared Nagaland as 'a people's sovereign republic'.[14] The Union government finally called in the army which resorted to the tactic of 'grouping villages' to break connections between the locals and the rebels fighting from the dense forests. Phizo soon escaped to London via East Pakistan on a fake passport.[15] This allowed the moderates (now led by Dr Imkongliba Ao) to take control of the NNC. They formed a reforming committee in February 1957 which was opposed to the method of violence and would seek a separate administrative unit in keeping with the Naga tradition within the framework of the Indian Union.[16]

In the 1957 general elections, three NNC members were elected to the Assam Assembly. However, many alliances broke and parties like the Mizo Union (MU) split. The Indian National Congress (INC) fared poorly across the autonomous districts. As a result, the chief minister of Assam, Bimala Prasad Chaliha of the INC, formed an alliance with the EITU by inviting its vice-president Captain Sangma to join his cabinet. This upset the MU—the leading political

---

[12] Sitlhou, 'Accord'.

[13] Ibid.

[14] B.B. Kumar, *Reorganization of North-East India: Facts and Documents* (India: Concept, 2017), p. 27.

[15] Sitlhou, 'Accord'.

[16] Chandrika Singh, *Naga Politics: A Critical Account* (India: Mittal Publications, 2004), p. 63.

party in the Mizo Hills District—who felt that their consistent support to the Congress had received an 'inadequate reward'[17].

*

Becoming Nagaland

In August 1957, Dr Ao of the NNC chaired a Naga People's Convention at Kohima, where he advocated negotiation over violence. In lieu of Naga independence, he instead asked for 'a single administrative unit comprising of Naga Hills district of Assam and Tuensang Frontier Division of NEFA'[18]. Tuensang had earlier been known as Naga Tribal Area. Prime Minister Jawaharlal Nehru accepted this demand when it was presented to him.

On 1 December 1957, the Naga Hills–Tuensang Area came into being as a new administrative unit in the state of Assam but under the direct control of the ministry of external affairs.[19] The unit was also simultaneously separate from Assam as it was governed by the Governor of Assam acting on behalf of the President of India.[20]

A second Naga People's Convention in May 1958 set up a draft committee that formulated a sixteen-point proposal to enable the establishment of Nagaland State within the Indian Union. The third Naga People's Convention in October 1959 adopted the proposal. Prime Minister Jawaharlal Nehru later accepted this proposal with slight modifications.[21] The state of Nagaland would become a reality following a three-year transitional period. An interim body was

---

[17]   Chaube, *Hill Politics*, p. 124.
[18]   Kumar, *Reorganization,* p. 29.
[19]   The Naga Hills–Tuensang Area Act, 1957.
[20]   Chandrika Singh, 'Nagaland: From A District To A State: Culmination Of Democratic Political Process,' *The Indian Journal of Political Science,* 41(4) (Dec 1980), pp. 822–23.
[21]   Ibid., pp. 823–25.

created consisting of forty-two members elected from Naga tribes, with Dr Imkongliba Ao as the chairman.

*

A Famine and the Imposition of Assamese

In the Mizo Hills, the periodic and deadly mautam famine—caused by a rat infestation corresponding to the flowering of bamboo trees—spread in 1959. As arguments over the distribution of the famine relief work escalated between Chief Minister Chaliha and the MU,[22] Laldenga—a clerk in the district council—formed a Mizo National Famine Front in 1960 to coordinate famine relief efforts.[23]

In April 1960, the Assam Pradesh Congress Committee (APCC) demanded the immediate introduction of Assamese as the official state language, despite it being spoken by only 57 per cent of the population who lived nearly entirely in the plains. Less than 1 per cent of the people in the hills spoke Assamese.[24] This demand revitalized the faltering hill state movement.

The EITU had split into two opposing factions, but they both opposed the imposition of Assamese. Captain Sangma called two All-Party Hill Leaders' Conferences (APHLC)—attended by parties across the spectrum, including even the District Congress Committees—where they issued an ultimatum to Chief Minister Chaliha to drop the language bill and to continue with English as the official language. Captain Sangma even resigned from his cabinet post in the Assam government. However, in a special sitting on 24 October 1960, the

[22] Chaube, *Hill Politics*, pp. 174–75.

[23] Sajal Nag, 'Bamboo, Rats and Famines: Famine Relief and Perceptions of British Paternalism in the Mizo Hills (India),' *Environment and History*, 5(2) (June 1999), pp. 245–52.

[24] Dilip Mukerjee, 'Assam Reorganization,' *Asian Survey*, 9(4) (April 1969), p. 299.

Assam Assembly passed the language bill. The APHLC demanded the immediate creation of a separate hill state as 'the only solution'[25].

In November 1960, Prime Minister Jawaharlal Nehru offered to increase the powers of the autonomous districts to include, among others, a separate budget, a separate cabinet minister and deputy ministers in the Assam government. Since it was modelled on the Committee for Scotland in the British House of Commons, this offer was known as the Scottish Plan.

However, the APHLC rejected this plan in April 1961 and called for a boycott of the 1962 general elections. The District Congress Committees did not agree. Instead, they held their own Assam Hills Peoples' Conference (AHPC) in July 1961 where they agreed to both accept Nehru's offer and contest the 1962 elections. This not only split the hill state movement again; it also forced the APHLC to contest the elections. At the same time, Laldenga converted the Mizo National Famine Front into a political party called the Mizo National Front (MNF).

The 1962 election results could be mapped geographically. The Congress won in Mikir and North Cachar Hills, and the APHLC triumphed in Garo, United Khasi–Jaintia, and Mizo districts. The APHLC believed it could use this electoral victory to reiterate its old demand of a separate hill state. When that was rejected again, they decided to withdraw from the Assembly. However, nearly half its elected members refused to resign, thereby damaging its reputation.

In September 1962, the Union government passed the State of Nagaland Act. The state of Nagaland officially came into being on 1 December 1963 and comprised the entire territory of the Naga Hills–Tuensang Area.

*

---

[25] Chaube, *Hill Politics*, p. 130.

Towards Greater Autonomy amidst Violence and Committees

The Chinese aggression in the region in October and November 1962 changed the flow of events. The hill state demand dissipated and parties split and realigned themselves. The expanded powers initially offered to the districts were increasingly pulled back in what was referred to as the Nehru Plan. Autonomy itself was now 'subject to a Commission being appointed to consider the whole thing'[26].

In May 1964, the Governor of Assam, Vishnu Sahay, constituted a committee led by Daying Ering, a member of Parliament (MP) nominated from NEFA to explore the feasibility of democratic decentralization in NEFA. The committee submitted its report containing certain landmark recommendations in January 1965, including the establishment of four organically-linked tiers of representative bodies in NEFA. Modelled along the lines of panchayati raj, these four tiers were Village (Gram Panchayats), Circle (Aanchal Samiti), District (Zilla Parishad), and Territory (Agency Council).[27]

Parliament passed the North-East Frontier Agency Panchayati Raj Regulation two years later, which incorporated most of the Ering Committee recommendations. This helped integrate the isolated NEFA better with the rest of the country by moving it under the care of the ministry of home affairs and introducing an integrated political system. It also gave NEFA a territorial identity and a people's forum[28]—'the nucleus of a separate state'[29].

In March 1965, the Pataskar Commission was appointed to study the administrative set-up of the hill districts of Assam, with

26   Chaube, *Hill Politics*, p. 134.

27   Swain, *Panchayati Raj*, pp. 47–49.

28   Aruna Gyati, 'Panchayat Raj Institutions in Arunachal Pradesh: A Historical Perspective,' *The Indian Journal of Political Science*, 72(4) (Oct.–Dec. 2011), pp. 1019–30.

29   Swain, *Panchayati Raj*, p. 49.

the objective of 'conferring full measure of autonomy'[30] while still preserving the unity of Assam. In its report, the Pataskar Commission refrained from commenting on the matter of conferring union territory or state status to any of the hill districts or of redrawing its boundaries. It did, however, recommend 'no basic change'[31] to the Sixth Schedule. The APHLC rejected the report and again demanded a separate hill state as well as a boycott of the 1967 general elections.

On the night of 28 February 1966, the MNF and its associated Mizo National Army (MNA) launched Operation Jericho. They attacked army posts and government buildings, took over communications and control of the district and declared Mizoram independent. On 2 March, the Union government declared the district a disturbed area under the Armed Forces Special Powers Act (AFSPA) 1958 and sent in the army and the air force.[32] Laldenga fled. In 1967, the Union government launched Operation Security, also known by the army as Operation Accomplishment, which involved forcibly grouping villages into smaller concentrations.[33]

*

Breaking an Impossible Deadlock

Prime Minister Indira Gandhi could not afford a boycott of the elections in a sensitive area of India. In January 1967, she met with Assam Chief Minister Chaliha and APHLC leaders and promised to reorganize Assam as a federated state 'comprising units of equal status not subordinate to

---

[30] Government of India. Report of the Commission on the Hill Areas of Assam, 1965–66, p. 5.

[31] Ibid., p. 127.

[32] Nandini Sundar, 'Interning Insurgent Populations: The Buried Histories of Indian Democracy,' *Economic and Political Weekly,* 46(6) (Feb. 5–11, 2011) p. 50.

[33] Ibid.

one another'[34]. While the overjoyed APHLC representatives accepted the proposal, the Assam Congress led by Chief Minister Chaliha rejected it, influenced by opposition dissent and public criticism.

In the 1967 elections, the APHLC won all the assembly seats in the Garo and United Khasi–Jaintia Hills, establishing their leadership in the region. However, the Assam Congress continued to reject the federated state idea.[35] Similar demands began to appear in other parts of Assam too. The Home Minister, Yashwantrao Balwantrao Chavan, put together a subcommittee headed by Asoka Mehta, the Union Minister for Planning, but the APHLC leaders boycotted it. In May 1968, all the elected APHLC members resigned their assembly seats. In September 1968, they started a non-violent satyagraha.

Finally, faced with an impossible deadlock, all sides agreed to reach a common middle ground. The compromise was worked around the subject of law and order—it would not be transferred to the new autonomous state within the state of Assam.

On 29 December 1969, Parliament passed the Assam Reorganisation (Meghalaya) Act. The autonomous state of Meghalaya would exist within Assam and comprise the districts of Garo Hills and United Khasi–Jaintia Hills. The districts of Mikir Hills and North Cachar Hills were given the option to join the new state, but they voted overwhelmingly to stay in Assam. Meghalaya came into existence on 2 April 1970.[36] Shillong became the capital of both Assam and Meghalaya.

*

Completing the Reorganization of Assam

In Mizo Hills District, a coalition executive council led by the MU came to power in the district council in 1971 and passed a resolution demanding a separate state of Mizoram within India as well as the

---

[34] Mukerjee, 'Assam Reorganization,' pp. 304–05.

[35] Ibid., p. 306.

[36] The Assam Reorganisation (Meghalaya) Act, 1969.

unification of all Mizo-inhabited areas. The Government of India offered to make Mizo Hills District a union territory, putting it under direct central authority. The district council welcomed it, but the Assam Congress refused to accept it 'even as a stepping stone'[37] and requested Prime Minister Indira Gandhi to continue the status quo. She refused.

The Union government reorganized Assam immediately after the 1971 Indo–Pakistan war that created Bangladesh. On 30 December 1971, Parliament passed the North-Eastern Areas (Reorganisation) Act, which came into effect on 21 January 1972. Meghalaya became a full-fledged state and Shillong became its capital the following year when Assam made Dispur its capital. Mizo Hills District became a centrally administered union territory called Mizoram, with C. Chhunga of the MU as its first chief minister. NEFA became a union territory called Arunachal Pradesh.

The reorganization of Assam was complete.

* *

[37] Chaube, *Hill Politics*, pp. 178–79.

BIHAR

On 22 March 1912, British India created possibly the earliest state
of modern India—Bihar and Orissa Province. 22 March is today
celebrated as 'Bihar Diwas' (Bihar Day). Orissa was later separated
into its own province on 1 April 1936, which it celebrates as
'Odisha Day'.

Bihar conducted elections in 1937 and 1946 as per the
Government of India Act 1935, resulting in the Indian National
Congress (INC) taking office and forming the government and
legislative assembly.

After India's Independence on 15 August 1947 and its creation
as a Republic on 26 January 1950, Bihar Province became Bihar
State and continued with the same boundaries as before. A few minor
princely states that fell within its boundaries merged into Bihar.

In 1953, when the States Reorganisation Commission
(SRC) was constituted to look into the matter of redrawing

state boundaries, Bihar and its neighbouring states put forth a number of claims regarding border adjustments, mostly on the east and south. These included the long-standing demand for the separation of the southern districts as the state of Jharkhand, and a number of claims and counterclaims with West Bengal on border districts.

In its 1955 report, the SRC dismissed all claims but one—the transfer of the Purulia district from Bihar to West Bengal. It did this for linguistic as well as developmental reasons. Purulia had the largest concentration of Bengali-speaking people outside West Bengal. Also, the river Kangsabati (Kasai) in the district was important to the implementation of a flood control and irrigation project in West Bengal.[1]

*

Bihar and Jharkhand

The idea of a separate state of Jharkhand as an adivasi[2] state had been floated as early as the 1920s. In the late 1930s, various adivasi organizations came together to form the Adivasi Mahasabha, led by the politician and tribal rights activist Jaipal Singh Munda.[3] After Independence, the Adivasi Mahasabha forwarded the demand for the state of Jharkhand. In November 1948, the constituent assembly suggested 'urgency of action'[4] from the state and Union governments on this issue.

---

[1]   Report of the States Reorganisation Commission, 1955, pp. 179–80.
[2]   Note: Adivasi literally means 'original dweller' and is usually collectively used to refer to members of tribes in India.
[3]   Louise Tillin, *Remapping India: New States and Their Political Origins* (New Delhi: Oxford University Press, 2013), pp. 70–71.
[4]   Final Report, Annexure VII, Appendix D, *Constituent Assembly Debates Official Report* (New Delhi: Lok Sabha Secretariat, 2014), p. 178.

In the 1951–52 elections, the Adivasi Mahasabha (renamed the Jharkhand Party) won thirty-two seats in the Bihar Assembly, making it the second-largest and main opposition party in the assembly to the INC.[5] This electoral verdict appeared to lend credence to the Jharkhand demand.

However, in its 1955 report, the SRC rejected the proposal on multiple grounds. The Jharkhand Party had not won a clear majority in the Chota Nagpur division and the Santhal Parganas in south Bihar. Tribals were not only a minority, making up only one-third of the total population, they were also spread across several language groups. Further, the industrial balance the region provided, due to its wealth of coal, minerals, steel and thermal power, only added to the volume of opposition to division from outside south Bihar. In lieu of statehood, the SRC recommended a special development board.[6]

After the Jharkhand Party merged with the INC, the Jharkhand Mukti Morcha (JMM) led the campaign for statehood through the 1970s and 80s. The JMM also pursued a wider agenda of social and economic activism, such as the 'dhan katao andolan' (cut down paddy movement) to reclaim tribal land and the 'jungle katao andolan' (cut down the forest movement) to protest against state forestry policies. These activities helped develop the consciousness of a political Jharkhand as a precursor to a territorial Jharkhand.[7]

In 1977, Bihar got a new chief minister, Karpoori Thakur of the Janata Party. Nationally, the Janata Party was vocal about the need to reorganize state boundaries, but in Bihar, the new chief minister was opposed to the idea of Jharkhand.[8] As a result, a rebel faction of politicians in Bihar set up a 'Sangharsh Samiti' (Struggle

---

[5]   Statistical Report on General Election, 1951, to the Legislative Assembly of Bihar, Election Commission of India.
[6]   Report of the States Reorganisation Commission, 1955, pp. 168–71.
[7]   Tillin, *Remapping India*, pp. 75–76.
[8]   Ibid., p. 79.

Committee) and passed a resolution in September 1977 calling for the establishment of Jharkhand.[9]

In 1980, the INC returned to power in Bihar and at the Centre. The Congress began to co-opt some of the JMM's platforms, and even agreed to a seat-sharing arrangement with its founder Shibu Soren, which led to a formal split in the JMM by the end of 1984. Rajiv Gandhi of the INC became India's new prime minister. Congress politicians from the Jharkhand region demanded union territory status as a first step towards eventual statehood.[10]

In June 1986, a more radical student wing of the JMM was established—the All Jharkhand Students Union (AJSU) led by Surya Singh Besra, a Santal adivasi. The following month, local activists established the Jharkhand Coordination Committee (JCC) to put Jharkhandi identity at the centre of the statehood conversation. A revivalist movement for recognizing Jharkhand as a cultural region emerged. Economics mixed with identity.[11]

By the late 1980s, the Bharatiya Janata Party (BJP) began to support the demand for Jharkhand statehood. However, they proposed the name Vananchal, after the 'van' (forests) and their dwellers in the region.[12] As a result, non-adivasi sections of society also began to support the demand for statehood.

The JCC then revived an older demand of Greater Jharkhand, which included twenty-one districts spread across Bihar, Madhya Pradesh, Orissa and West Bengal. Along with the AJSU, they pushed for statehood more aggressively, utilizing more direct-action methods like mass rallies, economic blockades and general strikes.[13] This forced the INC Union government to meet with the leaders of the movement. In August 1989, the Union government agreed to

---

[9]   Tillin, *Remapping India*, pp. 79–80.
[10] Ibid., pp. 81–82.
[11] Ibid., pp. 82–84.
[12] Ibid., p. 87.
[13] Ibid., p. 84.

establish the Committee on Jharkhand Matters (COJM) comprising representatives from Jharkhand, Bihar and the Centre. However, this was interrupted by the Lok Sabha elections later that year, which resulted in a new National Front coalition Union government, led by the Janata Dal and supported by the BJP. The eventual COJM report in 1990 recommended an elected Jharkhand General Council rather than a state as a way to achieve regional autonomy. This proposal was rejected by the members of the movement.

The National Front coalition soon fell and the INC then formed the government at the Centre. This did not suit the Janata Dal government in Bihar led by Lalu Prasad Yadav. As BJP leaders in Bihar began to demand the creation of Jharkhand more vociferously, the Congress government first demanded the withdrawal of their former ally, the JMM, from the state government. This split the JMM once again. In 1994, the Bihar state government agreed to establish a Jharkhand Autonomous Area Council (JAAC).[14]

In 1997, Lalu Prasad Yadav created a new political party called the Rashtriya Janata Dal (RJD) and his wife Rabri Devi took over as chief minister of Bihar. As a short-term tactical move to garner support from MLAs from the region, the RJD introduced a resolution supporting the creation of Jharkhand.[15]

In 1998, the BJP, led by Atal Bihari Vajpayee, headed a National Democratic Alliance (NDA) coalition government at the Centre. During its election campaign, the NDA had pledged the creation of Jharkhand as well as the imposition of President's rule in Bihar.[16] In September 1998, claiming a conspiracy to divide Bihar, the RJD withdrew its previous year's resolution to create Jharkhand and rejected the Bihar Reorganisation Bill.[17]

---

[14] Tillin, *Remapping India*, pp. 91–94.
[15] Ibid., p. 163.
[16] Ibid., p. 164.
[17] Ibid.

The BJP's influence grew significantly, and BJP politicians in north Bihar now began to actively support separation, arguing that the creation of Jharkhand would benefit industrial and agricultural development in north Bihar. In December 1998, a bill to create Jharkhand was tabled in the Lok Sabha. Despite a sudden general election in 1999, the BJP returned to form a more secure coalition government at the Centre.

In the Bihar assembly elections in February 2000, the RJD was re-elected with the support of the INC, who were also allied with the JMM in the Jharkhand region. This ensured that progress would be made towards the creation of the state of Jharkhand. In April 2000, the Bihar Reorganisation Bill was formally signed in the Bihar Legislative Assembly. The bill contained an amendment that would name the new state 'Jharkhand' and not 'Vananchal'.

In August 2000, the Bihar Reorganisation Act was passed by both the Lok Sabha and Rajya Sabha at the Centre and received Presidential assent. On 15 November 2000, the state of Jharkhand was born. It comprised eighteen districts from the southern region of the erstwhile Bihar State. Based on the results of the February 2000 Bihar elections, the BJP formed the first state government in Jharkhand with Babulal Marandi as the first chief minister.

*

CHHATTISGARH

> **Did You Know?**
>
> *Pre-Independence, the princely states in the region were also known as the Chhattisgarh states.*

At the time of India's independence, Chhattisgarh existed mostly in the form of fifteen minor princely states known as the Chhattisgarh states. They were a part of the Eastern States Agency which consisted of forty-two princely states. In August 1947, the members of the Eastern States Agency joined together to form the Eastern States Union—a motley of Odia- and Hindi-speaking states scattered across Orissa Province and Central Provinces. It was headed by Maharaja Ramanuj Pratap Singh Deo, the ruler of the princely state of Korea (now also spelled as Koriya).

However, two of the biggest states—Mayurbhanj and Bastar—along with some of the smaller states refused to join. Moreover, the Eastern States Union failed to gain recognition from the Union government due to linguistic and administrative irregularities. The States Ministry decided that the Orissa states would be merged into Orissa Province and the Chhattisgarh states into Central Provinces and Berar.

This decision split the rulers of the Eastern States Union into opposing camps. In the middle of December 1947, the head and the secretary of the States Ministry, Sardar Vallabhbhai Patel and V.P. Menon, respectively, first met the Orissa states rulers and then the Chhattisgarh states rulers. They apprised them of the law and order unrest that simmered in their states, the people's desire to have a responsible government which most states could not provide, and the possibility that the Union government would take over the states' administration if the situation worsened. Within a day, the rulers of all the Orissa states had signed the agreement, and the rulers of the Chhattisgarh states signed the following day. The fifteen Chhattisgarh states were then merged into Central Provinces and Berar.

In 1948, B.Y. Tamaskar, an opponent of the then-Premier of Central Provinces and Berar, Ravishankar Shukla, proposed statehood for Chhattisgarh for the first time. However, the proposal was neither seconded nor did it find mass appeal.[1] In 1951, Tamaskar joined what would eventually become the Praja Socialist Party (PSP), which became the first main political party to promote the idea of statehood.

In 1956, the larger state of Madhya Pradesh was formed by integrating the erstwhile Central Provinces and Berar, Madhya Bharat, Vindhya Pradesh and Bhopal State. The same year, Khubchand Baghel set up the Chhattisgarh Mahasabha, thereby becoming one of the foremost proponents of a separate Chhattisgarh. Baghel had also joined the PSP earlier in 1951. The Mahasabha furthered the idea of exploitation by outsiders through a number of movements and campaigns, including employment rights for locals and land rights for tribals.

In 1967, when Baghel felt that the movement against exploitation was weakening, he established the Chhattisgarh Bhratr Sangh to

---

[1]   Louise Tillin, *Remapping India: New States and Their Political Origins* (New Delhi: Oxford University Press, 2013), pp. 115–18.

rejuvenate the movement. However, the demand for statehood remained only an external pressure on the ruling Congress state government.[2]

In 1977, Purushottam Kaushik from the PSP contested the elections on a pro-statehood platform. He defeated Vidya Charan Shukla, the son of the first chief minister, and became a cabinet minister in the first non-Congress central government. To contest the 1980 Lok Sabha elections, Pawan Diwan established the Prithak Chhattisgarh Party.

From 1980 onwards, the movement for a regional Chhattisgarhi identity and Chhattisgarhi statehood gained new momentum, thanks largely to the new chief minister of Madhya Pradesh, Arjun Singh of the Indian National Congress (INC). He built and named universities, dams and statues after famous individuals from the region. He brought Pawan Diwan into the INC and established a development authority called the Chhattisgarh Vikas Pratikharan. He gave cabinet positions to a number of Other Backward Classes (OBC), Scheduled Castes (SC) and Scheduled Tribes (ST) MLAs from Chhattisgarh in his government, and established a state backwards classes commission. This new generation of OBC leaders, supported by Arjun Singh, not only began to promote the idea of statehood well into the early 1990s, but were at the forefront of the promotion of a Chhattisgarhi identity.[3]

In response, the Bharatiya Janata Party (BJP) intensified their efforts, both to represent OBCs as well as to support statehood for Chhattisgarh. In 1990, the BJP formed the government in Madhya Pradesh for the first time. Leaders from both the BJP and the INC set up all-party campaigns for the creation of Chhattisgarh. Ahead of the 1993 assembly elections, Chhattisgarhi statehood featured on the manifestos of both the INC and the BJP for the first time. In 1994, the new Madhya Pradesh Chief Minister, Digvijay Singh of the INC, passed a resolution in favour of statehood in the legislative assembly.

---

[2]   Tillin, *Remapping India*, pp. 119–23.
[3]   Ibid., pp. 130–31.

The BJP responded aggressively. They started to dominate the Chhattisgarh Rajya Nirman Manch (Chhattisgarh State Creation Committee), an all-party outfit set up just a few years earlier. In addition, they established a Chhattisgarh Nirman Samiti (Chhattisgarh Creation Committee) within the BJP and built the case for creation around development rather than social issues. The BJP's National Executive approved the demand for Chhattisgarh for the first time and it was included in the party's general election manifesto in 1996. In 1998, at an election rally, the BJP's prime ministerial candidate, Atal Bihari Vajpayee, promised to create Chhattisgarh if the party won all eleven seats in the region (they won seven).[4]

Finally, in August 2000, with the BJP in power at the Centre and the INC in power at the state, the Madhya Pradesh Reorganisation Act was passed. Chhattisgarh was born on 1 November 2000 comprising sixteen districts with its capital at Raipur. Based on the 1998 state elections, Ajit Jogi of the INC was invited to form the first government.

**

---

4   Tillin, *Remapping India*, pp. 137–38.

GOA

1947–61: Diplomacy Precedes Action

'At the stroke of the midnight hour, when the world sleeps, India will awake to life and freedom.'[1]

Except Goa.

In 1947, when India achieved independence from the British, Goa was under the occupation of a different colonial power. The Portuguese had a few holdings strung out along the west coast of India—Goa (the largest), Dadra, Nagar Haveli, Daman and Diu. And so, at the stroke of the midnight hour on 15 August 1947, these five territories simply continued to be a part of Portuguese India and did not become a part of the Union of India.

---

[1] Jawaharlal Nehru, 'Tryst With Destiny,' Speech delivered to the Indian Constituent Assembly, 15 August 1947.

Portugal viewed Goa as the 'Rome of the Orient'[2]—implying a timeless, eternal rule—but Indian nationalists viewed Portuguese India as a 'pimple'[3]—a temporary nuisance. Neither the local Goans nor the Government of India were all right with Portugal continuing this arrangement. Even before Independence, in June 1946, Dr Ram Manohar Lohia had led a disobedience movement and the Goan Political Conference had passed the 'Quit Goa' resolution.[4] In June 1949, both the Goan People's Party and the president of the Goan National Congress demanded the end to foreign rule and the establishment of democracy.[5] The same month, India established a diplomatic office in Lisbon, the capital of Portugal, and began to negotiate the withdrawal of Portugal from its colonies in India.[6]

Portugal refused to even discuss the issue. In the view of its dictator, António de Oliveira Salazar, these were not 'colonies' but parts of metropolitan Portugal.[7] Goa was 'the expression of Portugal in India'[8]. Goans were citizens of Portugal, represented in the Portuguese legislature and even in the cabinet.[9] Moreover, when Portugal had gained control over these territories in the early 16th century, there was no 'Republic of India', just a number of kingdoms. Further, in June 1951, Portugal amended its Constitution to change the status of its overseas colonies—

---

[2]   Philip Bravo, 'The Case of Goa: History, Rhetoric and Nationalism,' *Past Imperfect*, Vol. 7 (1998), p. 149.

[3]   Ibid., p. 149.

[4]   Sushila Sawant Mendes, 'Jawaharlal Nehru and the Liberation Struggle of Goa,' *Proceedings of the Indian History Congress*, 67 (2006-07), p. 550.

[5]   Russell H. Fifield, 'The Future of Portuguese India,' *Far Eastern Survey*, 19(7) (5 April 1950), p. 71. doi: 10.2307/3024038.

[6]   Bravo, 'The Case of Goa,' p. 133.

[7]   Andrew J. Rotter, *Comrades at Odds: The United States and India, 1947-1964.* (United Kingdom: Cornell University Press, 2000), p. 181.

[8]   D.P. Singhal, 'Goa—End of an Epoch,' *The Australian Quarterly*, Vol. 34, No. 1 (March 1962), p. 83.

[9]   Bravo, 'The Case of Goa,' p. 128.

including those in India—to provinces.[10] The question of transferring its territories to India simply did not arise. This didn't go down well with India. In June 1953, it withdrew its diplomatic mission from Lisbon[11] and instituted visa restrictions between Portuguese colonies and India.[12]

On 21 July 1954, a small party of Indian activists entered the Portuguese territory of Dadra and took over the administration. On 2 August, more activists entered and liberated Nagar Haveli without incident. Inspired by these developments, over a thousand satyagrahis attempted to cross into Goa and Daman on 15 August 1954 but were turned back at the border. A year later, on 15 August 1955, three thousand satyagrahis entered Goa, Daman and Diu in a similar attempt. This time, the Portuguese police and military met them with violence, resulting in deaths and injuries.[13]

Condemning the Portuguese firing, Prime Minister Nehru immediately broke off diplomatic relations with Portugal.[14] India closed its consulate in Goa, curtailed money order facilities, and instituted a travel and economic blockade against Goa, Daman and Diu.[15]

The issue now became internationalized. The Soviet Union and China backed India's stand, while Great Britain and other countries of the North Atlantic Treaty Organization (NATO, of which Portugal was a member) alliance supported Portugal. While

[10] Singhal, 'Goa—End of an Epoch,' p. 83.
[11] Mendes, 'The Liberation Struggle of Goa,' p. 551.
[12] Brigadier A.S. Cheema, VSM (Retd), 'Operation Vijay: The Liberation of 'Estado da India'—Goa, Daman and Diu,' *Journal of the United Service Institution of India,* Vol. CXLIII, No. 594 (October–December 2013).
[13] Administrative Reforms Commission. *Report, Study Team on Administration of Union Territories and NEFA,* 1968, pp. 172–73.
[14] Ibid.
[15] Archana Subramaniam, 'Goa Comes Home,' *The Hindu,* 17 December 2015.

the United States tried to remain neutral on the matter, it indirectly agreed that Goa was Portugal's province.[16] This greatly disappointed Nehru. However, this did not bring about any change in the status of Portuguese territories in India.

India tried a last-ditch effort to resolve the matter peacefully. In September 1960, it liberalized travel between Goa and India, and in April 1961, it removed the trade ban with Goa, Daman and Diu. Portugal did not reciprocate on both occasions.[17]

Through the second half of 1961, newly-independent post-colonial nations in Africa started applying greater pressure on India to resolve the Goa issue. At a seminar organized by the Indian Council for Africa in Delhi in October 1961, leaders of multiple African nations linked the immediate liberation of Goa as crucial to the success of ongoing independence movements in Africa.[18] Criticized for having too passive and soft a policy on Goa, Nehru said, 'We may even decide to send our armies.'[19] V.K. Krishna Menon, India's defence minister and the head of India's UN delegation, declared that India had not renounced 'the use of force'[20] in Goa. After fourteen years of attempting to persuade Portugal through patience and non-violence, armed conflict was now a real prospect for India.

*

November–December 1961: Military Action

By November 1961, the Portuguese had begun to reinforce their presence in Goa. Four thousand combat soldiers and two artillery

---

[16]   Rotter, *Comrades at Odds*, pp. 181–82.
[17]   Administrative Reforms Commission. *Report, Study Team on Administration of Union Territories and NEFA*, 1968, p. 173.
[18]   Singhal, 'Goa—End of an Epoch,' p. 87.
[19]   Rotter, *Comrades at Odds*, p. 182.
[20]   Ibid., p. 185.

units were stationed in Goa, and four frigates (small, fast military ships) patrolled Goa's coast. They also had over a thousand police officers and border guards as well as five merchant ships and two transport aircraft.[21] Roads leading into Goa were mined.[22]

The trigger came towards the end of November when the Portuguese fired unprovoked at an Indian steamer ship from Anjadip, an island they held just south of Goa. This resulted in injuries and deaths of Indian fishermen. India immediately deployed a destroyer and a frigate to patrol the Karwar coast south of Goa.

On 1 December, India began a surveillance and reconnaissance exercise called Operation Chutney.[23] Two frigates began to patrol the coast of Goa, and the Indian Navy mobilized sixteen ships, divided into four task groups. The Indian Air Force (IAF) began reconnaissance flights to lure any Portuguese fighter jets to reveal their positions. The Indian Army stationed troops around the borders of Goa, Daman and Diu. The army would lead Operation Vijay to liberate Goa, and the navy and the air force would support it.

Salazar attempted to garner international support, appealing to Great Britain and the United Nations Security Council and lodging protests through Brazil. Nehru postponed initiating military action twice after listening to the United States Ambassador, John Kenneth Galbraith, but it was just delaying the inevitable. On 10 December, Nehru declared that 'continuance of Goa under Portuguese rule is an impossibility'[24]. The escalating situation alarmed the European civilians in Goa. They began to evacuate, aided by the Governor-General of Portuguese India, Manuel António Vassalo e Silva.[25]

---

[21]   Brig Cheema (Retd), 'Operation Vijay'.

[22]   Rotter, *Comrades at Odds*, p. 185.

[23]   Cmde Srikant B. Kesnur and Lt Cdr Ankush Banerjee, 'How Indian Navy Helped in the Liberation of Goa,' *The Daily Guardian*, 25 December 2020.

[24]   Rotter, *Comrades at Odds*, p. 185.

[25]   'India: Intolerable Goa,' *Time*, 22 December 1961.

The first move came on 17 December. A unit of Indian troops captured the town of Maulinguém in north-east Goa after a brief skirmish. The operation began at four a.m. in the predawn darkness of 18 December, coordinated across Goa, Daman and Diu. Troops entered from the north, east and south, all aiming for the capital city of Panjim. They captured town after town with little resistance from the Portuguese forces, who blew up bridges as they retreated. The IAF ran morning bombing raids to destroy the runway at Dabolim airport and radio facilities at Bambolim and Mormugao harbour.[26] At noon, three Indian frigates stormed into Mormugao harbour to find a lone Portuguese frigate (the other three had sailed earlier to Portugal). In an exchange of fire lasting less than an hour, the Portuguese frigate was destroyed.[27]

Meanwhile, at Anjadip Island, the Portuguese falsely raised the white flag of surrender. They waited until the naval landing party approached the shore and then ambushed them with machine-gun fire. The Indian naval forces repelled the attack and won the island by the afternoon of 18 December, but suffered casualties.[28]

By the evening of 18 December, the towns of Margao and Dabolim had also fallen, and Indian Army troops had advanced up to the Mandovi River across from Panjim. The following morning, Indian troops marched into Panjim and captured Fort Aguada.

The Portuguese forces had been cornered into the town of Vasco da Gama, next to the Mormugao harbour. Salazar had ordered his troops to destroy Goa rather than surrender it to the Indians. However, the Governor-General Vassalo e Silva chose to not follow those orders. Instead, on the evening of 19 December, he offered

---

[26] Brig Cheema (Retd), 'Operation Vijay'.
[27] Cmde Kesnur and Lt Cdr Banerjee, 'How Indian Navy Helped'.
[28] Ibid.

to surrender.[29] About three-and-a-half thousand Portuguese soldiers were taken prisoner.[30]

Operation Vijay had concluded successfully. Goa, Daman and Diu had all been liberated. 451 years of Portuguese rule in India had ended.

*

1961–87: Too Big for a Union Territory, Too Small for a State

On the morning of 20 December 1961, Goa awoke to life as a union territory of India.

The Goa, Daman and Diu (Administration) Act, passed in March 1962 but valid retroactively from 20 December 1961, incorporated 'Goa, Daman and Diu' as the eighth union territory of India. All the three former Portuguese enclaves, 1400 km apart along the western coast, were combined into one union territory and granted representation in Parliament.

On 8 June 1962, the military governor, who had taken over administration in the immediate aftermath of Operation Vijay, gave way to a civilian lieutenant-governor. On 13 May 1963, the Government of Union Territories Act came into effect in Goa, Daman and Diu. This gave the union territory a legislature consisting of thirty members and a council of ministers.

However, Goa's existence was threatened almost immediately. Goa was economically much more prosperous than the border areas of both its neighbouring states—Maharashtra in the north and Mysore State in the east and south. As a result, both of those significantly larger states eyed Goa as a potential target for absorption.

---

[29] Brig Cheema (Retd), 'Operation Vijay'.
[30] Rotter, *Comrades at Odds*, p. 185.

Maharashtra had the upper hand as many Goan freedom fighters had been based out of Bombay City.

Many Hindu Goans supported a merger as an effective means of promoting national integration. They denied that Goans were distinguishable from their neighbours, despite the 'accident of history'[31] of 451 unbroken years of Portuguese rule and the fact that over a third of the Goan population at the time was Christian. At the other end of the spectrum, some Goans made a plea for independence before the United Nations, claiming distinctive historical, social and cultural patterns.[32]

In the election year of 1963, the Maharashtrawadi Gomantak Party (MGP)—led by Dayanand Bandodkar—was founded with the objective of 'the integration of Goa into the state of Maharashtra'[33]. While 95 per cent of Goans spoke Konkani, Marathi was widely used among the Hindus of Goa, leading the MGP to declare that 'the language of Goans is Marathi and Konkani is a dialect of Marathi'[34]. To protect their cultural identity and future, the Christian minority founded the United Goans Party (UGP), led by Dr Jack de Sequeira.

The third large party in the fray was India's biggest political party at the time—the Indian National Congress (INC). The Congress found itself in an unenviable position. It couldn't support the merger call with neighbouring states because Prime Minister Nehru had personally recognized Goa's distinctive personality and had pledged to maintain its separate identity.[35] At the same time, the INC also had to appease the powerful Congress state governments in Maharashtra and Mysore.

With the INC caught in the middle, the MGP won sixteen of the thirty seats—an absolute majority—in the December 1963

[31]   Arthur G. Rubinoff, 'Goa's Attainment of Statehood,' *Asian Survey*, 32(5) (May 1992), p. 473.
[32]   Ibid., p. 472.
[33]   Ibid., pp. 473–74.
[34]   Ibid., p. 474.
[35]   Ibid., p. 473.

assembly elections, while the UGP came in a close second with twelve. The INC won the seat in Daman and nothing in Goa, and an independent candidate won the seat in Diu.[36]

The MGP and its leader—now chief minister of the union territory—Dayanand Bandodkar interpreted the resounding electoral victory as a public endorsement of its call to merge Goa with Maharashtra and intensified measures to bring it to fruition. The new government promoted Marathi as the language of government and education. It passed a resolution in the Goa Assembly demanding the merger of Goa with Maharashtra and Daman and Diu with Gujarat. Maharashtrian civil servants began to be appointed into Goa's bureaucracy.[37]

Bandodkar's heavy-handedness had an unintended consequence. The Catholic and Brahmin Hindu communities that opposed the merger joined forces and formed a non-party Council of Direct Action to stage satyagrahas, marches and strikes.[38] By August 1966, these had begun to seriously disrupt daily life. The Union government, led by Indira Gandhi of the INC, was caught in the crossfire and unable to fully support or quell either motion. Eventually, in September 1966, it decided to settle the matter through a public vote. The people of Goa, Daman and Diu would decide the fate of Goa, Daman and Diu.

In December 1966, Parliament passed the Goa, Daman and Diu (Opinion Poll) Act to give legal standing to the poll. The Chief Election Commissioner would oversee the opinion poll and the results would be published in the official gazette. The Bandodkar government resigned and the territory was placed under President's rule so as to facilitate the conduct of the poll. The opinion poll was

---

[36] Ram Joshi, 'The General Elections in Goa', *Asian Survey,* 4(10) (October 1964), p. 1093. doi:10.2307/2642211

[37] Rubinoff, 'Goa's Attainment of Statehood,' p. 476.

[38] Ibid.

scheduled to be held on 16 January 1967 and would offer only two options: 'Merger' (symbolized by a flower) or 'Union Territory' (symbolized by two leaves)[39]. Both the pro-merger and anti-merger factions campaigned intensely in the month leading up to the vote.

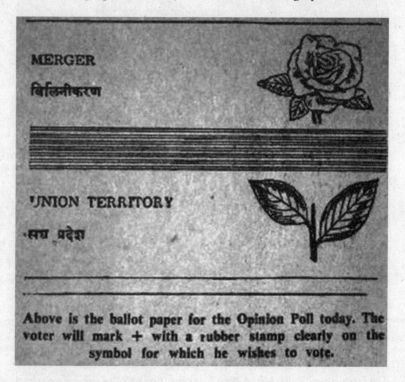

The ballot paper for the 1967 opinion poll in Goa, Daman and Diu[40]

Nearly 82 per cent of the eligible voters in Goa cast their votes. The majority chose for Goa to remain a 'Union Territory' (two leaves

[39] Sandesh Prabhudesai, 'The Historic Opinion Poll', *Goa News*, 20 July 2008.
[40] Aaron Pereira, 'What is Goa's 'Opinion Poll Day'?,' *The New Indian Express*, 18 January 2019.

symbol), which won by over 34,000 votes.[41] The union territory of Goa, Daman and Diu continued to exist in the Union of India as a separate entity. 16 January is observed every year in Goa as 'Asmitai Dis' (Self-identity Day).[42]

Portugal had refused to recognize India's sovereignty over all five territories all along. In 1974, it underwent a revolution that overthrew the regime and brought about democratic reforms. On 31 December 1974, Portugal and India signed a treaty that recognized that Goa, Daman, Diu, Dadra and Nagar Haveli had 'already become parts of India'[43] and that India had sovereign rights over them from the dates when they each became a part of India.

With the issues of integration and merger finally settled, politics in Goa went back to pre-referendum days. The MGP won the next four assembly elections and stayed in power for another twelve years. Dayanand Bandodkar died in office and was succeeded by his daughter, Shashikala Kakodkar, both as leader of the MGP and as chief minister of Goa.

The issue of Goa's statehood cropped up occasionally through the 1970s, but the demand was never forceful or urgent enough, not even after it became an election promise by the winning parties in the 1977 (MGP) and 1980 (Congress [U]) elections. Goa seemed to be stuck in an in-between ground between union territory and state requirements. For instance, while states were required to have assemblies with a minimum of sixty delegates, Goa needed just thirty for its small geographical size. And yet, economically, Goa regularly outperformed states that were many times larger. Moreover, granting

---

[41]   Rubinoff, 'Goa's Attainment of Statehood,' p. 477.
[42]   Prabhudesai, 'The Historic Opinion Poll'.
[43]   Treaty between the Government of India and the Government of the Republic of Portugal on Recognition of India's Sovereignty over Goa, Daman, Diu, Dadra and Nagar Haveli and Related Matters, 1974. http://www.liiofindia.org/in/other/treaties/INTSer/1974/53.html

statehood to Goa could have an effect on the statehood demands of other union territories, such as Delhi and Pondicherry.[44]

Since linguistics had been the basis of the States Reorganisation Act of 1956, pro-state advocates in Goa tried to get Konkani recognized as a national language. However, the Konkan regions were scattered along the western coast and creating a Konkan state would mean extensive redrawing of the state borders of Kerala, Karnataka and Maharashtra.[45]

The momentum really kicked in only in July 1986 when Luizinho Faleiro, the sole Goa Congress MLA, moved a bill to make Konkani the official language of Goa. This bill garnered support across communal lines, forcing the ruling INC government to endorse it. The all-India Congress Committee drafted a bill making Konkani the official language while assuring equal protection to Marathi.[46] This immediately set off violence between the pro-Marathi and pro-Konkani factions in Goa. Nevertheless, in February 1987, the Goa Assembly adopted the Official Languages Bill, making Konkani in Devanagari script the official language while keeping the use of Marathi.[47]

Curiously, this event propelled Goa along the path of statehood so rapidly that it became a state almost overnight. The INC at the Centre, seemingly inspired by granting statehood to both Arunachal Pradesh and Mizoram in February 1987, passed the Goa, Daman and Diu Reorganisation Act on 23 May 1987 to separate the state of Goa and the union territory of Daman and Diu. Small size? No problem! The Fifty-Sixth Amendment of the Constitution of India

---

[44] Rubinoff, 'Goa's Attainment of Statehood,' p. 483.

[45] NOTE: Konkani was given the status of a national language in India on 20 August 1992, through the 71st Amendment to the Eighth Schedule of the Constitution of India.

[46] Rubinoff, 'Goa's Attainment of Statehood,' p. 484.

[47] Ibid., p. 485.

allowed the Goa Legislative Assembly to have forty members instead of the minimum sixty.[48]

And so, on 30 May 1987, Goa awoke to life as the twenty-fifth and smallest state of India.

* *

---

[48] Government of India, Ministry of Law and Justice. The Constitution (Fifty-sixth Amendment) Act, 1987.

GUJARAT

Phase I: 1947–56: Small Pools Forming a Big Lake

At the time of Independence, Gujarat was home to about half of all the princely states in India, with many of them no larger than a city neighbourhood.[1] Even the name of the British agency administering the Gujarat region was an amalgamation of all the various agencies that had operated in the region until as recently as 1937—'The Baroda, Western India and Gujarat States Agency'.

The integration of Gujarat, like the integration of India, did not happen immediately or all at once. This slow process of coalescence happened across three roughly equal-sized regions in the south, the north and the east of Gujarat.

*

---

[1] V.P. Menon, *The Story of the Integration of the Indian States* (United Kingdom: Longmans, Green and Co., 1956), p. 123.

The Southern Third: Saurashtra State, 1948–56

At the time of Independence, 222 princely states dotted the region of Saurashtra (interchangeably known as Kathiawar). Many of them had more than one 'sovereign' or 'shareholder', meaning these princely states were further fragmented into 449 units. A number of these states had pockets of territories that were scattered across and separated by other states, leading to a further fragmentation into 860 jurisdiction areas.[2]

Sardar Patel, head of the States Ministry overseeing the integration of India, and his secretary, V.P. Menon, met the princely rulers and shareholders of Kathiawar in January 1948. They proposed the unification of all the princely states into the United State of Kathiawar, integrated with the Union of India. Sardar Patel emphasized that 'little pools of water tend to become stagnant and useless, but . . . if they are joined together to form a big lake, the atmosphere is cooled and there is universal benefit'.[3]

The rulers of Kathiawar, of large and small states, willingly signed the Covenant with just a few days of discussion and debate. The United State of Kathiawar came into being in February 1948— the first region where such a large-scale consolidation exercise was carried out. It was renamed as the United State of Saurashtra in November 1948. Maharaja Jam Sahib of Navanagar was appointed the Rajpramukh (Governor).

However, Junagadh—one of the three largest princely states in the Kathiawar region—didn't sign into the United State of Kathiawar. On 15 August 1947, the Nawab of Junagadh, Muhammad Mahabat Khanji III—whose coat of arms had the word 'Saurashtra' inscribed on it—announced his desire to accede to Pakistan, despite having

---

[2]   Ministry of States, Government of India. *White Paper on Indian States*, 1950, pp. 49–50.
[3]   Menon, *Integration*, p. 126.

earlier publicly announced his intention to join the United State of Kathiawar. Junagadh was situated at the extreme south of Kathiawar and was not contiguous to Pakistan. Junagadh's territories were also interspersed with other princely states of Kathiawar. The rulers of a couple of other smaller states too, like Manavadar and Mangrol, were considering acceding to Pakistan.[4]

This unforeseen decision of the Nawab of Junagadh resulted in rapid communication being exchanged by the governments of India, Pakistan and Junagadh. When no progress was made and the situation started jeopardizing the peace and tranquillity of the entire Kathiawar region, India moved troops into the princely states adjacent to Junagadh.

In September 1947, an Arzee Hukumat (Provisional Government) was formed on behalf of the people of Junagadh, who, it was believed, overwhelmingly wanted to join the Indian Union. This government was led by Samaldas Gandhi, who was Mahatma Gandhi's nephew. Traders began to refuse to risk any business with Junagadh. Revenues and food were hard to come by. The Nawab fled to Pakistan leaving his Dewan (chief minister) Shah Nawaz Bhutto in charge.

As the on-ground situation worsened through early November 1947, the Junagadh State Council decided it was necessary to have a 'complete reorientation'[5] of the state policy and revisit the earlier decision to accede to Pakistan. The dewan accordingly opened negotiations with India 'in order to avoid bloodshed, hardship, loss of life and property'[6].

When the representatives of the Indian government entered Junagadh to take over the administration, the dewan had already left for Pakistan. The Indian government conducted a plebiscite in

---

[4]   Menon, *Integration,* pp. 85–102.
[5]   Ibid., p. 98.
[6]   Ibid.

February 1948 asking the people of Junagadh whether they wanted to join India or Pakistan. Similar referendums were held at the same time in five other areas, including Mangrol and Manavadar. The people of all the regions voted almost unanimously to join India.[7]

On 20 February 1949, the administration of Junagadh as well as that of Mangrol and Manavadar were handed over to the government of the United State of Saurashtra, completing the unification of one of the most fragmented regions of the Indian Union, one that Prime Minister Jawaharlal Nehru called 'a crazy patchwork of states'[8].

*

The Northern Third: Kutch State, 1948–56

If Saurashtra was a crazy patchwork of states, Kutch was the very opposite. A large part of the Kutch region was a wide-open expanse of white salt flats and shallow wetlands that stayed under water for most of the year.

The Kutch princely state acceded to India. The States Ministry debated merging it with Saurashtra or with the princely states of Rajasthan, but ultimately decided that direct Union government control was needed for Kutch's geographic and economic requirements. Geographically, Kutch shared a border with Pakistan and formed an important link to the rest of Saurashtra. Given the prevailing turbulent situation in Junagadh, it was important to secure and stabilize Kutch. Economically, since the large harbour of Karachi had been allocated to Pakistan, there were plans to develop the Kandla port in Kutch along with railway lines and oil installations. Kutch became a Chief Commissioner's province on 1 June 1948.[9]

---

[7]   Menon, *Integration,* p. 101.
[8]   Balraj Krishna, *India's Bismarck, Sardar Vallabhbhai Patel* (India: Indus Source Books, 2007), p. 112.
[9]   Menon, *Integration,* p. 208.

In January 1950, when the Constitution of India came into force, Kutch State became a Part C state. This classification ensured that its administration remained under the direct control of the Union government of India.

*

The Eastern Third: Gujarat States (Bombay State), 1948–56

The Eastern Gujarat region was its own patchwork of states. 144 princely states, estates, talukas and thanas were further subdivided into 289 shareholders, all of them slicing across and interspersing each other, collectively known as 'Gujarat States'.[10]

The States Ministry believed that the future of the Gujarat States lay in merging it with the state of Bombay. However, after witnessing the seamless unification of the Saurashtra patchwork, the rulers of the Gujarat States hoped they could arrive at a similar arrangement, and thereby retain their separate existence. For this, they needed the ruler of the largest among them to agree to this union. They needed Sir Pratap Singh Gaekwar, the Maharaja of Baroda.

Unfortunately, Sir Pratap Singh didn't desire such a union. Instead, he desired to create and rule as an independent ally to India in Gujarat. When this was shot down by the States Ministry, he tried to create an independent state of Baroda. This was also declined by the ministry after studying its efficacy, including parameters like state of administration and revenues. Moreover, geographically, Baroda was split into multiple territories that were themselves surrounded by Bombay State.[11]

---

[10] Ministry of States, Government of India, *White Paper on Indian States*, 1950, pp. 42–43.
[11] Menon, *Integration*, pp. 285–97.

In March 1948, nearly all the Gujarat States signed the agreement to merge with Bombay State. The few stragglers followed soon after. Only Baroda remained. But Baroda resisted.

Right through 1948, there was a lot of communication between Sir Pratap Singh and the States Ministry, including worrying matters like the depletion of the state's treasury by the Maharaja. Finally, in January 1949, the ministry's efforts paid off as Sir Pratap Singh signed the merger agreement. Baroda was merged with Bombay State officially in May 1949, completing the integration of the Eastern Gujarat region.[12]

*

Phase II: Bilingual Bombay State, 1956–60

Right from Independence, a unified state of Gujarat was always on the cards, comprising Saurashtra, Kutch and the Eastern Gujarat States, all of which currently belonged to three different states. The term 'Mahagujarat' had been coined in 1937 to refer to a unification of all the Gujarati-speaking areas. With the setting-up of the States Reorganisation Commission (SRC) in December 1953 to look into the matter of reorganizing states on a linguistic basis, it appeared that Mahagujarat could become a reality.

However, the city of Greater Bombay presented a tough decision due to its demographics. Bombay had a sizable Gujarati population that had contributed significantly to building the economic might of the city. In the reorganization, Gujarat wanted Greater Bombay City.

The other linguistic group contesting for Bombay was the Marathis. Bombay not only had a larger Marathi population, the city geographically lay within Marathi-speaking areas and drew most of

---

[12] Menon, *Integration*, pp. 285–97.

its resources from the Maharashtra hinterland. Maharashtra believed that Bombay rightfully belonged to them.

The third option lay in spinning Bombay off as an independent city-state, belonging to the people of India rather than being hitched to any one state. This was also amenable to the Gujarati population as it would maintain the independence and cosmopolitan nature of the city and, more importantly, keep it out of Maharashtra.

The matter remained inconclusive and was left to the SRC to adjudicate upon. In its report in 1955, the SRC remarked about how previous linguistic commissions, namely, the Dhar Commission and the JVP Committee, had weighed in on the matter and had suggested constituting Bombay City into a separate unit. However, while it recognized Bombay's special position, the SRC determined that it would be better to feed the interests of all rather than satisfying any one group.[13]

The SRC recommended the creation of one large bilingual Bombay State that extended from the tips of Kutch and Saurashtra in the North-west, across the mainland of the Gujarat States, and all of present-day Maharashtra including Greater Bombay City. These recommendations went against the grain of the linguistic approach the SRC had taken for the rest of the country.

On 1 November 1956, the new bilingual Bombay State came into existence. It was by far the largest Indian state, covering over 5,00,000 sq. km. of land area—nearly one-sixth of all of India.[14] If it had been a country, Bombay State would have been among the fifty largest countries by land area.[15]

Suddenly, Gujarat, which had been on a straightforward course of coalescing and establishing its identity in the Indian Union,

---

[13] Report of the States Reorganisation Commission, 1955, pp. 112–21.
[14] Government of India, Census 2011.
[15] https://www.nationmaster.com/country-info/stats/Geography/Land-area/Sq.-km

had been subsumed. The state that had once housed the smallest princely state in India now formed the northern half of the largest state in the country.

*

Phase III: Unilingual Gujarat State, 1960 onwards

This solution failed to appease either linguistic group. Rather, it intensified their demands of unilingual bifurcation. The decision-making moved to the streets with the birth of two powerful movements in 1956: the Mahagujarat Andolan (Greater Gujarat Movement) led by Indulal Yagnik (popularly known as Indu Chacha), writer, film-maker and Independence activist, and the Samyukta Maharashtra Samiti (United Maharashtra Society) led by Keshavrao Jedhe, former Congress leader.

Finally, in December 1959, the Congress Working Committee passed a resolution recommending the bifurcation of Bombay State.[16] On 1 May 1960, bilingual Bombay State was separated into the two new unilingual states of Maharashtra and Gujarat. Bombay City became the capital of Maharashtra, while Ahmedabad, the largest city in Gujarat, became its capital. However, the city of Gandhinagar was planned and built right next to Ahmedabad. In 1970, Gandhinagar was declared as the state capital of Gujarat.

The journey of the state of Gujarat was finally realized—from a crazy patchwork containing the maximum number of princely states and jurisdictions to one contiguous administrative unit; from once containing the smallest princely state in the country to becoming the fifth largest state and enjoying the longest coastline in the Indian Union.[17]

* *

---

[16] Sadhna Sharma, *States Politics in India,* (India: Mittal Publications, 1995), pp. 189–91.
[17] Government of India, Census 2011.

HARYANA

Two Communities, One State

In 1947, Haryana formed the south-eastern region of East Punjab, which itself had been formed when Punjab Province was split due to Partition. East Punjab had been Hindu-dominant but the large-scale migration of Sikhs into East Punjab as a result of Partition altered the demographics of the state. In the North-western districts of East Punjab, Sikhs (and Punjabi in Gurmukhi script) formed the majority for the first time, while in the South-eastern districts, Hindus (and Hindi in Devanagari script) continued to form the overwhelming majority.[1]

---

[1]   Baldev Raj Nayar, 'Punjab,' in *State Politics in India*, ed. Myron Weiner (United States of America: Princeton University Press, 1968), p. 444.

There was a clear economic divide between the regions as well. Punjab Province had been the richest administrative province in British India.[2] However, in East Punjab, the North-western Punjabi-speaking region not only enjoyed a more favourable climate and soil fertility, they also had higher literacy and better-developed irrigation, transportation, educational and industrial facilities. The comparative economic backwardness of the Hindi-speaking region soon led to political grievances.[3]

To further complicate the situation, East Punjab itself was not a single compact unit. Eight princely states known as the East Punjab States lay strewn across East Punjab. Patiala was the largest, greater in area, population and revenue than all the rest of the East Punjab States put together. The States Ministry even deemed Patiala as viable to stand on its own.[4] To the States Ministry, the immediate merger of these eight princely states with the larger state of East Punjab appeared impractical and mistimed. Partition and the resulting two-way migration had strained East Punjab; its administration needed to reorganize and stabilize and deal with more pressing issues like law and order and refugees rather than amalgamation of new territories. Hence, the States Ministry decided that East Punjab and the East Punjab States would be kept as separate administrative units. Since Patiala was the largest among the East Punjab States, the resulting Union was called the Patiala and East Punjab States Union (PEPSU). It existed as 'five disconnected bits'[5] encased entirely within the territory of East Punjab. The Maharajas of Patiala and Kapurthala

---

[2]   Ian Copland, 'The Master and the Maharajas: The Sikh Princes and the East Punjab Massacres of 1947,' *Modern Asian Studies*, 36(3) (July 2002) p. 657.

[3]   Nayar, 'Punjab,' pp. 444–45.

[4]   V.P. Menon, *The Story of the Integration of the Indian States* (United Kingdom: Longmans, Green and Co., 1956), p. 164.

[5]   Report of the States Reorganisation Commission, 1955, p. 147.

were appointed the Rajpramukh (Governor) and Uprajpramukh (Deputy Governor). The Union was inaugurated on 15 July 1948.

However, the first call for splitting East Punjab into two separate states had already been made by the Punjabi-speaking region. In April 1948, Master Tara Singh, the president of the Shiromani Akali Dal (SAD), made the first demand for a consolidated Punjabi Suba (Punjabi Province) comprising the North-western districts that had a Sikh and Punjabi majority.[6] Founded in 1920, the SAD was the second-oldest political party in India after the Indian National Congress (INC). It was also the first state political party.

As a result, efforts to build a ministry in PEPSU failed. The two major political parties in the region, the INC and the SAD, were both seen to represent the Hindu and Sikh communities, respectively. Both parties wanted their candidate to be the Premier. The failure to reach a consensus twice resulted in the establishment of a caretaker government in PEPSU. Eventually, in early 1949, a ministry was established with members representing the various parties. Sardar Gyan Singh Rarewala, an independent politician, was accepted by all the parties to be the Premier of PEPSU.

Moreover, a new capital had to be decided for Punjab. Lahore, the erstwhile chief administrative and cultural city of undivided Punjab was now in Pakistan. In January 1948, Prime Minister Jawaharlal Nehru declared that there was the need for establishing new towns and cities considering the heavy inflow of refugees. In March 1948, the Union government officially decided to build the entirely new city of Chandigarh as the capital of Punjab.[7]

*

[6] S.S. Bal, 'Punjab After Independence (1947–1956),' *Proceedings of the Indian History Congress,* 46 (1985), p. 419.
[7] Meeta Rajivlochan, Kavita Sharma and Chitleen K. Sethi, *Chandigarh Lifescape: Brief Social History of a Planned City* (India: Chandigarh Government Press, 1999), p. 20.

Two Regions, One State

In October 1949, as a countermeasure to the Punjabi Suba demand
put forth by the SAD, the majority INC in East Punjab proposed
the division of the province into Punjabi and Hindi zones; the
dominant language would be the medium of instruction and the
other language would be a compulsory subject. This came to be
known as the Sachar Formula (or the Sachar–Giani Formula)
after Bhim Sen Sachar, the East Punjab Premier, and Giani Kartar
Singh, a SAD leader and a minister in the Sachar government.
'Devised by two Hindus and two Sikhs'[8], the Sachar Formula
sought to retain the bilingual character of East Punjab, but 'by
accident or design'[9], it sharpened the divide in the province along
linguistic and communal lines.

The Sachar Formula generated heated controversy. Bhim Sen
Sachar lost his premiership. The SAD reworked its demand for
autonomous status as a linguistic demand. The discord between the
two communities reached such a fever pitch that Prime Minister
Jawaharlal Nehru directed that no language be recorded in the 1951
census in Punjab State. Hence, the 1951 census showed 'Hindi/
Punjabi' as a joint option.[10]

On 21 September 1953, the capital of Punjab officially
moved from Shimla to Chandigarh.[11] A couple of months later,
at the end of 1953, the Union government created the States
Reorganisation Commission (SRC) to look into the multiple calls
for state reorganization across the country. The SAD reiterated its
demand for Punjabi Suba by merging the Punjabi-speaking region
with PEPSU. Haryana leaders asked for a separate Haryana State in
the Hindi-speaking region that included certain culturally-similar

---

8   Bal, 'Punjab After Independence,' p. 418.
9   Ibid.
10 Government of India, Census of India, 1951.
11 Rajivlochan, Sharma and Sethi. *Chandigarh Lifescape*, p. 12.

western districts of Uttar Pradesh; at the very least, they asked for separation from Punjab.[12]

These proposals to divide Punjab were met with vehement opposition. The State Congress proposed Maha Punjab by integrating Punjab, PEPSU and Himachal Pradesh. The Arya Samaj and the Jana Sangh, which were the leading political and social organizations representing Hindus across both regions, proposed an even larger amalgamation that included Delhi as well.[13]

In October 1955, the SRC released its report. It decreed that there was no real language problem and there were no distinctive cultural zones in Punjab; that in the 'battle of scripts', the superstructure of Punjabi was a dialect of western Hindi, and therefore the line of demarcation between Punjabi and Hindi was 'theoretical' and 'blurred'.[14] Noting a lack of general support of the people in the area, the SRC dismissed the demands for a separate Punjabi Suba and Haryana. Instead, it favoured an enlargement of Punjab by integrating both PEPSU and Himachal Pradesh into the state for advantages of economy and efficiency of administration. In effect, the SRC's recommendations were most like the Maha Punjab proposal.[15]

Displeased with the report, the SAD led by Master Tara Singh called for a conference in February 1956 in Amritsar to coincide with the INC conference in the city. Over one lakh Sikhs assembled in a disciplined, peaceful and purposeful manner in a massive show of unity, solidarity and strength.

Soon after, the two sides reached an agreement on a regional formula. Punjab and PEPSU would be merged but not Himachal Pradesh. Punjab would be a bilingual state demarcated as per the Sachar Formula into Punjabi- and Hindi-speaking regions; the dominant language would be the medium of instruction and

---

12   Nayar, 'Punjab,' pp. 450–51.
13   Ibid.
14   Report of the States Reorganisation Commission, 1955, p. 142.
15   Ibid., pp. 140–56.

the other language would be a compulsory subject. Two regional committees would be established in the state legislature having large powers in their respective regions.[16]

On 1 November 1956, Punjab and PEPSU merged to form the single state of Punjab. Patiala ceded its capital city status to Chandigarh. The SAD and the INC put aside their previous differences and began to work together. Their combined might returned a thumping majority in the 1957 legislative assembly elections in Punjab. The incumbent chief minister, Partap Singh Kairon of the INC, was reinstated.

*

Two States, Two Union Territories

The partnership between the SAD and the INC did not last long. The SAD was dissatisfied with both the working of the regional formula and the unwillingness of the INC state government to 'enhance the status of the Punjabi language'[17]. The SAD ended its partnership with the Congress and launched a renewed movement demanding Punjabi Suba in May 1960.

Meanwhile, the demand for a separate Haryana state also strengthened. In April 1961, the Haryana Lok Samiti was formed in association with the Arya Samaj to contest the upcoming general elections. Its campaign promoted Hindi and opposed the imposition of Punjabi as well as the economic discrimination of the region by the Punjab government.[18]

---

[16] Karnail Singh Doad, 'Punjabi Suba Movement,' in *The Encyclopaedia of Sikhism, Volume III M-R*, ed. Harbans Singh (India: Punjabi University, Patiala, 1997), pp. 392–94.

[17] Paul R. Brass, *Language, Religion and Politics in North India* (United States: iUniverse, 2005), p. 321.

[18] Ibid., p. 331.

At this point, the SAD went through an ideological split. Master Tara Singh's lieutenant Sant Fateh Singh began to take centre stage by presenting a more acceptable 'linguistic and only linguistic'[19] demand for Punjabi Suba, even to Prime Minister Jawaharlal Nehru, thereby allaying apprehensions of an autonomous Sikh state. Sant Fateh Singh then directly challenged the leadership of Master Tara Singh and formed a separate Akali Dal in 1962.

In 1964, the Congress leadership underwent major changes at the state and the Centre. Prime Minister Jawaharlal Nehru died in May. Chief Minister Partap Singh Kairon was removed on corruption charges in June; he was assassinated in February the following year.

In early September 1965, the Union government agreed to appoint a cabinet subcommittee to resolve the Punjabi Suba issue. This further galvanized leaders from the Haryana and hill regions to also demand for the reorganization of Punjab. However, later that month, war broke out between India and Pakistan, in which the Sikhs contributed immensely. Following this, a government-appointed parliamentary committee reported that 'an overwhelming majority'[20] now supported linguistic reorganization, noting also the rise in support in the Haryana region.

On 18 September 1966, the government passed the Punjab Reorganisation Act. Punjab was divided into four parts—two states and two union territories. The Hindi-speaking districts in the South-eastern plains formed the new state of Haryana, while the Punjabi-speaking North-western districts formed the new Punjabi Suba, the new state of Punjab. The North-eastern hill districts merged with the existing union territory of Himachal Pradesh. The city of Chandigarh

---

[19] Gurdarshan Singh Dhillon, 'Evolution of the Demand for a Sikh Homeland,' *The Indian Journal of Political Science,* 35(4) (Oct.–Dec. 1974), p. 371.
[20] Brass, *Language,* p. 331.

was reconstituted as a union territory. It was also named the joint capital of Punjab and Haryana and would house the common high court for all three territories.[21]

All four new territories came into being from 1 November 1966.

* *

---

[21] The Punjab Reorganisation Act, 1966.

HIMACHAL PRADESH

Did You Know?

For nearly twenty years after Independence, Himachal Pradesh existed as two separate parts.

The story of Himachal Pradesh is a story of small steps leading to a large result. Over the course of nearly twenty-four years, the region progressed stage by stage, from existing as two separate parts to witnessing multiple redesignations to its status to finally emerging as one whole state.

*

1947: A Confusion of Geographies (and Names)

When India gained independence in 1947, the present state of Himachal Pradesh existed in two parts. One, as the twenty-eight East Punjab Hill States (or the Shimla Hill States); two, as the hilly north-eastern part of East Punjab which sliced through the territories of the East Punjab Hill States, splitting them into two non-contiguous units. So, in a sense, it existed in three geographical parts. Well, four, actually, because the tiny princely state of Bilaspur was a separate administrative unit. It had previously been a part of the East Punjab Hill States, but had then been taken under the direct control of the Punjab States Agency before Independence.[1]

After Partition had cut through Punjab Province, Sikhs had migrated en masse into East Punjab, making them the majority community and Punjabi the majority language in the North-western districts for the first time. In the South-eastern districts, Hindus and Hindi formed the majority.[2] Eight princely states also lay strewn across East Punjab and were known as the East Punjab States, of which Patiala was the largest.

*

1948: Himachal Pradesh is Born . . . and Nearly Dissolved

In March 1948, a number of the rulers of the East Punjab Hill States signed agreements to cede authority, jurisdiction and governance to India. On 15 April 1948, the East Punjab Hill States were reborn as Himachal Pradesh. The only wish of the rulers had been for their territories to 'be consolidated into one unit'[3], which the Government of India had agreed to. However, even though it was now one administrative unit, Himachal Pradesh continued to exist in two non-contiguous geographical areas separated by East Punjab. The geographical consolidation would take another eighteen years.

---

[1]   Jaideep Negi, 'The Begar System in the Shimla Hill States during the British Period,' *Proceedings of the Indian History Congress*, 55 (1994), p. 693.
[2]   Baldev Raj Nayar, 'Punjab,' in *State Politics in India*, ed. Myron Weiner (United States of America: Princeton University Press, 1968), p. 444.
[3]   Ministry of States, Government of India, *White Paper on Indian States*, 1950, pp. 46–47.

The Government of India determined that Himachal Pradesh ought to be a centrally administered unit so as to exercise direct and strategic control, especially in matters of administration, resources and finances. Hence, it became a chief commissioner's province.[4]

In August 1948, the ruler of Bilaspur, which was geographically contiguous with the southern part of Himachal Pradesh, also signed the agreement to accede to India. However, instead of merging Bilaspur with Himachal Pradesh, the States Ministry decided to retain Bilaspur as a separate centrally administered province so as to pay direct attention to the planning of the large Bhakra Dam over the Sutlej River. On 12 October 1948, the Raja of Bilaspur, Anand Chand, was appointed as chief commissioner of Bilaspur.

In April 1948, Master Tara Singh, president of India's second-oldest political party, the Shiromani Akali Dal (SAD) in East Punjab, made the first demand for a consolidated Punjabi Suba (Punjabi Province) comprising the North-western districts of East Punjab that had a Sikh and Punjabi majority.[5]

V.P. Menon, secretary of the States Ministry, saw four options.[6]

1. Merge Himachal Pradesh, the East Punjab States and East Punjab, but without Patiala, which was already viable by itself.
2. Merge Patiala and Himachal Pradesh into one unit and the East Punjab States and East Punjab into another unit.
3. Bring just the East Punjab States together as a single union without Patiala or Himachal Pradesh.
4. Integrate all the East Punjab States, including Patiala.

---

[4] V.P. Menon, *The Story of the Integration of the Indian States* (United Kingdom: Longmans, Green and Co., 1956), p. 207.
[5] S.S. Bal, 'Punjab After Independence (1947–1956),' *Proceedings of the Indian History Congress*, 46 (1985), p. 419.
[6] Menon, *Integration*, p. 165.

The States Ministry narrowed its options through a process of elimination. It was important to keep Himachal Pradesh as a centrally administered unit, both to develop it into a self-reliant unit and to not mix the residents of the hills and the plains into one administrative system. The immediate merger of the princely states with the province appeared impractical and mistimed.

Hence, the States Ministry decided that East Punjab, Himachal Pradesh and the East Punjab States would be kept as three separate administrative units. The Patiala and East Punjab States Union (PEPSU for short) was created as 'five disconnected bits'[7] encased entirely within the territory of East Punjab. It was inaugurated on 15 July 1948.

*

1950–56: A Part C State Constantly Gaining Privileges

In 1950, when the Constitution of India came into force, Himachal Pradesh was redesignated as a Part C state. It continued to be centrally administered with no change to its territorial boundaries.

In September 1951, Parliament passed the Government of Part C States Act. This provided for a legislative assembly and council of ministers in Himachal Pradesh and Delhi.[8] Elections were then held to the legislative assembly. The Indian National Congress (INC) won a majority of the seats and Yashwant Singh Parmar was appointed as the first chief minister of Himachal Pradesh. The position of lieutenant-governor replaced that of chief commissioner as the agent acting on behalf of the President. Major-General Kumar Shri Himmatsinhji Jadeja became the first lieutenant-governor.

On 28 May 1954, the Union government passed the Himachal Pradesh and Bilaspur (New State) Act to merge the two centrally

---

[7]   Report of the States Reorganisation Commission, 1955, p. 147.
[8]   Administrative Reforms Commission, *Report, Study Team on Administration of Union Territories and NEFA*, 1968, pp. 7–8.

administered and contiguous Part C states. This did not affect the Union government's authority over the regions or over the Bhakra-Nangal Project. The new integrated state came into being on 1 July 1954.[9]

*

1956: A Union Territory with Lost Privileges

Towards the end of 1953, spurred by the multiple calls for state reorganization across the country, the Union government announced the creation of the States Reorganisation Commission (SRC) which invited memoranda from the public, individually and collectively.

The Punjab State Congress, Arya Samaj and Jana Sangh proposed Maha Punjab which would integrate Punjab, PEPSU and Himachal Pradesh (and Delhi in the latter two proposals). The SAD reiterated its demand for Punjabi Suba which would merge PEPSU with the Punjabi-speaking North-western districts of Punjab. Leaders from the Haryana region (the Hindi-speaking South-eastern districts of Punjab) also put forth a demand for a separate Haryana State.

In October 1955, the SRC released its report in which it dismissed the demands for Punjabi Suba and Haryana. The three members of the SRC, however, disagreed on how to proceed with Himachal Pradesh. Two members recommended integration with Punjab due to clear economic and administrative advantages and 'the mutual benefit of the people of the plains and of the hills'[10]. They dismissed the proposal for the formation of a larger hill unit consisting of the hill territories of Himachal Pradesh, Punjab, PEPSU and Uttar Pradesh as not forming an administratively viable unit. The proposed

---

[9]   Government of India. The Himachal Pradesh and Bilaspur (New State) Act, 1954.
[10] Report of the States Reorganisation Commission, 1955, p. 151.

state would consist of Punjab, PEPSU and Himachal Pradesh, but without Delhi and any western districts of Uttar Pradesh.

The Chairman of the SRC, S. Fazl Ali, took a different view. In a separate note, he recommended no change in Himachal Pradesh's current status as a separate unit under the direct control of the Union government. Invoking the views of the late Sardar Vallabhbhai Patel, head of the erstwhile States Ministry that had created Himachal Pradesh, Fazl Ali felt that a merger with Punjab would be locally unpopular. The hill state still needed support for development which had to be provided by the Centre and not by Punjab. Further, Punjab already had three distinct regions with its own language and communal issues which didn't exist in Himachal Pradesh.[11]

The SAD and the INC then agreed on a regional formula. PEPSU would be merged into Punjab, which would be a bilingual state demarcated into Punjabi- and Hindi-speaking regions. Haryana would not be created. Himachal Pradesh would continue to exist as before as two separate regions with no geographical boundary changes.[12]

The SRC also recommended doing away with the existing classification of states. Regarding Part C states in general, it observed that the arrangement was 'ad hoc . . . unsatisfactory and cannot be continued indefinitely'[13], and that they ought to either be centrally administered or merged with adjoining states. Regarding Himachal Pradesh specifically, the States Reorganisation Bill determined that 'while ultimately Himachal Pradesh has to form a part of the Punjab, it may for the present be continued as a centrally administered unit'.[14]

---

[11] S. Fazl Ali, 'Note on Himachal Pradesh,' Report of the States Reorganisation Commission, 1955, pp. 238–43.
[12] Karnail Singh Doad, 'Punjabi Suba Movement,' in *The Encyclopaedia of Sikhism, Volume III M–R*, ed. Harbans Singh (India: Punjabi University, Patiala, 1997), pp. 392–94.
[13] Report of the States Reorganisation Commission, 1955, p. 72.
[14] Manjit Singh Ahluwalia, *Social, Cultural, and Economic History of Himachal Pradesh* (India: Indus Publishing Company, 1998), p. 36.

On 1 November 1956, all Part C states, including Himachal Pradesh, were redesignated as union territories. The position of chief minister was abolished. Instead, charge was handed over to Lieutenant-Governor Raja Bajrang Bahadur Singh as the agent acting on behalf of the President of India.[15] Further, Parliament enacted the Territorial Councils Act which dissolved and replaced the legislative assembly in Himachal Pradesh with a territorial council. The council was meant to provide a measure of local self-government with powers over local affairs like education, public health and roads.[16]

*

1963: A First-class Union Territory

In 1961, the Centre constituted a committee headed by the Union Law Minister, Ashoke Kumar Sen, to study the administrative set-up in the union territories. In its June 1962 report, the committee recommended that 'the largest possible measure of autonomy should be granted'[17] while retaining Union control over finance and general policy. While it suggested the introduction of panchayati raj as well as the transfer of more subjects to the territorial councils, the union territories demanded legislative bodies.

In 1962, Goa, Daman & Diu and Pondicherry were integrated into India as union territories, and the State of Nagaland Act was passed. This inspired the Union government to go above and beyond the recommendations of the Ashoke Sen Committee. It passed the Constitution (Fourteenth Amendment) Act, 1962, and then the Government of Union Territories Act, 1963, which established legislative assemblies and councils of ministers and abolished

---

[15] Ahluwalia, *Himachal Pradesh.*

[16] Administrative Reforms Commission, *Report, Study Team on Administration of Union Territories and NEFA,* 1968, pp. 9–10.

[17] Ibid., pp. 11–13.

territorial councils in five union territories—Manipur, Tripura, Himachal Pradesh, Goa and Pondicherry. A throwback to the pre-SRC Government of Part C States Act of 1951, this Act created two classes of union territories. While the President still retained regulation-making powers over the second class[18], the first class, consisting of these five union territories, were seen as being independent stand-alone entities. Their legislative assemblies had powers and responsibilities similar to the state legislative assemblies, including the ability to make laws on subjects in the Union and Concurrent lists. They even had separate consolidated and contingency funds.[19] Yashwant Singh Parmar returned as chief minister of Himachal Pradesh. Statehood was now a distinct possibility.

*

1966: A Unified Territory

In March 1966, following a change in Congress leadership at the Centre and in Punjab as well as a war with Pakistan in September 1965 in which the Sikhs contributed immensely, the Union government appointed a Parliamentary Committee to look into reorganizing Punjab. The Committee reported that 'an overwhelming majority'[20] now supported linguistic reorganization, noting also the rise in support in the Haryana region.

On 18 September 1966, the government passed the Punjab Reorganisation Act. Punjab was divided into four parts—two states and two union territories. The Punjabi-speaking North-western

---

[18] Administrative Reforms Commission, *Report, Study Team on Administration of Union Territories and NEFA*, 1968, pp. 11–13.
[19] Ibid.
[20] Paul R. Brass, *Language, Religion and Politics in North India* (United States: iUniverse, 2005), p. 331.

districts formed the new Punjabi Suba, the new state of Punjab. The Hindi-speaking districts in the South-eastern plains formed the new state of Haryana. The North-eastern hill districts of Punjab were integrated into Himachal Pradesh, thereby approximately doubling the union territory's area and population. It also made Himachal Pradesh one contiguous unit—a geographically unified union territory for the first time in its history. The city of Chandigarh was reconstituted as a union territory and also named the joint capital of Punjab and Haryana.[21]

All four new territories came into being from 1 November 1966.

*

1971: Statehood

In 1965, before reorganization, the Pradesh Congress Committee of Himachal Pradesh had passed a resolution demanding statehood for the first time. In September 1966, while the Punjab Reorganisation Bill was being debated in Parliament, the lack of change in the status of Himachal Pradesh was raised. In July 1967, the Himachal Pradesh legislative assembly adopted a unanimous resolution asking for statehood as 'a just demand of the Himachalis'[22].

Eventually, on 25 December 1970, Parliament passed the State of Himachal Pradesh Act to grant statehood. On 25 January 1971, Himachal Pradesh's status was changed from union territory to state. The position of lieutenant-governor was replaced by that of Governor.

* *

---

[21]   Government of India. The Punjab Reorganisation Act, 1966.
[22]   Ahluwalia, *Himachal Pradesh*, p. 41.

JHARKHAND

Did You Know?

An official resolution supporting the creation of Jharkhand was passed three years before the state was created.

Early Demands and Refusals

In 1947, the present state of Jharkhand (literally meaning 'forest region'[1]) formed the southern half of the state of Bihar. The idea of a separate adivasi[2] state had been floated as early as the 1920s.

In the late 1930s, various organizations that promoted education and economic development among adivasis had come together to form the Adivasi Mahasabha, led by Jaipal Singh Munda, who was a tribal rights activist as well as an Olympic gold-medallist (and later

---

[1] Louise Tillin, *Remapping India: New States and Their Political Origins* (New Delhi: Oxford University Press, 2013), pp. 70–71.
[2] Note: Adivasi literally means 'original dweller' and is usually collectively used to refer to members of tribes in India.

a member of the constituent assembly).[3] After Independence, the
Adivasi Mahasabha ensured that the issue of Jharkhand was debated
and discussed in the constituent assembly. The constituent assembly's
scope of work did not include the creation of a separate state, but they
did invite 'urgency of action'[4] from the state and Union governments.
They felt that the problem of administration had to be dealt with
economically, educationally, politically, as well as psychologically.

As India's first elections approached in 1951–52, the Adivasi
Mahasabha was renamed the Jharkhand Party. It performed well,
winning thirty-two seats in the Bihar Assembly. As the second-largest
party in the assembly, it secured the position of the main opposition
party. The Indian National Congress (INC) formed the government
as the largest party in the assembly.[5] This electoral verdict seemed to
give weight to the proposal of a new state of Jharkhand.

However, the States Reorganisation Commission (SRC) rejected
the proposal in its 1955 report on numerous grounds. Electorally,
it cited the fact that the Jharkhand Party had failed to secure a clear
majority in the concerned regions of the Chota Nagpur division and
the Santhal Parganas in south Bihar. Demographically, it mentioned
that tribals made up only one-third of the total population and the
region consisted of several language groups, thereby making any
decision in favour of Jharkhand a minority-based one. Economically,
the region provided an industrial balance to the agriculture-
dominant plains in north Bihar as it contained coalfields, 40 per cent
of India's mineral wealth, a steel plant at Jamshedpur, and Bihar's
biggest thermal power plant at Bokaro, apart from a number of other
projects. Finally, it also referenced the volume of opposition outside
south Bihar to dividing the state. The SRC recommended that a

---

[3]   Tillin, *Remapping India*, pp. 70–71.
[4]   Final Report, Annexure VII, Appendix D, *Constituent Assembly Debates
Official Report* (New Delhi: Lok Sabha Secretariat, 2014), p. 178.
[5]   Statistical Report on General Election, 1951 to the Legislative Assembly
of Bihar Election Commission of India.

special development board, and not statehood, be considered for the region.[6]

*

A Political Jharkhand before a Territorial Jharkhand

In 1963, the Jharkhand Party merged with the INC and left a temporary vacuum in the campaign for Jharkhand statehood. In 1972, the Jharkhand Mukti Morcha (JMM) was established by A.K. Roy (a Bengali–Marxist trade unionist), Shibu Soren (a Santal tribal leader), and Binod Bihari Mahato (a Kurmi–Mahato leader). Through the 1970s and 1980s, the JMM led the campaign for statehood while also pursuing a wider agenda of social activism that focused on the marginalization of local people and the assertion of an adivasi identity. These included movements like the 'dhan katao andolan' (cut down paddy movement) to reclaim tribal land and the 'jungle katao andolan' (cut down the forest movement) to protest against state forestry policies. These activities helped develop the consciousness of a political Jharkhand as a precursor to a territorial Jharkhand.[7]

Political developments aided the consolidation of this idea. In 1977, the Janata Party came to power both in the state and at the Centre. The new Bihar chief minister, Karpoori Thakur, reserved a proportion of the posts in government and educational institutions for Other Backward Castes (OBCs). The Janata Party nationally had been vocal about the need to reorganize state boundaries so as to correct economic imbalances and enable administrative convenience, even calling for a second SRC. However, while his national leadership was for it, the chief minister himself was opposed to the idea of Jharkhand.[8] This resulted in a faction of party politicians

---

[6] Report of the States Reorganisation Commission, 1955, pp. 168–71.
[7] Tillin, *Remapping India*, pp. 75–76.
[8] Ibid., p. 79.

rebelling. The rebel faction set up a 'Sangharsh Samiti' (Struggle Committee) and passed a resolution in September 1977 calling for the establishment of a separate state in south Bihar.[9]

In 1980, the INC returned to power in Bihar and at the Centre. The Congress began to co-opt some of the JMM's platforms, and even agreed to a seat-sharing arrangement with Shibu Soren. This led to a formal split in the JMM by the end of 1984. The new Prime Minister of India, Rajiv Gandhi of the INC, appeared more sympathetic toward regional movements across the country. Congress politicians from the Jharkhand region raised a demand to declare the region as a centrally administered union territory—usually a possible first step toward eventual statehood. However, these Congress plans were quickly scuttled by a counter-movement that brought the question of statehood back to the fore.[10]

*

A Cultural Jharkhandi Identity

In the vacuum left by the splintering of the JMM, the All Jharkhand Students Union (AJSU) was established in June 1986. This was a more radical student wing of the JMM led by Surya Singh Besra, a Santal adivasi. In July 1986, local activists of diverse backgrounds established the Jharkhand Coordination Committee (JCC) to change the statehood conversation to a cultural Jharkhandi identity issue rather than a minority tribal question. A revivalist movement for recognizing Jharkhand as a cultural region emerged. Economics mixed with identity.[11]

By the late 1980s, the demand for Jharkhand statehood had attracted the attention and support of a rising national party—the Bharatiya Janata Party (BJP). The BJP proposed the districts in south

9   Tillin, *Remapping India*, pp. 79–80.
10 Ibid., pp. 81–82.
11 Ibid., pp. 82–84.

Bihar become the state of Vananchal, named after the 'van' (forests) and their dwellers in the region.[12] This also brought in support from non-adivasi sections of society, thereby helping create a convergence of regional opinion in favour of statehood.

The JCC then revived an older demand of the Jharkhand movement—Greater Jharkhand. They presented a memorandum to the President of India in December 1987 demanding twenty-one districts from the four surrounding states of Bihar, Madhya Pradesh, Orissa and West Bengal. Along with the AJSU, they pushed for statehood more aggressively, utilizing more direct-action methods like mass rallies, economic blockades and general strikes.[13]

The aggression paid off. In August 1989, following a series of meetings with leaders of the movement, the Congress government at the Centre agreed to establish the Committee on Jharkhand Matters (COJM) comprising representatives from Jharkhand, Bihar and the Centre. However, this was interrupted when the Rajiv Gandhi-led Congress government lost in the Lok Sabha elections later that year. A new National Front coalition government was formed, led by the Janata Dal and supported by the BJP. The eventual COJM report in 1990 acknowledged the near consensus on the need for regional autonomy, but recommended the formation of an elected Jharkhand General Council rather than a Jharkhand State. This proposal was rejected by the Jharkhand movement members.

*

A Political Tug-of-war

The first half of the 1990s was a period of political turmoil. After the BJP withdrew support to the National Front government at the centre, a Congress government came to power. This was not suitable

---

[12] Tillin, *Remapping India*, p. 87.
[13] Ibid., p. 84.

for the Lalu Prasad Yadav-led Janata Dal government in Bihar, which emboldened BJP leaders in Bihar to demand the creation of Jharkhand more vociferously. The Congress government, in turn, first demanded the withdrawal of their former ally, the JMM, from the state government. This led to a split in the JMM. In 1994, the Bihar State government agreed to establish a Jharkhand Autonomous Area Council (JAAC).[14]

Through the second half of the 1990s, the Bihar government was still formed by Lalu Prasad Yadav and his now-named Rashtriya Janata Dal (RJD). In 1997, his wife Rabri Devi took over as chief minister of Bihar and introduced a resolution supporting the creation of Jharkhand. This was meant to be a short-term tactical move in order to garner support from MLAs from the region.[15]

In 1998, the BJP led by Atal Bihari Vajpayee headed the National Democratic Alliance (NDA) coalition government at the Centre. Its election campaign had included the creation of Jharkhand as well as the imposition of President's rule in Bihar.[16] Claiming a conspiracy to divide Bihar, the RJD withdrew its resolution to create Jharkhand in September 1998 and rejected the Bihar Reorganisation Bill.[17]

Although the Union government had failed to impose President's rule in Bihar, the BJP's influence had grown significantly with the unravelling of the JMM. BJP politicians in north Bihar now began to actively support separation. They argued that the creation of Jharkhand would benefit north Bihar for industrial and agricultural development. In December 1998, a bill to create Jharkhand was tabled in the Lok Sabha. Despite a sudden general election in 1999, the BJP returned to form a more secure coalition government at the Centre.

---

[14]   Tillin, *Remapping India*, pp. 91–94.
[15]   Ibid., p. 163.
[16]   Ibid., p. 164.
[17]   Ibid.

In the Bihar assembly elections in February 2000, the RJD was re-elected with the support of the Congress, who were also allied with the JMM in the Jharkhand region. This three-way alliance enabled progress to be made towards the creation of the state of Jharkhand. In April 2000, the Bihar Reorganisation Bill was formally signed in the Bihar Legislative Assembly. The bill contained an amendment that would name the new state as 'Jharkhand' and not as 'Vananchal'.

In August 2000, the Bihar Reorganisation Act was passed by both the Lok Sabha and Rajya Sabha at the Centre and received Presidential assent. On 15 November 2000, the state of Jharkhand was born. It comprised eighteen districts from the southern region of the erstwhile Bihar state. Based on the results of the February 2000 Bihar elections, the BJP formed the first state government in Jharkhand with Babulal Marandi as the first chief minister.

* *

KARNATAKA

> **Did You Know?**
>
> *Karnataka did not have a coastline until 1956.*

The Jigsaw Puzzle of Karnataka

The different pieces that form the state of Karnataka came together physically over a period of nearly ten years. 150 years of divisive British administration policies in the region had scattered Kannada speakers over a wide number of different administrative regions— up to twenty, by some estimates. At the time of Independence in 1947, the five largest and most influential administrations that held Kannada speakers were (in no particular order):

- Mysore State (Kannada-dominant);
- Hyderabad State (Urdu- and Telugu-dominant);
- Madras Presidency (Tamil- and Telugu-dominant);
- Bombay Presidency (Marathi-dominant);
- Coorg (Kodava- and Kannada-dominant).[1]

---

[1] Government of India, Census India, Karnataka Administrative Divisions, 1872–2001.

However, while they had been physically separated, the singular thread of Kannada continued to bind them together. In 1920, the Ekikarana Movement, whose objective was the unification of all the Kannada-speaking regions, passed a resolution calling for the same. In the same year, the Indian National Congress (INC)—then the largest and most influential representative of the Indian people— accepted the linguistic redistribution of provinces as 'a clear political objective'[2] at its session in Nagpur. In 1927, the INC expressed the opinion that Andhra, Utkal, Sind and Karnataka could be constituted into separate provinces on the basis of the people speaking the same language and following the same traditions and culture.[3] At its Calcutta session in 1937 and in its 1938 Wardha resolution, the INC recommended the formation of Andhra and Karnataka and assured to undertake it as soon as they had the power to do so.[4] The linguistic and cultural basis for constituting administrative provinces was included in the Congress election manifesto of 1945–46.[5]

*

Piece 1/6: The Princely State of Mysore, 1947 (Nine Districts)

The most urgent matter at hand for the newly-birthed Union of India was to ensure accession and allegiance of all the princely states, since they had all been given the option to decide their own fate—to join India, to join Pakistan, or to remain independent.

The princely state of Mysore was one of the first to accede to integrate with the Union of India. The then-Maharaja,

---

[2]   Report of the States Reorganisation Commission, 1955, p. 13.
[3]   Ibid.
[4]   Ibid., p. 14.
[5]   Ibid.

Jayachamarajendra Wodeyar, twenty-eight years old at the time of Independence, signed in quick succession and with no fuss the Instrument of Accession and the Standstill Agreement. The constituent assembly set up to frame a constitution for the state recommended adopting the Indian Constitution.[6] The region was renamed Mysore State and was classified as a Part B state. Maharaja Jayachamarajendra Wodeyar was appointed Rajpramukh (Governor).

The first physical piece of Karnataka had been placed on the map, containing nine districts. Now, the other pieces needed to be attached to form a unified Karnataka. However, a problem arose. Mysore State no longer desired unification with the less-prosperous districts to its north.

*

Piece 2/6: Bellary, 1953 (One District)

The intellectual epicentres of the Ekikarana Movement were almost entirely in the arid districts situated in Bombay State and Hyderabad State, while the economic wealth rested in Mysore State in the south. Moreover, the two regions were split across religious lines, with Vokkaligas forming the majority in Mysore State and Lingayats forming the majority in the regions outside Mysore State. Hence, to avoid straining its resources and diluting its wealth and political influence, Mysore State advocated creating a separate Kannada State by combining all the northern districts, essentially creating two Karnatakas.

The unification of Karnataka was further hampered by the new position of the INC post-Independence. Prime Minister Jawaharlal Nehru maintained that 'this would obviously be the wrong time'[7]

---

6   V.P. Menon, *The Story of the Integration of the Indian States,* (United Kingdom: Longmans, Green and Co., 1956), pp. 203–05.

7   Ramachandra Guha, *India After Gandhi: The History of the World's Largest Democracy* (United Kingdom: Macmillan, 2017).

to form linguistic provinces, as desirable as they may be, since consolidation of the country was more important. In its December 1948 report, the Linguistic Provinces Commission, also known as the Dhar Commission, recommended against a linguistic reorganization. The JVP Committee set up to study the recommendations of the Dhar Commission also rejected a linguistic redrawing of the borders in April 1949. This committee carried considerable weight as its members were possibly the three most powerful people in the country then—Jawaharlal Nehru (Prime Minister of India), Vallabhbhai Patel (Deputy Prime Minister of India) and Pattabhi Sitaramayya (Congress President).

The 1951 election manifesto of the Congress declared that the wishes of the people concerned would play a major role in the decision to reorganize states, but so would non-linguistic factors, like economic, administrative and financial.[8] The reticence of Mysore State in integrating with the districts to its north stalled the proposal for the formation of a larger unified Karnataka State.

To the east of Mysore State, the Telugu population of Madras Presidency began to demand a separate state for themselves. Their protests succeeded and on 1 October 1953, the new Andhra State was created out of the eleven northern districts of Madras State. As a result of the creation of Andhra State, nearly the entire district of Bellary, which had been a part of Madras State, was integrated with Mysore State.[9] This gave Mysore State its tenth district as well as a state border with Hyderabad State.

The creation of Andhra State rippled across the country and led the government to set up a States Reorganisation Commission (SRC) a mere two months later to look into redrawing state boundaries for

---

[8]   Report of the States Reorganisation Commission, 1955, p. 17.
[9]   'Transfer of Territory from Madras to Mysore,' Section 4, The Andhra State Act, 1953.

the entire country. The SRC published its report towards the end of 1955 with recommendations for every state.

Regarding Mysore State (or what the SRC called 'Karnataka'), it viewed the opposition to unification as recent and tentative. Deeming that the majority were in favour of unification, it suggested the creation of a single unified Karnataka State. On the basis of this report, the States Reorganisation Act was passed and came into force on 1 November 1956, giving Mysore State its remaining jigsaw pieces from four different administrative regions. 1 November is also celebrated as Rajyotsava Day (State Festival Day) across the state to celebrate its formation.

*

Piece 3/6: Bombay Karnataka, 1956 (Four Districts)

The four districts of the Bombay–Karnataka region to be integrated were Belgaum, Bijapur, Dharwar and North Canara. These districts were some of the intellectual epicentres that had birthed and sustained the Ekikarana Movement, which had been instrumental in the birth of a unified Karnataka. Now, they formed the northern districts of Mysore State. The district of North Canara also gave the previously landlocked Mysore State its northern coastline.

*

Piece 4/6: Hyderabad Karnataka, 1956 (Three Districts)

When the States Reorganisation Act was enacted, the shape of nearly every state changed. Some got larger, some smaller, and some states ceased to exist entirely. Hyderabad State fell in the last category. It was apportioned into three sections and attached to neighbouring states. The Telugu-dominant southern districts went to Andhra State, the Marathi-dominant western districts went to Bombay State, and the three Kannada-dominant South-western districts of Raichur, Gulbarga and Bidar integrated with Mysore State.

In addition to celebrating Rajyotsava Day on 1 November, these districts also celebrate Liberation Day on 17 September every year to commemorate the date in 1948 when Hyderabad State was integrated into the Union of India. On the seventy-second Liberation Day in 2019, the name of the Hyderabad–Karnataka region was officially changed to Kalyana Karnataka.[10]

*

Piece 5/6: South Canara, 1956 (One District)

Madras State, which had already given Bellary to Mysore State in 1953, now also gave up South Canara district and a taluk of Coimbatore district. This gave Mysore State its southern coastline and took it from being a landlocked state to having the seventh-longest coastline in the country.

*

Piece 6/6: Coorg, 1956 (One District)

At the time of Independence in 1947, Coorg was a province. It continued as Coorg Province in the Union of India until 1950, when it became Coorg State in the Republic of India. It was given the status of a Part C state, meaning it would be centrally administered by the President of India through a chief commissioner appointed as an acting agent.

---

[10] B.S. Yediyurappa, 'Kalyana Karnataka: Harking Back to a Humanist History,' *The Hindu*, 17 September 2019, https://www.thehindu.com/news/national/karnataka/kalyana-karnataka-harking-back-to-a-humanist-history/article29433502.ece

The SRC grappled with the issue of Part C states as a whole, a set-up that they found unsatisfactory. Most Part C states were very small in size. While this gave them an advantage in running a more personal and nimble administration, that was outweighed by concerns of personal fiefdoms and heavier-than-required economic costs. In fact, the SRC felt that Coorg was the only Part C state that had been able to independently carry on 'a reasonable system of administration without central assistance'[11].

Further, most Part C states had a cultural, linguistic and economic link with an adjoining larger state. This was the case with Coorg as well. It was smaller and more lightly populated than many districts. Kannada-speaking people formed 35 per cent of its population, larger than even Kodava-speakers at 29 per cent (which was considered by some authorities to be a dialect of Kannada).[12] Culturally, Coorg was seen by the SRC to have more links with Karnataka than with Kerala (who had also put forward a claim on Coorg). Geographically, Coorg formed a part of Malnad which belonged essentially to Karnataka, in the view of the SRC. Moreover, the 1948 Dhar Commission had also suggested that a unified Karnataka State would help solve the problem of Coorg's 'difficult and isolated existence'[13].

And so, Coorg was integrated into Mysore State. To respect the distinct identity of its people, Coorg was demarcated as a separate district.

*

Naming Karnataka, 1973

Even though the state had been unified and the jigsaw puzzle completed, its official name was still Mysore State, named after the first piece of

[11] Report of the States Reorganisation Commission, 1955, p. 71.
[12] Ibid., p. 97.
[13] Ibid.

the jigsaw puzzle. After the States Reorganisation Act, 1956, the area of the state and the number of districts it contained had doubled. The name 'Mysore State' didn't resonate as much with the newer districts.[14] Moreover, the northern districts had been instrumental in founding and propagating the Karnataka Ekikarana Movement.

And so, on 1 November 1973, the eighteenth Karnataka Rajyotsava Day, Chief Minister Devaraj Urs renamed Mysore State as Karnataka.[15]

**

[14] 'Mysore, an Indian State, is Renamed as Karnataka,' *The New York Times*, 30 July 1972, p. 44, https://www.nytimes.com/1972/07/30/archives/mysore-an-indian-state-is-renamed-as-karnataka.html

[15] Bernard Weinraub, 'Indian State Sets New Course,' *The New York Times*, 2 Nov. 1973, p. 2, https://www.nytimes.com/1973/11/02/archives/indian-state-sets-new-course-pride-and-sentiment-area-has-rich-past.html

KERALA

As India's Independence approached, Kerala existed as three separate regions—Travancore, Cochin and Malabar. Although there was a general consensus that all three regions ought to be merged to form one state, the actual process of integration could occur only over two stages.

*

The United State of Travancore–Cochin

The princely state of Travancore was the southernmost of the three. Even though it was ruled by the young Sree Chithira Thirunal Balarama Varma, it already had an elected legislature with limited powers. On 11 June 1947, Travancore's chief minister, Dewan Sir C.P. Ramaswami Aiyar, announced that Travancore had decided to set itself up as an independent sovereign state. The secretary of the States Ministry, V.P. Menon, met Sir C.P. and impressed upon him the plan of accession on just three subjects without any other commitments. By the end of July, the Maharaja of Travancore had agreed to accept the Instrument of Accession and the Standstill Agreement.

To the north of Travancore lay the princely state of Cochin ruled by the aged Kerala Varma Thampuran. Cochin already had had a legislative council with an elected majority since the mid-1920s. On the eve of Independence, the Maharaja transferred greater areas of the administration to elected representatives. He also called for the formation of an Aikya Keralam (Unified Kerala) by merging the three regions that shared a common culture and language—Travancore, Cochin and Malabar.[1]

V.P. Menon felt similarly, noting that the people of Travancore and Cochin 'are of the same stock, speak the same language, and have a common culture and tradition'[2]. There were also geographical and commercial contiguities.

However, Aikya Keralam was not an immediate possibility, given the Centre's hesitance at the time in creating linguistic provinces. The Linguistic Provinces Commission—popularly known as the Dhar Commission after its chairman S.K. Dhar—set up in 1948 to explore the feasibility of reorganizing states linguistically, recommended postponing the matter for a few years. A follow-up JVP Committee—named after its members Prime Minister

---

[1] K. Pradeep, 'How the Cochin Maharaja, Aikya Keralam Thampuran Played a Pivotal Role in Unification of Kerala and of Cochin State's Accession to the Indian Union,' *The Hindu*, 15 Aug. 2019, https://www.thehindu.com/society/history-and-culture/how-the-cochin-maharaja-aikya-keralam-thampuran-played-a-pivotal-role-in-unification-of-kerala-and-of-cochin-states-accession-to-the-indian-union/article29099822.ece

[2] V.P. Menon, *The Story of the Integration of the Indian States* (United Kingdom: Longmans, Green and Co., 1956), p. 189.

Jawaharlal Nehru, head of the States Ministry Vallabhbhai Patel and Congress president Pattabhi Sittaramaya—also cautioned against the 'disintegrative effects of reorganisation'[3].

The States Ministry favoured the more immediate practical policy of forming unions of states. Hence, V.P. Menon began a series of meetings with the Maharajas of Travancore and Cochin to iron out all the issues that stood in the way of merging the two states. Even though Travancore and Cochin had been among the first states to accede to India, their union was among the last to be created.

The United State of Travancore–Cochin was inaugurated by V.P. Menon himself on 1 July 1949. The Maharaja of Travancore (the bigger state in revenue and status) became the Rajpramukh (Governor) while the Maharaja of Cochin became the Uprajpramukh (Deputy Governor). The city of Trivandrum (now officially known as Thiruvananthapuram) in Travancore became the capital while the high court sat in the city of Cochin (now officially known as Kochi).

*

1956: Aikya Kerala

Responding to multiple calls from across the country to redraw state boundaries, the Union government set up the States Reorganisation Commission (SRC) in 1953 to examine the issue. At the end of 1955, the SRC released its report and most of its recommendations were passed in 1956 in the States Reorganisation Act. The SRC considered language as the key factor in determining additions and subtractions to Travancore–Cochin State.

---

[3] Asha Sarangi and Sudha Pai, 'Introduction: Contextualising Reorganisation,' in *Interrogating Reorganisation of States: Culture, Identity and Politics in India,* ed. Asha Sarangi (India: Routledge, 2020), p. 7.

The coastal region of Malabar sat immediately north to Travancore–Cochin State but formed the 'somewhat isolated'[4] western part of Madras State. Since it shared much more with Travancore–Cochin State geographically, linguistically and commercially, the SRC recommended merging it to form a new state of Kerala. The Kasaragod taluk of South Canara was also transferred in, while five Tamil-speaking taluks in the extreme south were transferred out to Madras State.

The Amindivi island group, which today forms the northern part of the union territory of Lakshadweep, was administratively under South Canara. Meanwhile, the southern Laccadive island group was already a part of Malabar district. The SRC recommended putting both island groups under the administrative care of Kerala.[5] However, on considerations of security and development, the Union government decided to constitute the islands as a union territory under the direct care of the President of India who would act through an administrator. The jurisdiction of the Kerala High Court extended to the union territory, though.

The new state of Kerala came into being on 1 November 1956. Although the state was under President's rule at the time, the first assembly elections were held the following year. E.M.S. Namboodiripad of the Communist Party of India (CPI) was elected as the chief minister.

* *

---

[4]   Report of the States Reorganisation Commission, 1955, p. 85.
[5]   Ibid., p. 86.

MADHYA PRADESH

Did You Know?

The pre-Independence English name for the largest region in Madhya Pradesh also meant the same—'Central Provinces'.

Phase I: Bringing Together Central India

In 1947, central India was an intertwined mesh of a number of princely states and British provinces. The States Ministry's vision for the region was to 'have as large an administrative unit'[1] as possible. Over the course of the next ten years, the region coalesced into Madhya Pradesh—the largest Indian state by area. As a first step to begin the process, the States Ministry created four administrative regions that would, in some cases, unite quarrelling neighbours.

*

---

[1] V.P. Menon, *The Story of the Integration of the Indian States,* (United Kingdom: Longmans, Green and Co., 1956), p. 156.

Region 1: Central Provinces/Madhya Pradesh

The foundation of the large administrative unit the States Ministry hoped to establish in central India lay in the British province called 'Central Provinces and Berar'. Upon Indian Independence, all British provinces transferred directly to the Dominion of India, while the princely states had to be convinced. And so, Central Provinces and Berar transferred to India on 15 August 1947.

To the east of the Central Provinces lay a smattering of fifteen minor princely states, known as the Chhattisgarh states. They were a part of the Eastern States Agency which consisted of forty-two princely states. In August 1947, the members of the Eastern States Agency came together to form the Eastern States Union. However, two of the biggest states—Mayurbhanj and Bastar—along with some of the smaller states, refused to join. By November 1947, the States Ministry had decided that the Union government would not recognize the Eastern States Union due to linguistic and administrative irregularities. The Orissa states would be merged into Orissa Province, and the Chhattisgarh states into Central Provinces and Berar.[2]

This decision drew mixed reactions from the rulers of the Eastern States Union. In the middle of December 1947, Sardar Vallabhbhai Patel and V.P. Menon met first the rulers of the Orissa states and then the Chhattisgarh states. They apprised them of the law and order unrest in their states and the people's desire to have a responsible government. Within two days, all the rulers had signed the agreement. The fifteen Chhattisgarh states were merged into Central Provinces and Berar.[3]

On 26 January 1950, when the Indian Constitution came into force, Central Provinces and Berar was renamed as Madhya Pradesh. Nagpur was its capital.

*

---

[2]   Menon, *Integration*, pp. 106–15.
[3]   Ibid.

Region 2: Madhya Bharat

The first of the quarrelsome neighbours to be united were the important princely states of Gwalior and Indore, ruled by the Scindia and Holkar families, respectively. Both were highly ranked states under British rule, Gwalior being a twenty-one-gun salute state and Indore a nineteen-gun salute state. Both had managed their finances well enough to be self-sufficient, creating trusts and investment funds. The Maharaja of Gwalior, Sir George Jivaji Rao Scindia, was the first ruler among the five big states in India to agree to integration and to grant responsible government.

Another twenty-three smaller princely states interspersed the large tracts of land that comprised Gwalior and Indore, producing an 'extraordinary interlacing of jurisdictions', 'a veritable jumble'.[4] Together, these twenty-five princely states geographically occupied the plateau of Malwa. The prevailing language across all states was Hindi, and culturally and economically, too, Malwa formed one compact unit—'a homogeneous tract'.[5]

The scattered nature of the smaller princely states in the region made it impossible to integrate them into a cohesive, contiguous unit without involving the larger states of Gwalior and Indore. However, the States Ministry had already given an assurance that viable states that could stand independently would not be touched, and both Gwalior and Indore were viable states. Thus began a period of delicate diplomacy by the two stalwarts of the States Ministry— Sardar Vallabhbhai Patel and V.P. Menon.

First, V.P. Menon met the Maharaja of Gwalior in February 1948 where he pitched the idea of a combined Union, including Gwalior and Indore. Although the suggestion shocked the Maharaja at first, he saw the merit in the idea once V.P. Menon pointed out to him how a Union that had Indore but not Gwalior could only

---

[4]   Menon, *Integration*, p. 155.
[5]   Ibid.

be detrimental to Gwalior in the long run. Indore was in favour of joining the Union only if the capital was located at Indore. Menon organized a joint meeting with the two Maharajas, the first such after many years, where they accepted the proposed Union in principle.

However, following this, both Gwalior and Indore had second thoughts as they were worried about their respective states losing their identities in the new Union. Hence, their counter pitch was to form two separate Unions. Since both Gwalior and Indore were already viable states, the smaller states could be integrated into one or the other, thereby creating two larger and stronger Unions, an arrangement that could be reviewed after ten years.

Such an arrangement would have theoretically served the purpose of the States Ministry. However, the consequences of creating two Unions could have rippled through the country, with other similarly large states, such as Patiala, Bikaner and Udaipur, demanding Unions centred around themselves instead of integrating and merging into larger Unions. Moreover, one Union would result in better geographical integrity and administrative efficiency. Finally, the resistance to merging into one would be stronger after ten years of living separately. Hence, the States Ministry decided to push forward with creating a single Union.

This created a stalemate as the two states vehemently opposed merging into one. To break the deadlock, V.P. Menon now arranged for the two Maharajas to meet with Sardar Patel. This worked like a charm and both states accepted his advice to merge into one Union.

The new Union—the largest then created—was inaugurated by Prime Minister Jawaharlal Nehru on 28 May 1948. It was named 'United State of Gwalior, Indore and Malwa (Madhya Bharat)' in order to retain the identities of the two states. However, it was referred to primarily as 'Madhya Bharat' or 'Malwa Union'. The Maharaja of Gwalior was made the Rajpramukh (Governor) and the Maharaja of Indore, Sir Yeshwant Rao Holkar, was made the Senior Uprajpramukh (Senior Deputy Governor). Gwalior would be the winter capital for six-and-a-half months and Indore the summer capital for five-and-a-half months of the year.[6]

*

Region 3: Vindhya Pradesh

The second of the quarrelsome neighbours to be united were the thirty-five states of Bundelkhand and Baghelkhand. This was a region rich in agriculture and forest wealth but underdeveloped in terms of road and railway communications. Rewa was the largest, most populated, and most financially well-off state of Baghelkhand, so much so that it almost equalled all the Bundelkhand states put together. In fact, apart from Rewa, all the other states in the region were so small that even combining them all together would not have resulted in a viable Union.[7]

The States Ministry explored the possibility of merging these small states with United Provinces and Central Provinces. However, both those Provinces were already very large and had recently integrated a number of underdeveloped regions themselves. Adding these states to either of those provinces would weaken their financial and administrative capabilities.

This meant that the only feasible option left was to create a Union in the region that included Rewa. However, Rewa had already been declared a viable state and the States Ministry had promised on behalf of the Union government that 'the principle of merger would not be applied to viable states'[8].

Rewa itself offered a solution to the States Ministry's conundrum. In March 1948, the Maharaja of Rewa, the young Martand Singh, suggested to V.P. Menon a Union of the region built around Rewa.

---

[6]   Menon, *Integration*, p. 162.
[7]   Ibid., p. 145–46.
[8]   Ibid., p. 146.

This proactive initiative released the States Ministry from their promise to Rewa as a viable state. However, it also resulted in Rewa dictating conditions for the merger.

There were three parties in Rewa who influenced the terms of the merger—the young Maharaja, Martand Singh, the local leaders who led the discussions, and the deposed and exiled erstwhile Maharaja, Gulab Singh.

Rewa put forth conditions of the merger that didn't really exist in other parts of India. These included having the option to frame either a unitary or federal constitution, having the right to opt out of the proposed Union after its formation, and the creation of two separate ministries for Rewa and Bundelkhand. These were very generous concessions that added a sizable degree of uncertainty to the future of the Union. However, V.P. Menon believed it was more important to create the Union immediately and was confident that the States Ministry would be able to influence and control the future policy of the region.[9]

The new Union was named Vindhya Pradesh and was inaugurated in April 1948. After the experiment of having two separate ministries failed, they were fused into one composite ministry in July 1948. However, due to corruption, nepotism and infighting, Sardar Patel advised the ministers to resign. In April 1949, a year after its formation, the regional commissioner took charge as the chief minister.[10]

An inquiry in September 1949 revealed a grave administrative and political situation in Vindhya Pradesh. The state was on the verge of bankruptcy and the regional feuds between Bundelkhand and Baghelkhand were ongoing.

Sardar Patel, who had doubted the political future of Vindhya Pradesh from the start, demanded that the Union be dissolved and distributed between the two neighbouring states—United Provinces

---

9   Menon, *Integration*, p. 147.
10   Ibid., p. 149.

and Central Provinces. V.P. Menon felt it would be better to bring the region under direct central administration. Sardar Patel, however, did not believe Vindhya Pradesh had the ability to exist as a separate unit, and hence, his decision prevailed.

The States Ministry drafted a new agreement to abrogate the original covenant with effect from 26 December 1949. The rulers had to sign it before the new Constitution came into effect on 26 January 1950 because that would complicate the legal proceedings for such a move. They eventually signed it after much back-and-forth and convincing.

However, a further twist in the tale awaited. The Premiers of United Provinces and Central Provinces could not reach a mutual agreement regarding the distribution of Vindhya Pradesh among their regions. With the deadline fast approaching, the Government of India eventually decided to take over Vindhya Pradesh on 1 January 1950 as a centrally administered area.

*

Region 4: Bhopal State

The Nawab of Bhopal State, Sir Hamidullah Khan, acceded to the Indian Union at the time of Independence. In April 1948, in response to a growing demand within his state for responsible government, he constituted a ministry with popular leaders. However, there was also an agitation to merge Bhopal State with the newly-formed Madhya Bharat to its north and west. Finally, in January 1949, the nawab reached out to the States Ministry for advice.

The States Ministry held the opinion that Bhopal could not exist as a separate state and must merge with Madhya Bharat since it shared a common geographical, ethnic and cultural affinity with the states in the Malwa Union. Accordingly, the ministry resigned and a period of detailed discussions began between the nawab and V.P. Menon to determine the future of Bhopal State.

Eventually, they postponed the merger with Madhya Bharat. Instead, on 1 June 1949, Bhopal State was taken over by the Government of India as a centrally administered area. In 1950, it was declared a Part C state, governed by a chief commissioner appointed by the President of India, with a commitment that it would remain so for a period of five years.[11]

*

Phase II: Bringing Together Madhya Pradesh (1956)

The integration of Madhya Pradesh began with the separation of the eight Marathi-speaking districts of the Vidarbha region in the south-west of the state. The origins of the Maha Vidarbha movement can be traced back to 1905.[12] Vidarbha was mooted as an independent state in 1938 by a unanimous resolution passed by the Central Provinces Legislature.[13] In its 1955 report, the States Reorganisation Commission (SRC) recommended that Vidarbha be created as a separate state. However, during implementation in 1956, the region was integrated into the behemoth of a bilingual Bombay State.

The carving-out of the Marathi region led to a counter-demand for a consolidation of Hindi regions. Even though it noted that 'the area has never been administered together'[14], the SRC studied the feasibility of such a proposal.

First, it considered the two centrally administered areas. Bhopal State was already being considered for merger from as early as 1951. Vindhya Pradesh's dire political situation had barely

---

[11] Report of the States Reorganisation Commission, 1955, pp. 126–27.
[12] Ibid., p. 122.
[13] Ajit Kumar, 'Statehood for Vidarbha,' *Economic and Political Weekly*, 36(50) (15–21 Dec. 2001), p. 4614.
[14] Report of the States Reorganisation Commission, 1955, p. 126.

improved. Both would benefit greatly from merging into a larger, richly-endowed state.[15]

Then, the SRC looked at Madhya Bharat and found no strong reasons—developmentally, financially or administratively—to keep it separate. In fact, it felt that the ongoing rivalry between Gwalior and Indore would lessen considerably through the merger.[16]

On 1 November 1956, the newly-reconstituted state of Madhya Pradesh came into existence. It included Madhya Pradesh (without Vidarbha), Madhya Bharat, Vindhya Pradesh and Bhopal State. Since Nagpur had been lost with Vidarbha, Bhopal became the new capital of the state (even though the SRC had recommended the centrally-located city of Jabalpur).

Madhya Pradesh was the second-largest state in India, after the mammoth Bombay State. When Bombay State split on 1 May 1960, Madhya Pradesh became the biggest state in India by area and remained so for the next forty years until it also split in 2000.

*

Phase III: Separating Madhya Pradesh and Chhattisgarh (2000)

Statehood for Chhattisgarh was first proposed in 1948 by B.Y. Tamaskar, an opponent of the then-Premier of Central Provinces and Berar, Ravishankar Shukla. However, the proposal was neither seconded nor did it find mass appeal.[17] Tamaskar then joined what would eventually become the Praja Socialist Party (PSP) in 1951, which became the first of many political parties to promote the idea of statehood.

---

[15] Report of the States Reorganisation Commission, 1955, pp. 126–27.

[16] Ibid., pp. 128–29.

[17] Louise Tillin, *Remapping India: New States and Their Political Origins* (New Delhi: Oxford University Press, 2013), pp. 115–18.

Khubchand Baghel, also of the PSP, set up first the Chhattisgarh Mahasabha in 1956 and then the Chhattisgarh Bhratr Sangh in 1967, and also led a number of movements and campaigns to highlight the idea of exploitation by outsiders. However, the demand for statehood continued to remain only an external pressure on the ruling Congress state government.[18]

In both the 1977 and 1980 Lok Sabha elections, Chhattisgarhi statehood was a key issue, even securing Purushottam Kaushik of the PSP a cabinet berth in the first non-Congress Union government. From 1980 onwards, the movement gained new momentum. The new chief minister of Madhya Pradesh, Arjun Singh of the Indian National Congress (INC), established a development authority called the Chhattisgarh Vikas Pratikharan and built and named universities, dams and statues after famous individuals from the region. He gave cabinet positions to a number of Other Backward Classes (OBC), Scheduled Castes (SC) and Scheduled Tribes (ST) MLAs from Chhattisgarh and established a state backwards classes commission. This new generation of OBC leaders, supported by Arjun Singh, began to promote the idea of a Chhattisgarhi identity and Chhattisgarhi statehood.[19]

Chhattisgarh now became a central point for both leading political parties, the Bharatiya Janata Party (BJP) and the INC, and they set up all-party campaigns for the state's creation. During the 1993 assembly elections, Chhattisgarhi statehood featured for the first time on the manifestos of both parties. In 1994, the new chief minister of Madhya Pradesh, Digvijay Singh of the INC, passed a resolution in favour of statehood in the legislative assembly. The BJP established an internal committee called the Chhattisgarh Nirman Samiti and built a case around development rather than social issues. The BJP's National Executive approved the demand

---

[18]   Tillin, *Remapping India*, pp. 122–23.
[19]   Ibid., pp. 130–31.

for Chhattisgarh for the first time and it was included in the party's general election manifesto in 1996. In 1998, at an election rally, the BJP's prime ministerial candidate Atal Bihari Vajpayee promised to create Chhattisgarh if the party won all eleven seats in the region (they won seven).[20]

Finally, in August 2000, with the BJP in power at the Centre and the INC in power at the state, the Madhya Pradesh Reorganisation Act was passed. Chhattisgarh was born on 1 November 2000 comprising sixteen districts with its capital at Raipur. Based on the 1998 state elections, Ajit Jogi of the INC became the state's first chief minister.

**

---

[20] Tillin, *Remapping India*, pp. 137–38.

MAHARASHTRA

Perhaps no other state in India has gone through as massive a reorientation as the state of Maharashtra. Over the course of thirteen years, the state went through three shape-shifting avatars, each one more unrecognizable than the other.

*

Avatar 1: Bombay Province/State, 1947–56

Leading up to Independence in 1947, Bombay Province was one of British India's three large administrative regions—the others being Bengal and Madras. Bombay Province was an assortment of British-administered regions and princely states, staying true to the British approach of running two administrative systems in India.

Bombay Province started in the south bordering Mysore State and went north, around the Portuguese colony of Goa and through the heart of Bombay City. Then, it turned north-west and went across the princely states that littered the present state of Gujarat, crossed the Rann of Kutch, extended past Karachi and stretched out to the Upper Sind Frontier.

Independence in 1947, however, cut the north-western boundaries of Bombay Province, drawing the national borders around the Rann of Kutch. Bombay Province, with its capital at Bombay City, now had a strictly north–south orientation, hugging the western coast and dotted with princely states trying to determine their own future.

Over the next three years, one major princely state—Baroda State—and numerous minor ones merged with Bombay Province. This led to the creation of Bombay State in January 1950 when the Indian Union was created. Its capital was Bombay City.

*

Avatar 2: Bilingual Bombay State, 1956–60

Although Bombay State largely stretched down the coast, Marathi speakers spread deep into the hinterland. Movements to unify Marathi speakers into a single administrative unit had existed since 1918.[1] The movement began to tangibilize with the formation of the Samyukta Maharashtra Parishad in 1946.[2]

---

[1]   S.N. Jha, 'Historical Roots of Regional Variations in the Performance of Local Institutions of Development,' in *Public Governance and Decentralisation: Essays in Honour of T.N. Chaturvedi, Volume 1,* eds. S. N. Mishra, Anil Dutta Mishra and Sweta Mishra (India: Mittal Publications, 2003), p. 574.
[2]   Ramachandra Guha, 'Redrawing the Map (IV),' *India After Gandhi: The History of the World's Largest Democracy* (United Kingdom: Macmillan, 2017).

Four major regions were in contention for a united Maharashtra.

1. Vidarbha (the South-western districts of Central Provinces and Berar, which itself was known as Madhya Pradesh after 1950);
2. Marathwada (the North-western districts of Hyderabad State);
3. Greater Bombay City; and
4. Bombay State.

Vidarbha was first mooted as an independent state called Maha Vidarbha in 1938 through a unanimous resolution passed by the Central Provinces Legislature,[3] though the origins of the movement can be traced back to 1905.[4] However, in 1947, a week before Indian Independence, the Akola Pact was signed between the representatives of Bombay Province and those of Central Provinces and Berar. This pact was a step towards a unified Maharashtra. It envisaged both Bombay State and Vidarbha coexisting as 'a loose federation of two sub-provinces'[5] with a common governor but separate executive, judiciary, legislature and council of ministers.

In September 1953, three months before the States Reorganisation Commission (SRC) was constituted, the Nagpur Pact was signed between the representatives of three regions that represented contiguous Marathi-speaking districts—Bombay State, Vidarbha, and Marathwada. The Nagpur Pact proposed integrating the three regions to create a unified Marathi-speaking state, while also furthering the idea that the three regions would be treated as independent units for the purposes of development.

While the southern and eastern regions of the proposed unified Maharashtra State predominantly consisted of Marathi-speakers, the

---

[3] Ajit Kumar, 'Statehood for Vidarbha,' *Economic and Political Weekly* 36(50) (15–21 Dec. 2001), p. 4614.

[4] Report of the States Reorganisation Commission, 1955, p. 122.

[5] Kumar, 'Statehood for Vidarbha,' p. 4615.

northern regions going up from Greater Bombay City included a heavy Gujarati presence. Through the 1950s, Greater Bombay was caught in a tug-of-war between the Marathis and the Gujaratis. The heavy cosmopolitan composition of the city and its robust financial strength made it highly desirable to both communities, while their history in the city added a deep emotive element to the tussle.

The Marathi argument pointed out that Greater Bombay lay surrounded by Marathi districts and depended for much of its resources on the Marathi hinterland which was now coalescing into Maharashtra. Hence, they believed it was but natural for Bombay City to be the capital of the new unified unilingual Maharashtra.

The Gujaratis argued that not only was Bombay cosmopolitan but it was they—the Gujaratis—that had played possibly the largest role in developing the financial might the city boasted of. The unilingual approach could not be applied to the multilingual port city of Greater Bombay and it would strip the city of its very multifarious essence. They believed that a trifurcation was needed into the states of Maharashtra and Gujarat and the union territory of Greater Bombay—a city-state that belonged to India and its residents.

The matter remained inconclusive and was left to the SRC to adjudicate upon. In its report in 1955, the SRC remarked about how previous linguistic commissions, namely, the Dhar Commission and the JVP Committee, had weighed in on the matter and had suggested that Bombay City should be constituted into a separate unit. However, while it recognized Bombay's special position, the SRC determined that it would be better to feed the interests of all rather than satisfying any one group.[6]

The SRC recommended the creation of one large bilingual Bombay State that extended from the tips of Kutch and Saurashtra in the north-west to the edges of Marathwada in the south-east. Vidarbha was not included. Instead, it was to be carved out as a

---

[6]   Report of the States Reorganisation Commission, 1955, pp. 112–21.

separate Marathi-dominant state, given its potential for a balanced and prosperous economy and its 'deep-rooted regional consciousness'[7]. These recommendations went against the grain of the linguistic approach the SRC had taken for the rest of the country.

When the States Reorganisation Act was implemented in 1956, the large bilingual Bombay State was created but the specific recommendation about separating Vidarbha was disregarded. Vidarbha was integrated into the unified bilingual Bombay State to form its eastern section. Marathwada formed the south-eastern section. The four southern districts of Bombay State which were Kannada-dominant were added to Mysore State, cutting the state off at the Goa border. Bombay City would be the capital of the new bilingual Bombay State.[8]

On 1 November 1956, the new bilingual Bombay State came into existence. It was by far the largest Indian state, covering over 5,00,000 sq. km. of land area—nearly one-sixth of all of India.[9] If it had been a country, Bombay State would have been among the fifty largest countries by land area.[10]

*

Avatar 3: Maharashtra, 1960 onwards

The first chief minister of this bilingual Bombay State was the young Marathi Congressman, Yashwantrao Chavan. He was handed the reins from the previous chief minister, the Gujarati Congressman, Morarji Desai, seventeen years his senior.

---

[7] Report of the States Reorganisation Commission, 1955, p. 124.

[8] Ibid., pp. 112–21.

[9] Government of India, Census 2011.

[10] https://www.nationmaster.com/country-info/stats/Geography/Land-area/Sq.-km

The decision to create a bilingual Bombay State failed to satisfy or pacify either language group. Instead, it intensified demands for unilingual bifurcation. In 1956, two powerful movements came into being that would lead to the final avatars of Maharashtra and Gujarat. The Samyukta Maharashtra Samiti was led by Keshavrao Jedhe, former Congress leader. The Mahagujarat Andolan was led by Indulal Yagnik (popularly known as Indu Chacha), writer, film-maker and independence activist. The issue was debated heatedly in official buildings and on the streets. Demonstrations were large, meetings were mass, and protests were violent. Agitations and riots broke out often and invited an aggressive response from the police.

The 1957 elections for the Lok Sabha and the legislative assembly in Greater Bombay were touted as a referendum on bilingual Bombay State. The Congress wanted to continue the bilingual state, having brought it into existence. The Samyukta Maharashtra Samiti operated as a society with its core ideology of unilingual bifurcation bringing together multiple opposition political parties. Participation was enthusiastic, with voting numbers at nearly 66 per cent. The results were split down the middle. The Congress won twelve of the twenty-four seats (after losing a by-election) while the motley assembly of Samiti parties won the other twelve.[11] The results were similar across the rest of Bombay State, with the Congress doing better in the Gujarat regions and the Samiti doing better in the Maharashtra regions.

Quantitatively, the elections may not have delivered a clear result either for or against the unilingual bifurcation. However, ideologically, it certainly portended the direction the winds were blowing, one that the Congress could no longer ignore, despite forming the government in Bombay State.

---

[11]   Usha Mehta, 'The Second General Elections in Greater Bombay,' *The Indian Journal of Political Science*, 19(2) (Apr.–Jun. 1958), pp. 151–60.

The chief minister of Bombay State, Y. B. Chavan, impressed on the Union government the futility of continuing with the bilingual experiment. Given the continuous and widespread violence in the state on this issue as well as its own suddenly precarious political position, the Congress Working Committee passed a resolution in December 1959 recommending the bifurcation of Bombay State.[12]

On 1 May 1960, bilingual Bombay State was separated into the two new unilingual states of Maharashtra and Gujarat. Bombay City became the capital of Maharashtra.

* *

---

[12] Sadhna Sharma, *States Politics in India* (India: Mittal Publications, 1995), pp. 189–91.

MANIPUR

Democracy v/s Constitutional Monarchy

In 1947, Manipur was a princely state ruled by Maharaja Bodhachandra Singh. The demand for responsible government in Manipur had existed pre-Independence. In November 1938, hundreds of citizens signed and submitted a petition to the Maharaja requesting a legislative council.[1] A year later, the Nikhil Manipuri Mahasabha, which had earlier been patronized by the Maharaja as a cultural organization for Hindus, reoriented as a political party and submitted a petition to the Maharaja for a unicameral legislature.[2] In 1946, parties like the Kuki National Assembly and the Praja

---

[1] R.K. Jhalajit Singh, *A Short History of Manipur* (India: O.K. Store, 1992), p. 329.
[2] Ibid., pp. 325–29.

Sangha were founded to pursue democracy over monarchy.[3] Towards the end of 1946, the Nikhil Manipuri Mahasabha, the left-oriented Manipur Krishak Sabha, and the Youth Front founded the Manipur State Congress with the objective of securing responsible government in Manipur. The Manipur State Congress did not include the Praja Sangha.[4]

Prime Minister Jawaharlal Nehru wrote to Maharaja Bodhachandra Singh that 'the future of Manipur state obviously lies with the Union of India'[5] and wished for it to develop while retaining its distinct cultural entity. The Governor of Assam, Sir Muhammad Saleh Akbar Hydari, visited Manipur to explore the merger of the state with India and to campaign for the establishment of responsible government.[6] The Maharaja signed the Standstill Agreement and the Instrument of Accession with the Dominion of India just days before Indian Independence. This transferred control of Manipur's external affairs, defence and communication, but not internal administration. So, in order to create a constitutional monarchy, the Maharaja put together a Constitution Drafting Committee. The Manipur State Constitution Act, 1947, put the Maharaja at the constitutional head of the state. He appointed his younger brother, Priyobarta Singh, as

[3]   Thongkholal Haokip, 'Political Integration of Northeast India: A Historical Analysis,' *Strategic Analysis,* 36(2) (March 2012), p. 308, https://doi.org/10.1080/09700161.2012.646508.

[4]   Konthoujam Indrakumar, 'Colonialism and Movement for Democracy in Manipur,' in *Colonialism and Resistance: Society and State in Manipur,* eds Arambam Noni and Kangujam Sanatomba (New York: Routledge, 2016), pp. 67–68.

[5]   Haorongbam Sudhirkumar Singh, 'Socio-religious and Political Movements in Modern Manipur (1934–51),' *Doctoral Thesis submitted to Jawaharlal Nehru University* (2011), p. 137.

[6]   Ibid.

the chief minister and headed an assembly and a council of ministers.[7] Elections were held to the Manipur State Assembly in 1948.

The Manipur State Congress, meanwhile, campaigned for responsible government by launching a satyagraha movement (non-violent civil resistance). The Praja Sangha led a joint meeting of the representatives of nine political parties from across Manipur where they not only demanded full responsible government but also formed a United Manipur Front to keep the territorial integrity of Manipur.[8]

The political affiliations in Manipur were split down the middle. On one side, the Maharaja and his ruling party favoured an autonomous and sovereign Manipur led by a constitutional monarchy that maintained continuing relations with India. On the other side, the Manipur State Congress and other political parties demanded the integration and merger of Manipur with India.[9] One proposal suggested merging Manipur as a district in Assam, another suggested forming a separate Purbachal state that included—in various iterations—nearly every region around the Assam plains, and a third suggested creating an autonomous state of Manipur within the Union of India. There was even talk of attempting to integrate Manipur with the neighbouring country of Burma.

The matter of fully integrating Manipur with India still remained. For this, the Maharaja had to transfer the administration of Manipur to India. In September 1949, the Assam Governor, Sir Akbar Hydari, invited Maharaja Bodhachandra Singh to Shillong and pressed upon him to sign the Manipur Merger Agreement. Although the Maharaja refused at first, he eventually signed after

---

[7]   S.K. Banerjee, 'Manipur State Constitution Act, 1947,' *The Indian Journal of Political Science,* 19(1) (Jan.–Mar. 1958), pp. 35–38.
[8]   Priyadarshni M. Gangte, 'Political Climate of Manipur during the Transitionary Period, 1946–52: Some Reflections,' *Proceedings of the Indian History Congress,* 74 (2013), pp. 667–74.
[9]   Haokip, 'Political Integration of Northeast India,' p. 308.

some persuasion.[10] The agreement allowed him to keep his title and some ceremonial duties and earn a privy purse.[11]

On 15 October 1949, Manipur became a chief commissioner's province in the Union of India, through whom the Union government would directly administer the region. This also terminated the Manipur State Constitution Act and the previous legislative assembly and ministry in Manipur. The existing dewan, Major General Rawal Amar Singh, who had been appointed by the Union government to oversee the administration, was appointed as the chief commissioner.

On 26 January 1950, when India adopted its Constitution, Manipur was classified a Part C state, still kept under direct central administration. In September 1951, Parliament passed the Government of Part C States Act which provided for the constitution of a council of advisers to assist the chief commissioner in Manipur. A lieutenant-governor later replaced the chief commissioner.

*

Union Territory

In December 1953, the Union government set up the States Reorganisation Commission (SRC). Two years later, in its report, the SRC recommended that Manipur should continue to be centrally administered and not merged with Assam or a proposed Purbachal or hill state. The reasons included its importance as a border state, its economic development needs met by the Centre, and its racial and linguistic composition. Meitheis or Manipuris constituted two-thirds of the population, leading to a 'consciousness of a distinct linguistic and cultural individuality'[12]. However, the SRC also noted that Manipur could not maintain its separate existence for long and

---

[10] Haokip, 'Political Integration of Northeast India,' p. 308.
[11] Manipur Merger Agreement, 1949.
[12] Report of the States Reorganisation Commission, 1955, pp. 196–98.

the ultimate solution was to eventually merge it with Assam. When the States Reorganisation Act was passed in 1956, all Part C states, including Manipur, were redesignated as union territories, which continued to be centrally administered.

This was quickly followed by the Territorial Councils Act, 1956. Applicable to the union territories of Manipur, Tripura and Himachal Pradesh, this Act established territorial councils as a way to grant some autonomy in local affairs. This included education, public health, roads, animal husbandry and even levying taxes, subject to central approval.[13]

However, demands for greater autonomy kept growing in Manipur. In 1961, the Centre constituted a committee headed by the Union Law Minister, Ashoke Kumar Sen, which recommended 'the largest possible measure of autonomy'[14]. It suggested the introduction of panchayati raj as well as the transfer of more subjects to the territorial councils. However, what the union territories really wanted were legislative bodies.

In 1962, after Goa, Daman & Diu and Pondicherry were integrated into India as union territories, and the State of Nagaland Act was passed, the Union government decided to go above and beyond the recommendations of the Ashoke Sen Committee. It passed the Government of Union Territories Act, 1963, which was reminiscent of the pre-SRC Government of the Part C States Act, 1951. It established legislative assemblies and councils of ministers and abolished territorial councils in five union territories—Manipur, Tripura, Himachal Pradesh, Goa and Pondicherry.[15]

The Act also created two classes of union territories. These five union territories comprised the more advanced first class and were seen as being independent stand-alone entities. Their legislative

---

[13] Territorial Councils Act, 1956.
[14] Administrative Reforms Commission. *Report, Study Team on Administration of Union Territories and NEFA*, 1968. pp. 11–13.
[15] Ibid.

assemblies had powers and responsibilities similar to the state legislative assemblies, including the ability to make laws on subjects in the Union and Concurrent lists. They even had separate consolidated and contingency funds. Manipur got its first chief minister in Mairembam Koireng Singh of the Indian National Congress (INC). Rather than ultimately having to merge with Assam, statehood itself was now a possible future for Manipur.

In 1967, the state legislature passed the Manipur Hill Areas (Acquisition of Chiefs' Rights) Act, which authorized the government to acquire the rights of the chiefs over the land and compensate them in return. However, following protests by the chiefs, the Act was not implemented and chieftainship continued. Around the same time, public debates began in Manipur, especially among the youth, about the circumstances under which the Manipur Merger Agreement was signed in 1949.[16] This escalated into protests, eventually resulting in the imposition of President's rule in Manipur in October 1969.

*

Statehood

On 30 December 1971, Parliament passed the North-Eastern Areas (Reorganisation) Act, which brought into existence three new states—Meghalaya, Manipur and Tripura—and two new union territories—Mizoram and Arunachal Pradesh. On 21 January 1972, the full-fledged state of Manipur was born. In March, President's rule was revoked and Mohammed Alimuddin of the Manipur People's Party became the first chief minister of the new state of Manipur.

* *

---

16 Bhupen Sarmah, 'India's Northeast and the Enigma of the Nation-state,' *Alternatives: Global, Local, Political, Vol* 42, No. 3 (Aug. 2017), p. 172.

MEGHALAYA

Did You Know?

Meghalaya was India's first autonomous state within another state.

1947–52: Autonomous Districts and the Sixth Schedule

Meghalaya's push towards statehood came separately and collectively from all three of its regions—the Garo Hills, the Khasi Hills and the Jaintia Hills. All three regions shared a fundamental similarity of a matrilineal social system, helping them also bond emotionally on their distinct identity.[1] At the time of Indian Independence, these regions formed the south-western part of Assam bordering Bangladesh.

The constituent assembly set up a subcommittee to report and recommend on the 'excluded and partially excluded areas'—a term the British had used to denote areas that they had excluded from

---

[1]   Monirul Hussain, 'Tribal Movement for Autonomous State in Assam,' *Economic and Political Weekly,* 22(32) (8 August 1987), p. 1330.

direct purview. The subcommittee was headed by Gopinath Bordoloi, the Premier of Assam, and was hence referred to as the Bordoloi Committee. The committee included a Khasi leader, Reverend James Joy Mohan Nichols-Roy, along with a plains tribal leader and a social worker. The team toured all the hill districts of Assam and 'co-opted two members from the tribes'[2] in each of the districts. The Bordoloi Committee submitted its report in July 1947. It recommended that all the Khasi people be brought under a common administration and suggested a federation to bridge the gap between the states—which enjoyed certain rights—and the British portions, where there was no statutory local body for local self-government.[3]

By December 1947, all the siems (chiefs) of the Khasi Hill States had signed the Instrument of Accession to India, which pleased Sardar Vallabhbhai Patel, the head of the States Ministry.[4] The Khasi Siems and Jaintia Dolois (chiefs) demanded a joint federation and an Executive Council within Assam Province while also decreeing that the Assam Legislative Assembly would not have power to legislate on any subjects for Khasi–Jaintia Hills. Along the same lines, Garo National Union also demanded a Garo Hills Union and an executive council within Assam Province.[5]

The constituent assembly considered it 'desirable to preserve some of the tribal traditions and customs'[6]. Hence, instead of merging them outright with Assam, the three regions were included in the Sixth Schedule of the Constitution of India, which provided for district-level autonomy through the constitution of district councils.

---

[2]   S.K. Chaube, *Hill Politics in Northeast India,* (India: Orient Blackswan, 2012), p. 81.

[3]   Ibid., p. 84.

[4]   Ibid., p. 85.

[5]   B.B. Kumar, *Reorganization of North-East India: Facts and Documents* (India: Concept, 2017) pp. 15–16.

[6]   Ministry of States, Government of India. *White Paper on Indian States*, 1950, pp. 45–46.

Importantly, without the assent of the district councils, no act of the state legislature could apply to the autonomous districts, including on the use of land, management of forests, appointment of chiefs, marriage and social customs.

The Governor of Assam convened a durbar to prepare a Constitution for the Khasi States. Nichols-Roy, one of the people responsible for the Sixth Schedule, formed the Khasi–Jaintia Federated States National Conference. Opposing him and the Sixth Schedule was the Khasi States People's Union which included, importantly, the siems, who demanded the incorporation of their rights. When the durbar met in July 1949, the siems emerged stronger numerically. As a result, no instrument of merger was signed with the Government of India, and the Constitution of India put the Khasi siemships within Assam.[7]

When India adopted its Constitution on 26 January 1950, the Khasi Hill States and the Jaintia Hill District were constituted into a separate autonomous district in Assam known as United Khasi–Jaintia Hill District. Shillong, then the capital of Assam, fell in this district. Garo Hills was also constituted as a separate autonomous district in Assam. District councils were first elected in the 1952 general elections. However, when the United Khasi–Jaintia District Council was inaugurated on 27 June 1952, it was met with 'a big student and youth demonstration'[8].

*

1952–60: The Demand for a Unified Hill State

Meanwhile, the Khasi National Durbar—a social organization formed in the early 1920s—now moved to the political forefront.

---

[7]   Chaube, *Hill Politics*, pp. 89–90.
[8]   Ibid., p. 115.

Once a 'fortress of the siems' but now 'practically defunct',[9] the durbar was reorganized and revitalized. When Prime Minister Jawaharlal Nehru visited Shillong in October 1952, the durbar submitted a memorandum demanding, for the first time, the unification of all Assam hills under one administration. They also opposed the imposition of the Assamese language and demanded the full inclusion of Shillong in the United Khasi–Jaintia autonomous district.[10]

In December 1953, the Union government set up the States Reorganisation Commission (SRC) and invited written memoranda from the public. Delegates from the autonomous districts—Garo Hills, United Khasi–Jaintia Hills, North Cachar Hills, Mikir Hills and Mizo Hills (renamed from Lushai Hills)—first convened a meeting at Shillong in June 1954 and then held an Assam Hills Tribal Leaders' Conference at Tura in October 1954. They unanimously called for 'a separate State for the Autonomous Districts of Assam'[11] as well as an amendment of the Sixth Schedule, which conferred no real autonomy.

However, almost immediately after, differences began to crop up over which proposed amendments needed to be considered. The memorandum for the hill state was not signed by many tribal leaders and parties across the districts. As a result, the SRC declared in its September 1955 report that the demand for a hill state was 'confined virtually to the Garo and Khasi and Jaintia Hills'[12] and would be too expensive to create and maintain. It also refused to entertain any amendment to the Sixth Schedule and instead proposed constituting a separate body to study its working.[13]

At the end of October 1955, the hill leaders held another conference at Aijal where they created the Eastern India Tribal Union (EITU). However, the hill state movement began to splinter

---

[9]   Chaube, *Hill Politics*, p. 115.
[10] Ibid.
[11] Ibid., p. 119.
[12] Report of the States Reorganisation Commission, 1955, p. 188.
[13] Ibid., p. 189.

as internal political dynamics shifted and hardened. Some parties, including the Garo National Conference, refused to merge with the EITU as it was heavily backed by the siems, thereby confining it to the Khasi–Jaintia Hills. Other leaders changed parties. In the 1957 general elections, many alliances broke and parties like the Garo National Conference stood and won independently in their districts; the Indian National Congress (INC) fared poorly across the Autonomous Districts. Nichols-Roy died and two new organizations cropped up in the Garo Hills. The EITU itself split into two opposing factions. The Union's president B.M. Pugh was expelled, but he had the backing of vice-president Captain Williamson Ampang Sangma, who was also the head of the Garo National Council and a cabinet minister in the Assam government. The other faction was headed by Theodore Cajee and backed by the Khasi National Durbar.

The faltering hill state movement was revitalized in April 1960 when the Assam Pradesh Congress Committee (APCC) demanded the official state language be Assamese—a language of the plains, not of the hills.[14] The two EITU factions held separate conferences in April and June 1960 where they both opposed the imposition of Assamese. In July 1960, Captain Sangma called the first All-Party Hill Leaders' Conference (APHLC), which was presided over by Pugh and was attended by parties across the spectrum, including the District Congress Committees. Their primary demand was not for a hill state but for the language bill to be dropped and for English to continue as the official language. In August, the APHLC issued an ultimatum to the Assam chief minister, Bimala Prasad Chaliha of the INC, after their second conference held in Shillong. In October, Captain Sangma protested by resigning his cabinet post in the Assam Government and the APHLC staged a demonstration in Shillong. However, on 24 October 1960, the Assam Assembly passed the

---

[14] Dilip Mukerjee, 'Assam Reorganization,' Asian Survey, 9(4) (April 1969): p. 299.

language bill in a special sitting. At their third conference in Haflong in November, the APHLC declared that the immediate creation of a separate hill state was 'the only solution'[15].

*

1960–66: Scottish Plan and Nehru Plan

In November 1960, Prime Minister Jawaharlal Nehru offered a 'Scottish pattern' of government to the Autonomous Districts modelled on the Committee for Scotland in the British House of Commons. The powers of the Districts would be increased to include, among others, a separate budget, a separate cabinet minister and deputy ministers in the Assam government, and final decision on legislative matters in the Assam Assembly. A commission to review the provisions of the Sixth Schedule would also be appointed.

However, the APHLC rejected Nehru's Scottish plan at its fourth session in April 1961 in Shillong. They also called for a boycott of the 1962 general elections. This once again split the hill state movement. The District Congress Committees did not agree with this response and they stayed away from the APHLC's fifth session. Instead, in July 1961, along with B.M. Pugh, they held their own Assam Hills Peoples' Conference (AHPC) where they agreed to both accept Nehru's offer and contest the 1962 elections. This forced APHLC's hand; at their sixth session at Aijal in October 1961, they too decided to contest the 1962 elections.

The 1962 election results were cleanly split by geography. The Congress won in Mikir and North Cachar Hills, while the APHLC won in Garo, United Khasi–Jaintia, and Mizo Districts. When the APHLC tried to use this numerical strength to reiterate its old demand of a separate hill state, it was rejected again. Hence, they decided

---

[15] Chaube, *Hill Politics*, p. 130.

to withdraw from the assembly. However, nearly half its elected members refused to resign, damaging its reputation. Simultaneously, India went to war with China. The tide had turned.

Further discussions with Nehru were no longer held directly but through various interlocutors. The expanded powers initially offered to the districts were increasingly pulled back in what was referred to as the Nehru Plan. For instance, the whole cabinet could now initiate, consider and approve legislation related to the districts, while the districts' views would only have special importance instead of being the final decision. Autonomy itself was now, as Nehru told an APHLC member of the Lok Sabha, 'subject to a Commission being appointed to consider the whole thing'[16].

In March 1965, the Pataskar Commission—appointed to study the autonomous demands of Assam's hill districts—refrained from commenting on union territory or state status or the redrawing of boundaries. Instead, it recommended 'no basic change'[17] to the Sixth Schedule. The APHLC rejected the report and again demanded a separate hill state as well as a boycott of the 1967 general elections.

*

1966–72: An Extraordinary Experiment

Meanwhile, the Union government went through a drastic leadership change. Prime Minister Jawaharlal Nehru died in May 1964 and his successor Lal Bahadur Shastri died in January 1966. The new Prime Minister, Indira Gandhi, could not afford a boycott of the elections in a sensitive area of India. In January 1967, she met with Assam Chief Minister Chaliha and APHLC leaders and promised a plan that had never been seen before in

---

[16] Chaube, *Hill Politics*, p. 134.
[17] Ibid., p. 127.

India—to reorganize Assam as a federated state 'comprising units of equal status not subordinate to one another'[18]. In other words, to create an autonomous state within the state of Assam. Overjoyed, the APHLC representatives accepted the proposal. The Assam Congress led by Chief Minister Chaliha rejected it.

In the 1967 elections, the APHLC won all the Assembly seats in the Garo and United Khasi–Jaintia Hills, establishing their leadership in the region. However, the Assam Congress, bolstered by support from Congress leaders in other states, refused to back down and rejected the federated states idea 'in categorical terms'[19]. In May 1968, all the elected APHLC members resigned their assembly seats. In September 1968, they started a non-violent satyagraha. Finally, all sides agreed to compromise—law and order would not be transferred to the new autonomous state.

On 29 December 1969, Parliament passed the Assam Reorganisation (Meghalaya) Act. The autonomous state of Meghalaya would exist within Assam and comprise the districts of Garo Hills and United Khasi–Jaintia Hills. Meghalaya came into existence on 2 April 1970. Captain Williamson A. Sangma of the APHLC became Meghalaya's first chief minister.[20]

The creation of Meghalaya was historic and unprecedented because it established a new tier in India's state structure. Autonomous states now existed alongside full-fledged states and union territories. Similar in structure to the autonomous republics of the former Union of Soviet Socialist Republics (USSR), Meghalaya was considered an 'extraordinary experiment'[21]. In practice, Meghalaya functioned almost as a full-fledged state. It had powers to make laws on sixty-one out of

18   Mukerjee, 'Assam Reorganization,' pp. 304–05.
19   Ibid., p. 306.
20   The Assam Reorganisation (Meghalaya) Act, 1969.
21   Hussain, 'Tribal Movement,' p. 1330.

sixty-six subjects in the state list, and it contained autonomous district councils. Shillong became the capital of both Assam and Meghalaya.

The new Meghalaya state government continued to push for full-fledged statehood, pausing only for India's 1971 war with Pakistan, which resulted in the creation of Bangladesh. On 30 December 1971, Parliament passed the North-Eastern Areas (Reorganisation) Act, which brought into existence three new states—Meghalaya, Manipur and Tripura—and two new union territories—Mizoram and Arunachal Pradesh.[22]

On 21 January 1972, the full-fledged state of Meghalaya was born. Its creation was all the more remarkable because it had been achieved with little to no violence. In 1973, Assam shifted its capital to Dispur and Shillong remained the capital of Meghalaya.

**

---

[22] The North-Eastern Areas (Reorganisation) Act, 1971.

MIZORAM

1947–52: A District Council within India

In 1947, the present-day state of Mizoram was known as Lushai Hills District, named by the British as an administrative unit. Lushai Hills was an excluded area as demarcated by the British in order to exclude it from direct purview. As a result, the Lals (chiefs) of various tribes—Lushai, Chin, Kuki, Hmar, Pawi, Lakher and others—continued to be the dominant force in society after the British.

After the Second World War, a new class of elites began to rise in society. They had money and education and 'rose in revolt'[1] against the rule of the chiefs. Mizoram's first political party, the Mizo Union (MU), was formed in 1946 with the aim

---

[1] Suhas Chatterjee, *Mizo Chiefs and the Chiefdom* (India: M.D. Publications, 1995), p. 2.

to abolish chieftainship.[2] The name Mizo (Mi is Man, Zo is Hill) was chosen to reflect 'the typical integrationist aspiration of the middle class'[3].

At its first general assembly in September 1946, the MU boycotted the failed district conference idea of the district's British superintendent. Instead, they chose to join India while giving themselves the right to review the situation and reconsider independence after ten years. This created two factions within the MU. The founder president and second president, both seen to be influenced by the British superintendent, were removed from their posts in November 1946.

Meanwhile, the constituent assembly had set up a subcommittee to report and recommend on the excluded and partially excluded areas. The subcommittee was headed by Gopinath Bordoloi, the Premier of Assam, and was hence referred to as the Bordoloi Committee. When the subcommittee arrived in Lushai Hills in 1947, both factions of the MU appeared together.

The Bordoloi Committee eventually created the Sixth Schedule in the Indian Constitution. This made Lushai Hills an autonomous district in Assam with its own district council, which would have the power to legislate on the usage of land, management of forests, establishment of town councils and inheritance of property, among others.

In July 1947, around the time the Bordoloi Committee submitted its report, one faction of the MU broke off and founded the United Mizo Freedom Organisation (UMFO) to try and merge the district with Burma. The Chin chiefs in the south-eastern part of the district formed a Pawi-Lakher Tribal Union along similar lines and even secured a Regional Council. However, all talks of merging

---

[2]   Chatterjee, *Mizo Chiefs*, p. 2.
[3]   S.K. Chaube, *Hill Politics in Northeast India* (India: Orient Blackswan, 2012), p. 171.

with Burma ended when the district superintendent told the MU in October 1947 that Burma was severing connections with the British Empire and that India was the future of the Mizos.[4]

At its next conference, the MU demanded the setting up of district councils within two months as well as the 'abolition of the oppressive practices'[5] that were pro-chief and anti-people. When the Government of Assam did not respond favourably, the MU started a civil disobedience movement against the chiefs in late 1948.[6] In response, the government implemented the Sixth Schedule early in the Lushai Hills District, giving it an advisory council before a district council. The name of Lushai Hills District was then changed to Mizo District.

In April 1952, after India's first general elections, in which the MU won all three seats in Mizo Hills, the Mizo District Council was formed. This effectively ended the practice of chieftainship, which was eventually abolished in 1954 with the Assam Lushai Hills District (Acquisition of Chiefs' Rights) Act.

*

1953–59: An Attempted Hill States Movement

In December 1953, the Union government set up the States Reorganisation Commission (SRC) and invited written memoranda from the public. Delegates from the autonomous districts—Garo Hills, United Khasi–Jaintia Hills, North Cachar Hills, Mikir Hills and Mizo Hills—first convened a meeting at Shillong in June 1954. Then, they held an Assam Hills Tribal Leaders' Conference at Tura in October 1954 where, although the Mizo Hills was not represented, suggestions were sent by the UMFO. The hill leaders

---

4   Chaube, *Hill Politics*, p. 173.
5   Ibid., pp. 173–74.
6   Ibid., p. 174.

called for a separate state for the autonomous districts of Assam as well as an amendment of the Sixth Schedule as it conferred no real autonomy.[7] However, almost immediately after, differences began to crop up over which proposed amendments needed to be considered. The memorandum for the hill state was not signed by many tribal leaders and parties across the districts. As a result, the SRC declared in its report the following year that the demand for a hill state was 'confined virtually to the Garo and Khasi and Jaintia Hills'[8] and would be too expensive to create and maintain. It also refused to entertain any amendment to the Sixth Schedule and instead proposed constituting a separate body to study its working.[9]

At the end of October 1955, the MU hosted another conference of the hill leaders at Aijal. The Eastern India Tribal Union (EITU) was born at this conference. However, while the UMFO joined the EITU, the MU, which had hosted the conference, refused to join. Some other leaders too refused to merge their parties with EITU as it was heavily backed by the siems (Khasi chiefs). This confined EITU to the Khasi–Jaintia Hills.[10]

In the 1957 general elections, many alliances broke and parties like the UMFO stood independently in their districts. The MU split when the MU (Right Wing) left. The EITU tried, and failed, to reorganize itself by amalgamating parties across various regions, including the MU, MU (Right Wing), and UMFO. The EITU itself then split into two opposing factions.

The Indian National Congress (INC) fared poorly in the 1957 elections across the autonomous districts. As a result, the chief minister of Assam, Bimala Prasad Chaliha of the INC, formed an alliance with the EITU by inviting its vice-president Captain Sangma

---

[7]   Chaube, *Hill Politics*, p. 119.
[8]   Report of the States Reorganisation Commission, 1955, p. 188.
[9]   Ibid., p. 189.
[10] Chaube, *Hill Politics*, pp. 121–23.

to join his cabinet. This upset the MU, who felt that their consistent support to the Congress had received an 'inadequate reward'[11].

In 1959, the periodic and deadly mautam famine ravaged the Mizo Hills. It occurred approximately every fifty years and was caused by a rat infestation that corresponded to the flowering of a particular species of bamboo trees. Chief Minister Chaliha and the MU sparred over the distribution of the famine relief work, deepening the rift and lack of trust between the two.[12] Frustrated by the lack of support, Laldenga—a clerk in the district council—formed a Mizo National Famine Front in 1960 to coordinate famine relief efforts.[13]

In April 1960, the Assam Pradesh Congress Committee (APCC) demanded the immediate introduction of Assamese—a language of the plains—as the official state language. The two EITU factions opposed this demand at separate conferences in April and June 1960. In July 1960, Captain Sangma called the first All-Party Hill Leaders' Conference (APHLC), which was attended by the MU, the UMFO, and other parties across the spectrum, including even the District Congress Committees. They demanded the language bill be dropped and English continue as the official language.

Following a second conference in Shillong in August, the APHLC issued an ultimatum to Chief Minister Chaliha. In October, Captain Sangma resigned from his cabinet post in the Assam Government and the APHLC staged a demonstration in Shillong. However, in a special sitting on 24 October 1960, the Assam Assembly passed the language bill. In response, at their third conference in Haflong in November, the APHLC demanded the immediate creation of a separate hill state as 'the only solution'[14].

---

[11]   Chaube, *Hill Politics*, p. 124.

[12]   Ibid., pp. 174–75.

[13]   Sajal Nag, 'Bamboo, Rats and Famines: Famine Relief and Perceptions of British Paternalism in the Mizo Hills (India),' *Environment and History*, 5(2) (June 1999), pp. 245–52.

[14]   Chaube, *Hill Politics*, p. 130.

Prime Minister Nehru then proposed a Scottish pattern of government to the autonomous districts. Modelled on the Committee for Scotland in the British House of Commons, he offered a separate budget, cabinet minister and deputy ministers in the Assam government, as well as final decision on legislative matters concerning the districts.

However, at its fourth session in April 1961 in Shillong, the APHLC not only rejected Nehru's Scottish plan, they also called for a boycott of the 1962 general elections. This once again split the hill state movement as the District Congress Committees disagreed. They stayed away from the APHLC's fifth session and held their own Assam Hills Peoples' Conference (AHPC) in July 1961. They agreed to both accept Nehru's offer and contest the 1962 elections, thereby forcing APHLC's hand. At APHLC's sixth session at Aijal in October 1961, they too decided to contest the 1962 elections. Meanwhile, Laldenga converted the Mizo National Famine Front into a political party called the Mizo National Front (MNF).

The APHLC won all three seats in the Mizo Hills—two by MU and the third by UMFO. When they tried to use this numerical strength to reiterate their old demand of a separate hill state, it was again rejected. Hence, they decided to withdraw from the assembly. However, nearly half its elected members from across the region refused to resign, including one MU MLA who then joined the Congress. The MNF then won the by-elections to the other two seats that had been resigned by the MU and the UMFO.

*

1963–66: Attempts to Unify Mizos

In June 1963, with the demand for the hill state all but over, the MU attempted to regain its standing. At a conference at Aijal, it demanded a Mizo State that also included 'the contiguous Mizo-inhabited areas of Assam, Tripura and Manipur'[15]. In October 1963,

---

[15]   Chaube, *Hill Politics*, p. 175.

the Tribal Union in the southern Pawi–Lakher region split ahead of the regional council elections. The new chief executive member of the council, L. Chinza, led the founding of the Chin National Front (CNF) as an alternative to MNF and to reunite the Pawi and the Lakher. In January 1965, the MU led an all-party meet at Churachandpur which raised the demand for 'the unification of all Mizos'[16]. Laldenga even demanded for 'union with the Mizos of Burma and Pakistan'[17], a demand that raised his profile during the India–Pakistan war of 1965. He was arrested and released only after he promised good conduct.

In March 1965, the Pataskar Commission was appointed with the objective of 'conferring full measure of autonomy'[18] to the hill districts while still preserving the unity of Assam. The Mizo District Council controlled by the MU wanted to discuss nothing less than the creation of a separate state of Mizoram. The Pataskar Commission in its report refrained from commenting on the status or boundaries of any of the hill districts, but it did, however, recommend 'no basic change'[19] to the Sixth Schedule. The APHLC rejected the report and again demanded a separate hill state as well as a boycott of the 1967 general elections.

*

1966: MNF insurgency begins

Meanwhile, the MNF began to intensify their hostilities. In response, the Union government sent in a battalion of the Assam Rifles as reinforcements. The Assam Governor, Vishnu Sahai, and the Pataskar Commission separately visited the Mizo Hills in early

---

[16] Chaube, *Hill Politics*, p. 175.
[17] Ibid., pp. 175–76.
[18] Government of India. Report of the Commission on the Hill Areas of Assam, 1965–66, p. 5.
[19] Ibid., p. 127.

February 1966. A week later, a Joint Intelligence Committee report warned of violence, but only after the district council elections more than a year later.[20] It got the date wrong.

Less than two weeks after the report, on the night of 28 February 1966, the MNF and its associated Mizo National Army (MNA) launched Operation Jericho in a bid for Mizo independence. They attacked army posts and government buildings and took over communications and control of the district and declared Mizoram independent. On 2 March, the Indian government declared the district 'a disturbed area'[21] under the Armed Forces Special Powers Act (AFSPA) 1958 and sent in the army. The Indian Air Force aerially strafed Aizawl on 5 and 6 March and burnt down its biggest market.[22] It was the first time the Indian government had bombed its own citizens.[23] Prime Minister Indira Gandhi and Assam Chief Minister Bimala Chaliha both denied the bombing, saying instead that 'the air force had been used to drop men and supplies'[24]. Laldenga fled. In 1967, the Indian government launched Operation Security, also known by the army as Operation Accomplishment, which involved forcibly grouping villages into smaller concentrations.[25]

During the 1970 district council elections, the INC advocated for a political settlement with the MNF, despite them pursuing opposing stances on Mizo independence. As a result, the Congress won the

---

[20] Vijendra Singh Jafa, 'Ten o'clock to Bed: Insouciance in the Face of Terror,' *Faultlines: Writings on Conflict & Resolution* Vol. 5 (May 2000).

[21] Nandini Sundar, 'Interning Insurgent Populations: The Buried Histories of Indian Democracy', *Economic and Political Weekly,* 46(6) (5–11 Feb. 2011), p. 50.

[22] Ibid.

[23] Government of India. Ministry of Information & Broadcasting, Films Division. *MNF: The Mizo Uprising,* 2014.

[24] Sundar, 'Interning Insurgent Populations', p. 50.

[25] Ibid.

elections from the MNF-strong remote areas while the MU did well in the regrouped villages. However, within a year, the Congress-led executive council was toppled twice. A coalition executive council led by the MU came to power and passed a resolution demanding a separate state of Mizoram within India as well as the unification of all Mizo-inhabited areas.

*

1971–87: First a Union Territory, then the State of Mizoram

In July 1971, the Government of India offered to make Mizo Hills District a union territory, putting it under direct central authority. This polarized Mizo Hills. The district council welcomed it, but the state Congress in Assam refused to accept it 'even as a stepping stone'[26] and met with Prime Minister Indira Gandhi to request her to continue the status quo. She refused.

On 30 December 1971, Parliament passed the North-Eastern Areas (Reorganisation) Act, which brought into existence three new states—Meghalaya, Manipur and Tripura—and two new union territories—Mizoram and Arunachal Pradesh. Mizo District was separated from Assam and was reconstituted as Mizoram. On 21 January 1972, Mizoram was born as a union territory with C. Chhunga of the MU as the first chief minister. The MU eventually dissolved and its members joined the INC.

Then began a long period of parleys between the Union government and the MNF, whose leader Laldenga was still in hiding. In July 1976, the two parties signed a peace accord at Delhi, according to which the MNF would give up violence and surrender its arms to the Indian government in a bid to work politically within

---

26   Chaube, *Hill Politics*, pp. 178–79.

the framework of the Indian Constitution.[27] However, the promised MNF surrender never came.[28] The government eventually called off the talks in frustration in March 1978.

In July 1979, the MNF served a 'Quit Order' on vais (non-Mizos), asking them to leave Mizoram immediately. As the violence escalated, a large number of vais began to leave Mizoram.[29] This alarmed the Union government. The MNF was declared unlawful and Laldenga was arrested.[30]

In November 1979, when Laldenga tried to reopen talks with the government, the Home Minister Y.B. Chavan demanded the implementation of the 1976 Delhi peace accord and the surrender of all arms by the MNF. However, the Union government changed in January 1980. Indira Gandhi of the INC returned as prime minister and withdrew all the pending criminal cases against Laldenga, who in turn publicly declared that he was willing to settle the Mizo problem within the framework of the Indian Constitution.[31] In addition, the Mizoram Chief Minister, Brigadier Thenpunga Sailo (Retd), offered to step down from office to aid in bringing about the settlement.

On 30 June 1986, a Memorandum of Settlement (also known as the 'Mizoram Accord') was signed between the Government of India, the Government of Mizoram and the MNF. While the MNF promised to help in the restoration of normality and to work within the Constitution of India, the Union government promised statehood to Mizoram.[32]

---

[27] 'Mizos: Return of the Hostile Prodigals,' *India Today*, 15 July 1976.

[28] Hamlet Bareh, *Encyclopaedia of North-East India: Mizoram* (India: Mittal Publications, 2001), p. 194.

[29] Ibid., pp. 200–01.

[30] Ibid., pp. 201–02.

[31] Ibid., p. 171.

[32] Government of India: Memorandum of Settlement (Mizoram Accord), 1986.

On 14 August 1986, Parliament passed the State of Mizoram Act to convert the union territory of Mizoram into a state. The chief minister, Lal Thanhawla of the INC, resigned and Laldenga was appointed in his place. Mizoram was born as a state when the Act came into effect on 20 February 1987. Laldenga became the first chief minister of Mizoram State.[33]

* *

[33]   Government of India. The State of Mizoram Act, 1986.

NAGALAND

1947–50: Independent or in India?

In 1947, as India was approaching Independence, the people of Nagaland were considering their own independence.

The Naga Hills District had been demarcated as 'Naga Hills Excluded Areas' by the British in 1935, thereby excluding the territories from direct British purview. This was in part due to the memorandum put forth by the Naga Club, a motley crew of forty-two tribes banding together after World War I to protect their identities and to rehabilitate the war-devastated areas of Naga Hills.

In the mid-1940s, the Naga Club transformed into the Naga National Council (NNC), a political organization with Imti Aliba Ao as its secretary. They first sought local autonomy and a separate electorate while being 'constitutionally included in an autonomous

Assam'[1] but quickly graduated to self-determination for the Nagas based on ethnic, social and religious distinctiveness. However, in August 1946, Jawaharlal Nehru, the future prime minister of India, wrote that the Naga territory was 'much too small to stand by itself'.[2]

In May 1947, the NNC submitted another memorandum to the British government requesting an interim government of the Naga people in Naga Hills for ten years.[3] This would give them full power over legislative, executive and judicial matters, while allowing a 'Guardian Power' to maintain a force in the hills for defence matters. In June, the Governor of Assam, Sir Akbar Hydari, representing the Government of India, signed a nine-point agreement with the NNC largely along similar lines. However, the two parties interpreted the last point about reviewing the situation after ten years differently. Some Naga leaders interpreted it to mean they could still opt out of India after ten years, while the Government of India determined that they could only explore options within the framework of the Union of India. Jaipal Singh Munda—a politician, tribal rights activist, Olympic gold-medallist and a member of the constituent assembly—told the assembly in July 1947 that there was 'no question of secession'[4] since the Naga Hills had always been part of India.

On 14 August 1947, on the eve of India's Independence, Zapu Phizo, an Angami leader, declared Nagaland an independent Christian republic, just as he had told Mahatma Gandhi he would a month earlier. The Government of India did not recognize this declaration. The constituent assembly had already set up an advisory

---

[1]   B.B. Kumar, *Reorganization of North-East India: Facts and Documents* (India: Concept, 2017), p. 22.

[2]   Makepeace Sitlhou, 'Accord,' *Fifty-Two* (27 Nov. 2020), https://fiftytwo.in/story/accord/

[3]   Chandrika Singh, 'Nagaland: From a District to a State: Culmination of Democratic Political Process,' *The Indian Journal of Political Science*, 41(4) (Dec. 1980), p. 816.

[4]   Sitlhou, 'Accord'.

committee on tribal areas, which in turn had set up a subcommittee with the chief minister of Assam, Gopinath Bordoloi, as its chairman. The Bordoloi Committee reported that the Naga Hills were on 'a totally different footing' and must be 'treated separately from the rest'.[5]

As it turned out, the Hydari Agreement didn't make it to ten years. Imti Aliba Ao quit politics for a posting in the Indian Frontier Administrative Service. Zapu Phizo wrested the post of president of the NNC in November 1949 and 'decisively rejected'[6] the Hydari Agreement. The drafters of the Indian Constitution 'simply ignored'[7] the Hydari Agreement and created the Sixth Schedule based on the Bordoloi Committee's recommendations.

*

1950–56: A Violent Struggle for Naga Independence

The Sixth Schedule constituted the Naga Hills as an autonomous district in Assam. It had its own district council with the power to legislate on a number of matters, including the usage of land, the management of forests and the inheritance of property, among others. However, compromises were said to have been made with the traditional institutions.[8]

In response, the NNC conducted a plebiscite in 1951 and 'claimed that 99.9 per cent of Nagas had voted in favour of independence'[9]. In 1952, the Nagas boycotted India's first general elections. They began a non-cooperation movement and blocked the formation of

---

[5] Singh, 'Nagaland', pp. 818–19.
[6] S.K. Chaube, *Hill Politics in Northeast India,* (India: Orient Blackswan, 2012), p. 154.
[7] Sitlhou, 'Accord.'
[8] Chaube, *Hill Politics,* pp. 105–06.
[9] Sitlhou, 'Accord.'

the district council. The Assam Government then had to administer the Naga Hills directly.

When the States Reorganisation Commission (SRC) was constituted in December 1953 to redraw India's state borders, the NNC stood apart from all the other hill districts mentioned in Part A of the Sixth Schedule. While the hill districts put forth a demand for their unification, the NNC continued to seek 'independence from Assam and India'.[10]

In September 1955, the SRC released its report. It dismissed the demand of a separate hill state as well as that of a separate Nagaland. Citing the past violence in the Naga Hills district, as well as the recent relative peace, it recommended no change to the area's status.

This did not go down well with the Nagas and violence escalated across the region. The government tried to quell it first by recruiting armed village guards and then by deploying the police. Eventually, it passed the Assam Disturbed Areas Act. The NNC split into two 'irreconcilable'[11] camps—the extremists (led by Zapu Phizo) pursuing Naga independence, and the moderates (led by T. Sakhrie) trying to find a Naga future within the Indian Constitution. In January 1956, Sakhrie was killed, allegedly by Phizo's extremist faction, as a way to hamper peace negotiations.[12] This led to a political and personal rivalry between the two clans that often turned violent and spanned generations.

In March, Phizo declared Nagaland as 'a people's sovereign republic'[13]. He founded the Federal Government of Nagaland with its own national flag and Constitution. The Union government finally called in the army. In order to break connections between the

---

[10]   Report of the States Reorganisation Commission, 1955, p. 184.
[11]   Sitlhou, 'Accord.'
[12]   Ibid.
[13]   Kumar, *Reorganization*, p. 27.

locals and the rebels in the forests, the Army resorted to the tactic of 'grouping villages'. Before the end of the year, Phizo escaped to London via East Pakistan on a fake passport.[14]

*

1957–63: A Negotiated Journey to Statehood

Phizo's exit changed the flow of events. The moderates under the leadership of Dr Imkongliba Ao took control of the NNC and formed a reforming committee in February 1957. The committee was opposed to the method of violence, preferring a separate administrative unit keeping with the Naga tradition within the framework of the Indian Union.[15] The Nagas participated in the general elections held in early 1957 and elected three members to the Assam Assembly.

In August 1957, Dr Ao chaired a Naga People's Convention at Kohima which was attended by thousands of people across all Naga tribes (except the underground extremists). Advocating negotiation over violence, the convention formally gave up the demand for Naga independence and instead asked for 'a single administrative unit comprising of Naga Hills district of Assam and Tuensang Frontier Division of NEFA'[16] (North-East Frontier Agency). Tuensang (earlier known as Naga Tribal Area) lay just north of Naga Hills District. It was a 'frontier division'—an administrative unit—of NEFA, which was constitutionally a part of Assam. A nine-member delegation led by Dr Ao presented this resolution to the Governor in Shillong and then the prime minister in New Delhi in September.

---

[14] Sitlhou, 'Accord.'

[15] Chandrika Singh, *Naga Politics: A Critical Account* (India: Mittal Publications, 2004), p. 63.

[16] Kumar, *Reorganization,* p. 29.

This proved successful as Prime Minister Nehru accepted the delegation's demands.

On 1 December 1957, the Naga Hills–Tuensang Area came into being as a new administrative unit in the state of Assam but under the direct control of the ministry of external affairs.[17] The unit was also simultaneously separate from Assam as it was governed by the Governor of Assam acting on behalf of the President of India.[18]

While the moderates considered the establishment of the separate Naga Hills–Tuensang Area as a victory and a first step towards statehood, the underground extremists saw it as a consolidation of the Indian government in the Naga Hills and ramped up the violence. To keep their momentum going, the moderate leaders organized a second Naga People's Convention at Ungma in May 1958. This convention, again well-attended, set up a draft committee that formulated a sixteen-point proposal to enable the establishment of the state of Nagaland within the Indian Union. The third Naga People's Convention at Mokokchung in October 1959 adopted this proposal. In July 1960, a fifteen-member delegation led by Dr Ao presented this proposal to Prime Minister Nehru, which he later accepted with slight modifications.[19] The state of Nagaland would become a reality.

A three-year transitional period was put into effect for 'the regulation of Nagaland'[20] until its creation. An interim body was created consisting of forty-two members elected from Naga tribes, with Dr Imkongliba Ao as the Chairman. Five of these members were also appointed by the Governor to an advisory executive council with P. Shilu Ao as the chief executive councillor. These two bodies worked as the de facto legislature and cabinet.

---

[17]   The Naga Hills–Tuensang Area Act, 1957.
[18]   Singh, 'Nagaland', pp. 822–23.
[19]   Ibid., pp. 823-25.
[20]   Ibid., p. 825.

However, the underground extremist faction refused to recognize the sixteen-point accord and intensified their violent struggle. Dr Imkongliba Ao, chairman of the interim body, was assassinated in August 1961. Undeterred, the interim body elected T.N. Angami as the chairman and continued on the path of transition.

In September 1962, the Union government passed the State of Nagaland Act. The new state comprised the entire territory of the Naga Hills–Tuensang Area. It would have three districts—Kohima, Mokokchung and Tuensang.[21] The Constitutional Amendment also included Section 371A that sought to protect the religious and social practices, customary laws, and land ownership of the Nagas.[22]

The state of Nagaland officially came into being on 1 December 1963. P. Shilu Ao of the Naga Nationalist Organisation was the first chief minister.

**

---

[21] The State of Nagaland Act, 1962.
[22] The Constitution (Thirteenth Amendment) Act, 1962.

ODISHA

Did You Know?

Odisha was the first modern Indian state to be created on a linguistic basis.

Odisha was born on 1 April 1936, a date which is celebrated every year as 'Utkala Dibasa' (Odisha Day), making Odisha one of only two states in India to have a formation day pre-dating Independence. It was created as Orissa Province in 1936 following an elaborate enquiry by three separate committees spread over thirty years.[1] It was also created on a linguistic basis, comprising an amalgamation of Odia-speaking districts from the existing Bihar and Orissa Province (42 per cent of land area and 66 per cent of population), Madras Province (53 per cent of land area and 31.7 per cent of population), and Central Provinces (5 per cent of land area and 2.3 per cent of population).[2]

---

[1] Report of the States Reorganisation Commission, 1955, p. 199.
[2] Bandita Devi, *Some Aspects of British Administration in Orissa, 1912–1936*, (India: Academic Foundation, 1992), pp. 213–14.

At the same time, in keeping with the British two-tiered system of administration, forty-two princely states in the region were grouped under the Eastern States Agency. This included twenty-six princely states of Orissa.[3]

And so, at the time of Independence in 1947, Odisha existed in two parts—Orissa Province and a large part of the Eastern States Agency. Due to the provincial elections held in January 1946, Orissa Province already had a chief minister—Harekrushna Mahatab of the Indian National Congress (INC).

*

Unifying Orissa

In August 1947, the members of the Eastern States Agency made a play to form their own state. They joined together to form the Eastern States Union, headed by Maharaja Ramanuj Pratap Singh Deo, the ruler of the princely state of Korea (now also spelled as Koriya). However, two of the biggest states—Mayurbhanj and Bastar—along with some of the smaller states, refused to join. The Union was a motley of Odia-speaking states and Hindi-speaking states scattered across Orissa Province and Central Provinces. By November 1947, the States Ministry had decided that the Union government would not recognize the Eastern States Union due to linguistic and administrative irregularities. The Orissa princely states would be merged into Orissa Province, and the Chhattisgarh states into Central Provinces.[4]

The States Ministry's decision split the rulers of the Eastern States Union into opposing camps. At Cuttack in the middle of December 1947, Sardar Vallabhbhai Patel and V.P. Menon first met the rulers

---

[3]   Devi, *British Administration in Orissa*, pp. 213–14.
[4]   V.P. Menon, *The Story of the Integration of the Indian States* (United Kingdom: Longmans, Green and Co., 1956), p. 106–115.

of the smaller class B and C states, and later of the larger class A states. They apprised them of the law and order unrest that simmered in their states, the people's desire to have a responsible government which most states could not provide, and the possibility that the Union government would take over the states' administration if the situation worsened. Within a day, all the rulers signed the agreement merging their Orissa states with Orissa Province. The following day, the rulers of the Chhattisgarh states signed a similar merger agreement. The Eastern States Union was dissolved. By the end of the month, the Orissa government was given the power to administer the states.[5]

In May 1948, two states—Seraikela and Kharsawan—were shifted from Orissa to Bihar as they were exclaves within Bihar. On 17 October 1948, the Maharaja of Mayurbhanj, who had independently attempted to run a responsible government and had failed, signed an Instrument of Merger with India. On 1 January 1949, the States Ministry merged Mayurbhanj with Orissa as it was 'linguistically and culturally linked'[6]. This completed the process of the creation of the state of Orissa.

*

Orissa to Odisha

Odisha is the Odia spelling and pronunciation of the state. However, the state was known as Udisa in Hindi and Orissa in English. Similarly, the state language is Odia, while it was known as Udiya in Hindi and Oriya in English. In 2008, the state government passed a proposal to introduce a bill to standardize all the spellings and pronunciations to Odisha and Odia.[7]

---

5   Menon, *Integration*, pp. 106–15.
6   Menon, *Integration*, pp. 116–17.
7   Press Trust of India, 'Orissa Wants to Change its Name to Odisha', *Rediff News*, 10 June 2008, https://www.rediff.com/news/2008/jun/10orissa.htm.

Eventually, in September 2011, Parliament passed the Orissa (Alteration of Name) Act at the Centre. From 1 November 2011, the official nomenclature became Odisha and Odia.[8]

* *

---

[8]   Government of India. The Orissa (Alteration of Name) Act, 2011.

PUNJAB

Did You Know?

Punjab shared an international border with China for nearly twenty years.

1947: Multiple Geographies, Communities and Names

Punjab Province had been the richest administrative province in British India.[1] With Independence, the Radcliffe Line cut through Punjab Province. 62 per cent of the land formed Muslim-dominant West Punjab and became a part of Pakistan, while 38 per cent formed Hindu-dominant East Punjab and became a part of the Dominion of India.[2] The Sikhs had been a numerical minority in undivided Punjab Province but had 'virtually held

---

[1]   Ian Copland, 'The Master and the Maharajas: The Sikh Princes and the East Punjab Massacres of 1947,' *Modern Asian Studies,* 36(3) (July 2002), p. 657.

[2]   S.S. Bal, 'Punjab After Independence (1947–1956),' *Proceedings of the Indian History Congress,* 46 (1985), p. 416.

the balance in the politics'[3] of the region. Partition resulted in a large-scale migration of Sikhs into East Punjab, consolidating their community. As a result, three distinct geographical and demographical regions began to emerge in East Punjab post-Partition. State boundaries would be drawn and redrawn across these three regions over the following twenty years.

In the North-western districts of East Punjab, Sikhs formed the majority for the first time. In the South-eastern districts, Hindus formed the majority.[4] The hilly north-eastern part of East Punjab cut through the territories of thirty East Punjab Hill States (or the Shimla Hill States) and split them into two chunks.

Eight princely states in the region had been a part of the erstwhile Punjab States Agency under the British administration. These princely states were known as the East Punjab States and they lay strewn across East Punjab. Patiala was the largest, greater in area, population and revenue than all the rest of the East Punjab States put together. The States Ministry deemed Patiala as viable to stand on its own.[5]

Finally, the tiny princely state of Bilaspur sat surrounded by both East Punjab and the East Punjab Hill States. It had previously been a part of the latter, but had then been taken under the direct control of Punjab States Agency before Independence.[6]

*

[3]   V.P. Menon, *The Story of the Integration of the Indian States* (United Kingdom: Longmans, Green and Co., 1956), p. 163.

[4]   Baldev Raj Nayar, 'Punjab,' in *State Politics in India*, ed. Myron Weiner (United States of America: Princeton University Press, 1968), p. 444.

[5]   Menon, *Integration*, p. 164.

[6]   Jaideep Negi, 'The Begar System in the Shimla Hill States during the British Period,' *Proceedings of the Indian History Congress*, 55 (1994), pp. 693–97.

1948: The First Movement

In March 1948, the rulers of the East Punjab Hill States signed accession agreements with India citing only one request—that their territories 'be consolidated into one unit'[7]. On 15 April 1948, the East Punjab Hill States were consolidated into Himachal Pradesh, a chief commissioner's province. Being a centrally administered unit allowed the Government of India to exercise direct and strategic control, especially in matters of administration, resources and finances. Himachal Pradesh was also non-contiguous as it continued to be separated by East Punjab.

In August 1948, the ruler of Bilaspur also signed the agreement to accede to India. Bilaspur was retained under central administration in order to pay direct attention to the planning of the large Bhakra Dam over the River Sutlej. On 12 October 1948, the Raja of Bilaspur, Anand Chand, was appointed as chief commissioner. Bilaspur was eventually integrated into Himachal Pradesh in 1954 as the two regions were geographically contiguous.

In April 1948, Master Tara Singh, the president of the Shiromani Akali Dal (SAD), made the first demand for a consolidated Punjabi Suba (Punjabi Province) comprising the North-western districts that had a Sikh and Punjabi majority.[8] Founded in 1920, the SAD was the second-oldest political party in India after the Indian National Congress (INC). It was also the first state political party.

Contemplating the dilemma before the States Ministry, V.P. Menon, who was secretary of the States Ministry, said:

'There were four alternatives before us. Firstly, we could amalgamate Himachal Pradesh and the East Punjab States with East Punjab, leaving out Patiala which had been declared

---

[7]   Ministry of States, Government of India, *White Paper on Indian States*, 1950, pp. 46–47.

[8]   Bal, 'Punjab After Independence,' p. 419.

a viable unit. Secondly, we could amalgamate Patiala together with Himachal Pradesh and the East Punjab States with the province. Thirdly, we could leave Himachal Pradesh and Patiala alone and amalgamate the States of Kapurthala, Nabha, Jind, Malerkotla and Faridkot into a single Union. Fourthly, we could integrate all the Punjab States, including Patiala, into one Union.'[9]

The States Ministry narrowed its options through a process of elimination. It was important to keep Himachal Pradesh as a centrally administered unit, both to develop it into a self-reliant unit and to not mix the residents of the hills and the plains into one administrative system.

The immediate merger of the princely states with the province appeared impractical and mistimed. Partition and the resulting two-way migration had strained East Punjab; its administration needed to reorganize and stabilize and deal with more pressing issues like law and order and refugees rather than amalgamation of new territories. Hence, the States Ministry decided that East Punjab, Himachal Pradesh and East Punjab States would be kept as three separate administrative units.

A Union of East Punjab States needed Patiala in order to be feasible. V.P. Menon met with the Maharaja of Patiala, Yadavindra Singh, and impressed upon him the merits of such a Union, including stability and the position of Patiala as well as the crucial aspiration of building Sikh politics, both in the Union and in the province.

The Union was called the Patiala and East Punjab States Union (PEPSU). It existed as 'five disconnected bits'[10] encased entirely within the territory of East Punjab. The Maharajas of Patiala and

---

9   Menon, *Integration*, p. 165.
10 Report of the States Reorganisation Commission, 1955, p. 147.

Kapurthala were appointed the Rajpramukh (Governor) and Uprajpramukh (Deputy Governor). The Union was inaugurated on 15 July 1948.

However, efforts to build a ministry failed. The two major political parties in the region, the INC and the SAD, were both seen to represent communities—Hindus and Sikhs, respectively. Both parties wanted their candidate to be the Premier. The failure to reach a consensus twice resulted in the establishment of a caretaker government in PEPSU. Eventually, in early 1949, a ministry was established with members representing the various parties. Sardar Gyan Singh Rarewala, an independent politician, was accepted by all the parties to be the Premier.

Further, a new capital had to be decided for Punjab. Lahore, the erstwhile chief administrative and cultural city of undivided Punjab, was now in Pakistan. In January 1948, Prime Minister Jawaharlal Nehru declared that there was the need for establishing new towns and cities considering the heavy inflow of refugees. In March 1948, the Union government officially decided to build the entirely new city of Chandigarh for the capital of Punjab.[11]

*

1949–56: The Second Movement

In October 1949, as a countermeasure to the Punjabi Suba demand put forth by the SAD, the majority INC in East Punjab presented what became known as the Sachar Formula (or the Sachar–Giani Formula). This was named after Bhim Sen Sachar, the East Punjab Premier, and Giani Kartar Singh, a SAD leader and a minister in the Sachar government. The Sachar Formula 'devised by two Hindus

---

[11] Meeta Rajivlochan, Kavita Sharma and Chitleen K. Sethi, *Chandigarh Lifescape: Brief Social History of a Planned City* (India: Chandigarh Government Press, 1999), p. 20.

and two Sikhs'[12] sought to retain the bilingual character of East Punjab by dividing the province into Punjabi and Hindi zones where the dominant language would be the medium of instruction and the other language would be a compulsory subject. However, 'by accident or design'[13], it sharpened the divide in the province along linguistic and communal lines.

The Sachar Formula generated heated controversy. Bhim Sen Sachar lost his premiership. The SAD capitalized on the formula recommendations by demanding autonomous status for the Punjabi-speaking region, presenting it as a linguistic demand. The discord between the two communities reached such a fever pitch that Prime Minister Jawaharlal Nehru directed that no language be recorded in the 1951 census in Punjab State (renamed from East Punjab after India adopted its Constitution on 26 January 1950). Hence, the 1951 census showed 'Hindi/Punjabi' as a joint option.[14]

In the 1952 legislative assembly elections, the INC romped home with a huge majority in Punjab. In PEPSU, however, no party gained a clear majority. Even though the INC was the single largest party, the SAD built a coalition called the United Democratic Front (UDF) with other parties and formed a non-Congress government in PEPSU in April 1952.

Between October and December 1952, SAD leaders Hukam Singh and Master Tara Singh proposed the creation of a Punjabi Suba by merging the Punjabi-speaking region of Punjab State with PEPSU. This would create a Punjabi- and Sikh-majority state. This proposal was bolstered both by the imposition of President's rule in PEPSU in March 1953 and by the creation of Andhra State on a linguistic basis in October 1953.

---

[12]   Bal, 'Punjab After Independence,' p. 418.
[13]   Ibid.
[14]   Government of India, Census of India, 1951.

Meanwhile, on 21 September 1953, the capital of Punjab officially moved from Shimla to Chandigarh.[15]

Towards the end of 1953, spurred by the multiple calls for state reorganization across the country, the Union government announced the creation of the States Reorganisation Commission (SRC) which invited memoranda from the public, individually and collectively. By May 1954, the SAD, the Congress, the Arya Samaj and the Jana Sangh had submitted separate memoranda for the reorganization of Punjab. The SAD reiterated its demand for Punjabi Suba, merging the Punjabi-speaking region with PEPSU and excluding much of the south-eastern region of Punjab known as Haryana. It built a linguistic argument that Punjabi was a distinct language recognized in the Indian Constitution with its own Gurmukhi script that was not derived from the Hindi Devanagari script.[16]

On the other hand, the State Congress proposed Maha Punjab by integrating Punjab, PEPSU and Himachal Pradesh. The Arya Samaj and Jana Sangh went a step further by including Delhi as well in the proposed amalgamation.[17]

In October 1955, the SRC released its report. It decreed that there was no real language problem and there were no distinctive cultural zones in Punjab; that in the 'battle of scripts', the superstructure of Punjabi was a dialect of western Hindi, and therefore the line of demarcation between Punjabi and Hindi was 'theoretical' and 'blurred'.[18] The SRC felt that the creation of a unilingual state where Gurmukhi was imposed when Devanagari proved just as suitable for writing Punjabi may create more problems than it would solve. Noting also that the entire area would still be bilingual since Hindi would not be unimportant and would continue to exist and

---

[15] Rajivlochan, Sharma, and Sethi, *Chandigarh Lifescape,* p. 12.
[16] Bal, 'Punjab After Independence,' pp. 424–25.
[17] Report of the States Reorganisation Commission, 1955, p. 147.
[18] Ibid., p. 142.

develop side-by-side with Punjabi, the SRC decided that it would be impossible to create a compact unilingual state, especially one which also lacked the general support of the people in the area. The SRC also dismissed the demand for Haryana.[19]

The SRC did view PEPSU as very much a part of Punjab, physically and geographically. Given PEPSU's extremely small size and lack of geographical contiguity, the SRC saw advantages of economy and efficiency of administration in merging it with Punjab. Patiala had to cede its capital city status to the newly planned under-construction city of Chandigarh.

On the matter of Himachal Pradesh, the three members of the SRC disagreed on how to proceed. Two members recommended integration with Punjab due to clear economic and administrative advantages and 'the mutual benefit of the people of the plains and of the hills'[20]. They dismissed the proposal for the formation of a larger hill unit consisting of the hill territories of Himachal Pradesh, Punjab, PEPSU and Uttar Pradesh as not forming an administratively viable unit. Hence, in effect, they backed the proposal of Maha Punjab as the most satisfactory solution. The proposed state would consist of Punjab, PEPSU and Himachal Pradesh, but without Delhi and any western districts of Uttar Pradesh. The chairman of the SRC, S. Fazl Ali, however, recommended no change in Himachal Pradesh's current status as he felt that a merger with Punjab would be locally unpopular. The hill state still needed support for development which had to be provided by the Centre and not by Punjab.[21]

Displeased with the report, the SAD led by Master Tara Singh arranged for a series of parleys with the Government of India starting in October 1955. More emphatically, in February 1956,

---

[19] Report of the States Reorganisation Commission, 1955, pp. 140–56.

[20] Ibid,. p. 151.

[21] S. Fazl Ali, 'Note on Himachal Pradesh,' Report of the States Reorganisation Commission, 1955, pp. 238–43.

the SAD called for a conference in Amritsar on the same days as the INC conference in the city. Over one lakh Sikhs assembled in a disciplined, peaceful and purposeful manner in a massive show of unity, solidarity and strength.

Soon after, the two sides reached an agreement on a regional formula through sustained efforts by leaders including Giani Kartar Singh, Sardar Hukam Singh and Gian Singh Rarewala, among others. Punjab and PEPSU would be merged but not Himachal Pradesh. Punjab would be a bilingual state demarcated as per the Sachar Formula into Punjabi- and Hindi-speaking regions where the respective language would be the medium of instruction and the other language would be a compulsory subject. Two regional committees would be established in the state legislature having large powers in their respective regions.[22]

On 1 November 1956, Punjab and PEPSU merged into one state of Punjab. Himachal Pradesh continued under direct central authority and became known as a union territory. The SAD and INC put aside their previous differences and began to work together. Their combined might returned a thumping majority in the 1957 legislative assembly elections in Punjab. The incumbent chief minister, Partap Singh Kairon of the INC, was reinstated.

*

1960–66: The Third Movement

The partnership between the SAD and the INC did not last long. The SAD was dissatisfied with both the working of the regional formula and the unwillingness of the INC state government to 'enhance the

---

[22] Karnail Singh Doad, 'Punjabi Suba Movement,' in *The Encyclopaedia of Sikhism, Volume III M-R*, ed. Harbans Singh (India: Punjabi University, Patiala, 1997), pp. 392–94.

status of the Punjabi language'[23]. The SAD ended its partnership with the Congress and launched a renewed movement demanding Punjabi Suba in May 1960.

At this point, an ideological split began to form in the SAD. Master Tara Singh's approach had created apprehensions of an autonomous Sikh state. His lieutenant Sant Fateh Singh, however, was given direct access to Prime Minister Jawaharlal Nehru where he maintained that the demand for Punjabi Suba was 'linguistic and only linguistic'[24] and it didn't matter whether Hindus or Sikhs were in the majority. He also used pressure tactics like embarking on a fast-unto-death and threatening self-immolation. This promotion emboldened Sant Fateh Singh to directly challenge the leadership of Master Tara Singh and form a separate Akali Dal in 1962.

Meanwhile, the demand for a separate Haryana state also strengthened. In April 1961, the Haryana Lok Samiti (Haryana People's Society) was formed in association with the Arya Samaj to contest the upcoming general elections. Its campaign promoted Hindi and opposed the imposition of Punjabi as well as the economic discrimination of the region by the Punjab government.[25]

In 1964, the Congress leadership underwent major changes at the state and the Centre. Prime Minister Jawaharlal Nehru died in May. Chief Minister Partap Singh Kairon was removed on corruption charges in June; he was assassinated in February the following year. The Punjab Congress splintered and 'lacked the will or the leadership'[26] to oppose the Punjabi Suba demand.

---

[23] Paul R. Brass, *Language, Religion and Politics in North India* (United States: iUniverse, 2005), p. 321.
[24] Gurdarshan Singh Dhillon, 'Evolution of the Demand for a Sikh Homeland,' *The Indian Journal of Political Science,* 35(4) (Oct.–Dec. 1974), p. 371.
[25] Brass, *Language,* p. 331.
[26] Ibid., p. 322.

In 1965, Sant Fateh Singh's breakaway Akali Dal wrested control of the Shiromani Gurdwara Parbandhak Committee (SGPC, Supreme Gurdwara Management Committee), which has been described as 'a government within the government' and the 'source of legitimacy and authority for the Sikh community'.[27] Having received this mandate, Sant Fateh Singh engaged with the new Prime Minister Lal Bahadur Shastri of the INC on the demand for Punjabi Suba. In early September 1965, the Union government agreed to appoint a cabinet subcommittee to resolve the Punjabi Suba issue. This further galvanized leaders from the Haryana and hill regions to also demand for the reorganization of Punjab.

Later in September 1965, war broke out between India and Pakistan. The immense contribution of the Sikhs in this war proved to be the final incentive the government needed to concede the Punjabi Suba demand and solve the political unrest in Punjab. In March 1966, the government appointed a parliamentary committee to look into reorganizing Punjab. The committee reported that 'an overwhelming majority'[28] now supported linguistic reorganization, noting also the rise in support in the Haryana region.

On 18 September 1966, the government passed the Punjab Reorganisation Act. Punjab was divided into four parts—two states and two union territories. The Hindi-speaking districts in the South-eastern plains formed the new state of Haryana. The North-eastern hill districts merged with the existing union territory of Himachal Pradesh. The Punjabi-speaking North-western districts formed the new Punjabi Suba, the new state of Punjab. The city of Chandigarh was reconstituted as a union territory; Chandigarh was also named

---

[27] Brass, *Language,* p. 313.
[28] Ibid., p. 331.

the joint capital of Punjab and Haryana and would house the common high court for all three territories.[29]

All four new territories came into being from 1 November 1966.

* *

---

[29] The Punjab Reorganisation Act, 1966.

RAJASTHAN

At the time of Independence, the current state of Rajasthan was almost wholly contained in the Rajputana Agency, a political office of the British Indian Empire. It consisted of twenty-two princely states and estates. Less than twenty-two months later, all twenty-two of them had assimilated into the largest state in India—Rajasthan. It was done in a step-by-step manner.

*

Step 1: Matsya Union (March 1948—May 1949)

The States Ministry believed that the four princely states of Alwar, Bharatpur, Dholpur and Karauli, clustered together in the eastern edge of Rajputana, had 'natural, racial and economic affinities'[1] with each other and, hence, could be integrated into a Union. Accordingly, Matsya Union was inaugurated on 18 March 1948. The Maharaja of Dholpur, the oldest of the four rulers, was named Rajpramukh (Governor).

At the time of formation itself, the understanding was that Matsya Union was a temporary arrangement as it was not large enough or financially self-supporting to continue being an independent Union. When the time came, it would have to join either Rajasthan or United Provinces.

While the rulers and representatives of Alwar and Karauli unanimously favoured integration with Rajasthan, the preference was less clear in Bharatpur and Dholpur. Hence, a three-member committee was formed to ascertain public opinion in the latter two states through questionnaires and public meetings; majority opinion in both states favoured integration with Rajasthan. And so, on 15 May 1949, less than fourteen months after it was created, Matsya Union was dissolved and its four princely states joined the newly-formed Greater Rajasthan Union.[2]

*

Step 2: Rajasthan Union (March 1948—March 1949)

Almost parallelly, the idea of a state of Rajasthan began to take shape in the south-east of Rajputana. Ten princely states considered merging to form a Union. An alternative to merge them with the proposed state of Madhya Bharat was also mooted, but then it was decided that 'the natural affinity of these states was more with Rajputana'[3].

---

[1]   V.P. Menon, *The Story of the Integration of the Indian States* (United Kingdom: Longmans, Green and Co., 1956), p. 175.
[2]   Ministry of States, Government of India. *White Paper on Indian States*, 1950, pp. 53–55.
[3]   Ibid.

Udaipur (also known as Mewar), which was the biggest of the ten, suggested that all the states should merge into Udaipur. However, this idea of a larger state swallowing smaller states, and therefore also their identity and existence, ran counter to the idea of integration that the Union was trying to achieve. As a result, the nine smaller states decided to go ahead and form the Union themselves, leaving Udaipur out.

On 25 March 1948, the Rajasthan Union was inaugurated. The Maharao of Kotah, Bhim Singh II, was designated as the Rajpramukh. He had been exploring the possibility of a Union since 1946, when he had convened a conference with neighbouring states.

The Maharana of Udaipur officially decided to join the Rajasthan Union three days after its inauguration. As a result, a new covenant to reconstitute the Union had to replace the existing agreement. After discussions with the other nine states, it was decided that the Maharana of Udaipur, Bhupal Singh Bahadur, would become the Rajpramukh for life, while the Maharao of Kotah would be elected as the Senior Uprajpramukh (Senior Deputy Governor). The capital, which was currently at Kotah, would be moved to Udaipur. However, the legislature would hold at least one session every year in Kotah, and one commissioner's administrative division would be in Kotah. A number of institutions would remain or be located in Kotah, including the Forest School, the Police Training College and the Aeronautical College, as well as any other institutions 'which could conveniently be at Kotah'[4].

This second Rajasthan Union was inaugurated by Prime Minister Jawaharlal Nehru on 18 April 1948.

*

Step 3: Greater Rajasthan (March 1949 onwards)

While all the smaller states had merged to form Matsya Union in the east and Rajasthan Union in the south-east, the four largest states

---

4   Menon, *Integration*, p. 179.

that comprised most of Rajputana still remained independent. These were Jaipur, Jodhpur, Bikaner and Jaisalmer.

The latter three all shared a national border with Pakistan. V.P. Menon, secretary of the States Ministry, suggested integrating these three states into a centrally administered area under a chief commissioner.[5] If Kutch State (currently in northern Gujarat) was also included in this scheme, then all of the central and southern border with Pakistan would be under the direct control of the Government of India. However, this idea did not have many backers and Menon gave it up. The alternative was to merge the four states of Jaipur, Jodhpur, Bikaner and Jaisalmer individually into the newly-formed Rajasthan Union. This solution found favour with Sardar Vallabhbhai Patel, the head of the States Ministry.[6]

Discussions began in January 1949. In principle, the four states agreed immediately to the integration. This allowed Sardar Patel to announce the impending reality of Greater Rajasthan on 14 January. Then, the parties settled down to discuss the details of the integration.

The Maharana of Udaipur, Bhupal Singh Bahadur, expressed his desire to be Rajpramukh of the new Union. He was the Rajpramukh of the previous Union and the senior most among all the rulers at sixty-four years of age. However, considering his declining health, it was instead decided to create an honorary position for him of Maharajpramukh (Great Governor) that would be outside the general administrative set-up.

Jaipur was picked as the capital of the new Union and the Maharaja of Jaipur, Sawai Man Singh II, was selected as Rajpramukh. He was thirty-six years old. The rulers of Jodhpur and Kotah would be the Senior Uprajpramukhs and the rulers of Bundi and Dungarpur would be the Junior Uprajpramukhs.

---

5   Menon, *Integration*, p. 181.
6   Ibid.

Greater Rajasthan was inaugurated by Sardar Vallabhbhai Patel on 30 March 1949. This date is still celebrated as 'Rajasthan Day' every year.

On 15 May 1949, Matsya Union—which had been the first step in the creation of a single unified Rajasthan—merged with Greater Rajasthan and ceased to exist.

*

1956: Minor Changes

On 1 November 1956, the States Reorganisation Act resulted in a few minor changes to the state of Rajasthan. First, the States Reorganisation Commission (SRC) rejected a latent idea of splitting the state up into three parts—Western Rajasthan (or Maru Pradesh), Eastern Rajasthan and Southern Rajasthan. Their reasoning was that such a move would financially weaken the units, especially the largely desert border region of Maru Pradesh, and it would run counter to the 'substantial measure of agreement in 1948 and 1949 in support of the mergers'[7].

Ajmer was a small Part C state that existed independently in central Rajasthan. Given its linguistic, cultural and geographical links with Rajasthan and the absence of any discernible reason for Ajmer to continue being an independent state, it was integrated into Rajasthan as a district.

In 1950, the Abu Road taluk of Sirohi district had been sliced and included in Bombay State. However, Rajasthan maintained their claim on the taluk, citing both local feeling and that Rajasthani was the mother tongue of 65 per cent of the local population. Even the Government of India had reopened this question and reconsidered their decision in 1952. Hence, in 1956, the Abu Road taluk was re-integrated with Sirohi district and Rajasthan State.[8]

---

[7] Report of the States Reorganisation Commission, 1955, pp. 135–39.
[8] Ibid.

The enclave of Sunel was received from Madhya Pradesh while the enclave of Sironj was given to Madhya Pradesh due to ease of geography and administration.

Today, Rajasthan is the largest state in India by area, covering over 10 per cent of the country.

* *

SIKKIM

> **Did You Know?**
>
> *Sikkim was officially not a part of the Indian Union until 16 May 1975.*

Different from Other Indian States

As India's Independence approached, a unique future was being debated for the princely state of Sikkim—whether to be included in the Union of India or not.

The head of the States Department, Sardar Vallabhbhai Patel, and the constitutional adviser to the constituent assembly, B.N. Rau, wanted the Chogyal (king) of Sikkim, Tashi Namgyal, to sign the Instrument of Accession with India, like the other princely states were doing. After all, Sikkim was a member state of the Chamber of Princes and of the constituent assembly, and the States Ministry hence viewed Sikkim as an Indian state.

However, Sikkim also had a unique past under British rule, as did Bhutan and Nepal, the other two monarchies that formed the mountainous buffer states between British India and China. The British had established a formal protectorate over Sikkim in the nineteenth century but continued to remain ambiguous about Sikkim's status. It was not a feudatory native state like the other princely states in British India and its relations were conducted through the government's external affairs department, but neither was it independent nor internally autonomous.[1]

As a result, when the time came for soon-to-be-independent India to determine its stand on Sikkim, the future prime minister of India, Jawaharlal Nehru, wanted to respect Sikkim's unique status and treat it as a special case. During a constituent assembly meeting on 22 January 1947, Nehru remarked on the need of examining the special problems of Bhutan and Sikkim and noted the difference between the two princely states. Bhutan was, he observed, 'an independent state under the protection of India' while Sikkim was 'an Indian state but different from others'.[2]

On 3 June 1947, a meeting was held between representatives of the Indian States Ministry and ministry of external affairs and those of Sikkim and Bhutan. The Sikkim delegation was led by Maharaj Kumar Palden Thondup Namgyal, the son and heir-apparent of the Sikkim Chogyal Tashi Namgyal. Sikkim's proposal was that it be placed on the same footing as Bhutan even though it had so far been treated as an Indian state. V.P. Menon, the secretary of the States Ministry, offered Sikkim the regular Instrument of Accession where India would take over control of three subjects—defence, external affairs and communication—but he also specified that the choice of accession to India was up to Sikkim to make. Until this was finalized and concluded, Sikkim would have to sign a Standstill Agreement

[1]   Leo E. Rose, 'India and Sikkim: Redefining the Relationship,' *Pacific Affairs,* 42(1) (Spring 1969), p. 32. doi:10.2307/2754861
[2]   G.B.S. Sidhu, *Sikkim: Dawn of Democracy* (India: Penguin Random House India Private Limited, 2018), p. 39.

with India to maintain the status quo. This Standstill Agreement was signed on 27 February 1948 and contained eleven subjects, including internal infrastructure, external affairs and defence.[3]

Sikkim had three major communities—Bhutia, Lepcha and Nepalese—in order of political and societal power, but not in terms of size. The Nepalese community formed three-fourths of the population and was about six times as large as either of the other two equally sized communities.[4] This played out in a curious manner in the political landscape.

The Sikkim State Congress (SSC) was the largest political party and was led by Tashi Tshering, a Bhutia. The Praja Mandal was led by Kazi Lhendup Dorji Khangsarpa, a Lepcha, and the Praja Sudharak Samaj was led by Dhan Bahadur Chhetri, a Nepali. Both these parties soon merged into the SSC. On 5 December 1947, the three parties—the bulk of whose membership consisted of Nepalese—met in Gangtok and passed a resolution demanding a popular government (or an interim government until then), the abolition of landlordism, and accession to India. The smaller pro-Nepalese Sikkim Rajya Praja Sammelan (SRPS) went further, demanding an outright merger with India and the creation of a larger Nepalese state within India. Meanwhile, to counter the pro-democracy SSC, Maharaj Kumar Thondup set up his own party to pursue an independent Sikkim and oppose accession to India—the Sikkim National Party (SNP), whose membership was restricted to Bhutias and Lepchas.

In late 1948, the SSC took out pro-democracy rallies and demonstrations. A delegation including Tashi Tshering and Kazi Dorji met Prime Minister Jawaharlal Nehru to draw his support for Sikkim's accession. However, Nehru suggested that Sikkim,

---

[3]   Sidhu, *Sikkim*, p. 55.
[4]   Ranjan Gupta, 'Sikkim: The Merger with India,' *Asian Survey*, 15(9) (September 1975), p. 790. doi:10.2307/2643174

like Bhutan and Nepal, should be allowed to 'grow according to its own genius'[5]. In early 1949, the SSC launched a state-wide 'no-rent no-tax' campaign against the exploitation of land cultivators in the form of discriminatory rents, which led to the arrests of its party workers. Thousands of SSC followers marched to the palace on 1 May 1949. Over the following days, the durbar (king's court) sought the intervention of India's resident political officer and promised to form an interim popular government with Tashi Tshering as the chief minister. However, less than a month later, the Maharaja dismissed the interim government. In its place, an Indian officer was appointed as diwan (chief minister) along with an advisory committee that contained representatives from both SSC and SNP.

On 5 December 1950, the Government of India and Maharaja Tashi Namgyal signed the Indo–Sikkim Treaty. Sikkim would be a protectorate of India with autonomy in internal affairs—'a non-sovereign state attached to India'[6]. India would be responsible for Sikkim's defence, external affairs and strategic communications. India also secured exclusive rights for building infrastructure in Sikkim. Sikkimese travelling abroad would be treated as Indian protected persons holding Indian passports. Unrestricted free movement was allowed between India and Sikkim, and the Chief Justice of India would preside over disputes regarding this treaty. In terms of democratic reform, directly elected panchayats were established but not a representative government. In a follow-up explanatory letter again signed by both parties, the tenth and last clause gave India overriding powers in the event of a serious internal security threat. This clause would be invoked more than twenty years later.

*

5   Sidhu, *Sikkim*, p. 56.
6   Nirmal Chandra Sinha, 'The Sikkim Agreement 1973,' *India Quarterly*, 29(2) (April–June 1973), pp. 155–158.

Strengthening the Chogyal's position

On 15 May 1951, Maharaj Kumar Thondup signed an agreement with SSC leaders that brought a 'parity formula' into force. The formula gave an equal number of seats in the state council (the assembly) to the Nepalese and Bhutia–Lepcha communities, even though the former was three times as large as the latter. Along with the power to nominate an additional five members, Maharaj Kumar Thondup could thus maintain control over the council free from the consequences of demographic spread or universal adult franchise.

On 23 March 1953, the Chogyal Namgyal issued a royal proclamation that strengthened his powers and limited the councils' functioning further. Some subjects were reserved for the Chogyal's decision alone, like his constitutional position and treaty relations with India. His principal adviser, the diwan, also became the head of the executive council (the cabinet). In the first state council elections held in 1953, the SSC and SNP split the twelve seats, and Maharaj Kumar Thondup's nominations tilted the balance in his favour.

This political manoeuvring caused the SSC leadership to disagree and split. The SSC president Tashi Tshering wanted his six elected members to boycott the council and the parity formula. However, he was in the minority. The majority faction led by Kazi Dorji wanted to continue in the council without challenging the parity formula. As a result, the SSC replaced Tshering with Kazi Dorji as president and Kashiraj Pradhan as vice-president. Tashi Tshering died soon after on 9 May 1954.

The new leadership of the SSC again tried various methods to gain India's support and introduce democratic reforms in Sikkim, ranging from establishing party-to-party relations with the Indian National Congress (INC) to asking that India's five-year plans be applied to Sikkim as well to demanding full-fledged responsible government in place of the current diarchy to seeking the status of centrally administered area for Sikkim. However, all their efforts were rebuffed as India worked to support Chogyal Namgyal and his governance. The demand for accession to India faded.

After the 1958 council elections, internal disagreements resulted in the ouster of the presidents of both the SSC and the SNP. The ousted presidents, Kazi Dorji and Sonam Tshering, along with dissidents from other parties, formed the Sikkim National Congress (SNC) in May 1960. They demanded democratic reforms afresh—a responsible government, a new constitution and universal adult franchise.

*

Like Monaco or Luxembourg?

The decade of the 1960s resulted in large shifts in the on-ground situation of and the relationship between India and Sikkim.

In July 1961, in a bid to further strengthen his powers, Maharaj Kumar Thondup both passed the Sikkim Subjects Regulation and strengthened the Sikkim Guards. The regulation laid down stringent requirements for being recognized as a subject (citizen) of Sikkim, which adversely affected a large section of the Nepalese population. This drew strong reactions from the pro-reforms political parties in Sikkim.

The 1962 council elections were postponed due to the war between India and China in October 1962. In March 1963, Maharaj Kumar Thondup married Hope Cooke, an American. This marriage catapulted Sikkim into international media attention for the rest of the decade. The reclusive Chogyal Tashi Namgyal died in December 1963. Maharaj Kumar Thondup, who had already been running the affairs of the state for much of the previous two decades, was crowned as the new Chogyal Palden Thondup Namgyal in April 1965. Meanwhile, Prime Minister Jawaharlal Nehru died in May 1964, India fought another war with Pakistan in mid-1965, and the second prime minister, Lal Bahadur Shastri, died in January 1966. Indira Gandhi became India's new prime minister.

The new Chogyal Thondup leveraged this period of change and uncertainty to try and secure Sikkim's independence. He had always sought to remove the word 'protectorate' from the 1950 Indo–Sikkim Treaty. Now, he began to desire a new treaty to be signed between two 'sovereign' states. He began projecting a separate identity for Sikkim in political, diplomatic and social circles in India and globally.

Meanwhile, in India's 1967 general elections, Indira Gandhi and the INC turned in their worst performance since Independence, barely winning a majority. Although she was still the prime minister, her position had weakened considerably. Skirmishes with Chinese troops took place in Sikkim in September and October 1967. Chogyal Thondup utilized this opportunity to assert his importance to India's security and defence strategy, and India began to offer him allowances it had never done before.

For instance, Prime Minister Indira Gandhi received him and his family at the airport, a courtesy normally extended to visiting heads of state of friendly countries. Deputy Prime Minister Morarji Desai agreed to return the excise duty—a central government tax—levied on Sikkim, an indirect admission of Sikkim's separate status. External Affairs Minister Dinesh Singh bantered with Chogyal Thondup on whether Sikkim was more like Monaco, a sovereign city-state that had observer status in the United Nations, or like Luxembourg, a landlocked independent country in Europe. By September 1970, a revised treaty had already been drafted by India's foreign secretary which upgraded Sikkim's status from 'protectorate' to 'permanent associate', changing the relationship from protection to more of a partnership between a major nation and a minor political territory.[7]

---

[7] Sidhu, *Sikkim*, pp. 105–07.

However, for the next two years, despite repeated efforts from India, Chogyal Thondup refused to accept the revised treaty, believing that 'permanent association' was one step shy of merger. Instead, encouraged by India's support for Bhutan's membership at the United Nations in 1971, he demanded the inclusion of phrases like 'Sikkim in full sovereign rights', 'separate', and 'countries', as well as references to the United Nations, all of which were unacceptable to India. He also let go of his India-appointed diwan (referred to by the Tibetan equivalent 'sidlon') and left the position vacant, desiring a Sikkimese to fill it.

This proved to be a point when India's policy towards Sikkim changed course. By the end of 1972, Prime Minister Indira Gandhi decided that India would no longer support Chogyal Thondup and would instead back the pro-democracy forces like Kazi Dorji. This policy shift 'acted like a spark'[8] that dramatically and immediately altered the course of Sikkim's future.

*

1973–74: Chogyal Gives Way to Chief Minister

In the 1973 state council elections held in January and February, the pro-Chogyal parties won nine seats; with his additional nominations, their number swelled to fifteen in a twenty-four-member house. This strengthened his belief that independent status for Sikkim was now just a matter of time. However, the anti-Chogyal and pro-democracy forces now began to grow in strength and confidence, encouraged and supported clandestinely by Indian intelligence teams.[9] The SNC and the Janata Congress allied with each other and formed a Joint Action Committee (JAC) by the end of March

---

[8] Sidhu, *Sikkim*, p. 141.
[9] Ibid., p. 134.

1973 to demand democratic reforms, including a constitution, an independent judiciary, and a replacement to the Indo-Sikkim Treaty of 1950. Large-scale demonstrations against Chogyal Thondup were planned so as to coincide with his fiftieth birthday celebrations on 4 April 1973.

Frustration had been building up among much of the Sikkimese population. Their socio-economic and political status was poor and three-quarters were even denied citizenship. Hence, when the pro-democracy parties began to take out anti-Chogyal speeches and rallies, they found an empathetic populace eager to participate in order to improve their living conditions. Demonstrators started arriving in Gangtok from the last week of March. Violent anti-Chogyal protests began to break out in parts of Sikkim. Chogyal Thondup tried last-minute appeasement tactics but it was too late. On 4 April, thousands of protesters marched to the palace demanding reforms. Law and order broke down across Sikkim, resulting in the tenth clause of the 1950 Indo–Sikkim Treaty being invoked and giving India overriding powers. On 7 April, Chogyal Thondup handed over the maintenance of law and order to the resident India political officer, and on 8 April, he handed over administration of the government. On 9 April, Kazi Dorji called off the agitation. The SNC and Janata Congress also wound up the JAC and merged their parties to form the Sikkim Congress led by Kazi Dorji.

A month later, on 8 May 1973, a tripartite agreement was signed between the Government of India, Chogyal Thondup, and the leaders of the Sikkim Congress and the SNP. It provided for elections (supervised by the chief election commissioner of India) to the state council (legislative assembly) on the basis of universal adult franchise. An Indian-appointed chief executive became the speaker of the assembly and a virtual chief minister, with the Indian government taking the final decision on any disputes. The legislative powers of the executive council (cabinet) were expanded significantly.

Guided by officials from the Indian government, assembly elections were held across Sikkim in mid-April 1974, a year after the anti-Chogyal demonstrations. The pro-democracy Kazi-led Sikkim Congress swept the elections, winning thirty-one of thirty-two seats. Soon after, on 11 May, the new assembly passed a resolution requesting the Government of India to aid in the creation of a constitution, further strengthen the Indo-Sikkim relationship, and enable Sikkim's participation in the political and economic institutions of India.

On 4 July 1974, in what was seen as 'a significant milestone'[10] and 'a red-letter day'[11] in the history of Sikkim, the Sikkim Assembly passed the Government of Sikkim Act, duly signed by Chogyal Thondup. This was immediately followed by the promulgation of a new constitution and the formation of a five-member cabinet with Kazi Dorji as the first popularly-elected chief minister of Sikkim. In the first week of September 1974, India's Lok Sabha and Rajya Sabha passed the Constitution (Thirty-Fifth Amendment) Act which 'associated'[12] Sikkim with the Union of India and allowed for one member from the state to be elected to both Sabhas.

*

1975: Merger and a New Great Experiment of Democracy

On 9 April 1975, the Sikkim Congress declared that 'the people of Sikkim can realize their full rights only if Sikkim becomes a unit of the Union of India'[13]. Chief Minister Kazi Dorji also sent a formal request to Prime Minister Indira Gandhi requesting the removal of Chogyal Thondup. The same day, the Indian Army disarmed the

---

[10]   Sidhu, *Sikkim*, p. 273.
[11]   Ibid., p. 263.
[12]   The Constitution (Thirty-Fifth Amendment) Act, 1974.
[13]   Sidhu, *Sikkim*, p. 310.

Sikkim Guards as a precautionary measure. The following day, at an emergency session of the Sikkim Assembly, two resolutions were unanimously passed—to abolish the institution of the Chogyal and to merge Sikkim with India. To gain public approval, a referendum (public vote) was held four days later on 14 April through a single question. Nearly two-thirds of eligible Sikkimese voted and an overwhelming 97 per cent of them favoured the abolition of the institution of the Chogyal and the merger of Sikkim with India.[14]

Within a week, the minister of external affairs for India, Yashwantrao Balwantrao Chavan introduced the Constitution (Thirty-Sixth Amendment) Bill in the Indian Lok Sabha seeking to incorporate Sikkim as a state in the Union of India, calling it a 'revolutionary political situation'[15]. The bill was passed nearly unanimously in both Sabhas and the President of India, Fakhruddin Ali Ahmed, gave his assent. The Act came into effect on 16 May 1975 and Sikkim began what Prime Minister Indira Gandhi called its 'new great experiment of democracy'[16] as the twenty-second state of India.

**

---

[14] Sidhu, *Sikkim*, pp. 302–13.
[15] Ibid., p. 314.
[16] Ibid., p. 263.

TAMIL NADU

Did You Know?

Until 14 January 1969, Tamil Nadu was known as Madras State.

Madras Province was one of British India's three main Presidencies, along with Bombay and Calcutta. Madras Province (Madras State from 1950) covered such a large part of south India that it contained within its boundaries all the major language groups of south India.

*

Telugu

Telugu was the linguistic majority in the northern districts of Madras State while Tamil was the linguistic majority in the southern districts starting from, and including, the city of Madras. This was a curious arrangement, for Telugu was the second-largest language spoken in independent India. According to the 1951 census, which combined Hindi, Urdu and Punjabi into the single-largest language, Telugu was spoken by 9.24 per cent of the Indian population while Tamil was fourth, after Marathi, spoken by 7.43 per cent of the population.[1] Rarely does it transpire that a majority faction has to petition for its own space.

The petition came in the form of Potti Sriramulu, a 51-year-old former sanitary engineer, railway-man, and an acolyte of Gandhi's Sabarmati Ashram. After a lot of talking from both the pro- and anti-Andhra State factions but little discernible progress, Sriramulu began a fast-unto-death in Madras, a tactic he had used with little success for other causes in the past. Starting on 19 October 1952, his fast fast-tracked the demands for statehood by the Telugu population, adding a sense of emotional urgency to the protests.

The city of Madras fell on the linguistic border. The Tamils considered the city theirs, while the Telugus believed they could claim Madras since they had a significant demographic and economic presence in the city. However, the Tamils had the explicit support of both the Union and state government heads. In a report released in April 1949, the centrally constituted JVP Committee, named after its committee members Jawaharlal Nehru (Prime Minister), Vallabhbhai Patel (Deputy Prime Minister) and Pattabhi Sitaramayya (Congress president)—then possibly the three most powerful people in the country—stated 'Andhra Province could be formed provided the Andhras give up their claim on the city of Madras'.

And so, Andhra lost its first capital city, Madras, even before the state came into being. But while the capital city might have been lost, the state was about to be won in a swift and decisive manner.

Sriramulu's death on 15 December 1952—on day fifty-eight of his fast—blew the lid off the anger and resentment simmering in the pro-Andhra camp. In the Andhra region, government offices were

---

[1]   Government of India. Census of India, 1951.

attacked, public transportation was set upon with a vengeance, and millions of rupees' worth of public property was damaged.

The terms of discussion of Andhra statehood had shifted irrevocably from the rational to the emotional. Nehru had wanted to settle the issue with 'facts, not fasts' but Sriramulu's death-by-fasting not only changed the narrative, it wrested the decision from him and placed it firmly with the people.

Two days after Sriramulu's death, on 17 December 1952, Nehru gave in and announced that the state of Andhra would indeed become a reality. On 1 October 1953, just under a year after Sriramulu began his history-making fast and just over four years after the declaration by the JVP Committee, the new Andhra State was inaugurated as a Part A state at its capital city of Kurnool. In attendance were both C. Rajagopalachari and Nehru, the latter as the chief guest.

*

Kannada and Tulu

The creation of Andhra State isolated the district of Bellary from the rest of Madras State. Bellary was not included in Andhra as it contained a Kannada-speaking majority. Hence, Bellary was integrated with Mysore State in 1953, along with the creation of Andhra State.[2]

The separation of Andhra State from Madras State also led the Centre to set up the SRC to look into the matter of redrawing state boundaries. In its 1955 report, the SRC recommended transferring the Kollegal taluk of Coimbatore district and the western coastal region of South Canara to Mysore State.

*

---

[2] 'Transfer of Territory from Madras to Mysore,' Section 4, The Andhra State Act, 1953.

Malayalam

The coastal region of Malabar formed the 'somewhat isolated'[3] western part of Madras State. Since Malabar shared much more with Travancore–Cochin State geographically, linguistically and commercially, the SRC recommended merging them to form a new state of Kerala. The Kasaragod taluk of South Canara was also transferred to Kerala while five Tamil-speaking taluks in the extreme south were transferred out to Madras State.

*

1969: Madras State to Tamil Nadu

Soon after the redrawn Madras State came into being on 1 November 1956, a movement began to rename the state to Tamil Nadu. It was led chiefly by C.N. Annadurai, the leader of the Dravida Munnetra Kazhagam (DMK), which was in the opposition in the assembly. However, multiple motions to rename the state failed to secure a majority vote.

In the 1967 assembly elections, the DMK won a resounding majority. This brought Annadurai as chief minister of Madras State. In July 1967, the legislative assembly and legislative council of Madras State unanimously passed a resolution demanding the change in nomenclature. It was forwarded to the Union government two months later.[4]

In December 1968, Parliament passed the Madras State (Alteration of Name) Act. On 14 January 1969, Madras State was renamed as Tamil Nadu.

* *

---

[3]   Report of the States Reorganisation Commission, 1955, p. 85.
[4]   The Madras State (Alteration of Name) Act, 1968.

TELANGANA

Did You Know?

Telangana was earlier a part of the princely state of Hyderabad.

I: Hyderabad State

In 1947, Telangana formed the southern and south-eastern Telugu-dominant region of the princely state of Hyderabad. Ruled by the Nizam, Mir Osman Ali Khan, Hyderabad was among the largest and premier princely states in India, with its own coinage, currency and stamps. It sat squarely at the heart of the country as a melting pot of languages and religions. Urdu was spoken in the capital region, Marathi was spoken in the north, Kannada in the south-west, and Telugu in the south and south-east. The population was largely Hindu, but the government bodies, such as the legislative assembly, the civil services, the police and the army, had a Muslim-majority.[1]

---

[1] V.P. Menon, *The Story of the Integration of the Indian States,* (United Kingdom: Longmans, Green and Co., 1956), p. 219.

When the plan to partition India was announced on 3 June 1947, the Nizam of Hyderabad declared his intention to join neither dominion and to remain an independent sovereign dominion, a member of the British Commonwealth of Nations. However, Governor-General Louis Mountbatten dashed this hope saying that Britain would not accept Hyderabad as an independent member of the Commonwealth and that it could join only as a part of India or Pakistan.

The States Ministry, headed by Sardar Vallabhbhai Patel and executed by V.P. Menon, then began endless rounds of discussions with the delegation from Hyderabad regarding the state's accession to India. The Hyderabad delegation was headed by Lieutenant-Colonel Muhammad Ahmed Said Khan (generally referred to as the Nawab of Chhatari), who was the president of the Nizam's executive council. The States Ministry wanted Hyderabad to accede, like every other princely state, on the three subjects of external affairs, defence and communications, without any financial commitments. However, the Nizam was unwilling to compromise his sovereignty and even kept open the option of joining Pakistan.

With 15 August looming, the Nizam did not look any closer to signing the Instrument of Accession. Hence, an extension of two months was given to continue negotiations. Through multiple rounds of discussions, the Nizam and the Nawab made multiple demands, all of which were unacceptable to the States Ministry—a separate tripartite negotiating committee with Hyderabad, India and Pakistan; a conditional treaty with India that ensured that Hyderabad maintained a degree of say over its foreign policy, defence and communications; signing the Standstill Agreement without the Instrument of Accession; and renaming the Instrument of Accession as Articles of Association. They also rejected the idea of a referendum (public vote).

Meanwhile, an external influence on the Nizam began to grow stronger. Kasim Razvi was the leader of a Muslim communal organization called the Ittehad-ul-Muslimeen (supported by the Nizam). He also commanded a private militia called the Razakars. By late October 1947, negotiations between India and Hyderabad had reached a stalemate, and India had to urgently deal with the invasion in Kashmir. Kasim Razvi chose this moment to begin playing a more direct role in Hyderabad's future. He influenced the Nizam to replace the Nawab and other members of the executive council with his choices, such as Mir Laik Ali, the former representative of Pakistan to the United Nations, and Nawab Moin Nawaz Jung, the brother-in-law of Laik Ali. The Hyderabad government began to reach out to Pakistan more often and tried to procure arms and ammunition from abroad. The dangers of communal violence in Hyderabad began to increase. Kasim Razvi now effectively ruled Hyderabad.

In order to gain some stability and make some progress in the negotiations with Hyderabad, India agreed to sign the Standstill Agreement without the Instrument of Accession. The Agreement was signed on 29 November 1947 and would remain in force for one year. Or as Prime Minister Jawaharlal Nehru remarked, 'peace for one year'.[2]

However, almost immediately, the Hyderabad government began to repeatedly violate the terms of the Standstill Agreement. It restricted the export of precious metals to India and declared Indian currency as not legal tender in the state. It had already advanced a loan to Pakistan and had appointed a public relations officer in Karachi with plans to install more agents in other foreign nations. The violent activities of the Razakars too began to increase in intensity, and the state forces were strengthened.[3]

Through the first half of 1948, tensions rose through multiple rounds of failed discussions, unreasonable demands and broken promises. Leaders from the Razakars and the government in

---

[2] Menon, *Integration*, p. 230.
[3] Ibid., pp. 232–33.

Hyderabad began to speak openly of large-scale communal violence and war with India, and even began border raids with Madras and Bombay Provinces.[4] India stationed troops around Hyderabad's borders and began to prepare for military intervention.[5] The Hyderabad government began to reach out to the United Nations and the United States of America to arbitrate.[6] In the middle of June 1948, Mountbatten completed his term as Governor-General and left India for good, unable to resolve the Hyderabad crisis before leaving. Chakravarti Rajagopalachari replaced him as Governor-General.

By the end of August and early September 1948, the law and order situation in Hyderabad and its borders had escalated to anarchy levels, with murder, rape, looting and train attacks becoming frighteningly regular.[7] After endless demands by the Indian government—and dismissals by the Hyderabad government—to ban and disband the Razakars and bring the law and order situation under control, India decided to employ military force.

On 9 September, India officially launched Operation Polo, referred to more commonly as 'police action'. On 13 September, Indian forces entered Hyderabad. On the evening of 17 September, the Hyderabad army surrendered and the cabinet resigned. Kasim Razvi was arrested on 19 September. The Indian government took over administration in Hyderabad but decided to carry it out in the name of the Nizam so as to maintain stability.

When India adopted its Constitution on 26 January 1950, Hyderabad State was classified as a Part B state[8]. The Nizam,

---

4 Menon, *Integration*, p. 238.
5 Narayani Basu, *V.P. Menon: The Unsung Architect of Modern India*, (India: Simon & Schuster India, 2020), pp. 348–49.
6 Menon, *Integration*, pp. 254–55.
7 Ibid., p. 255.
8 Note: In 1950, the Constitution of India specified three classifications of States. Part B states were former princely states and had a Rajpramukh (Governor) and an elected state legislature.

Mir Osman Ali Khan, was appointed the Rajpramukh and M.K. Vellodi the first chief minister.

*

II: Andhra Pradesh

In December 1953, the Indian government set up the States Reorganisation Commission (SRC) to look into the matter of redrawing state boundaries. In its September 1955 report, the SRC took cognisance of the growing demand to disintegrate Hyderabad State and merge it with its neighbouring states so that progress could reach the people of 'an artificial political unit'[9] with an undemocratic tradition that needed to be liquidated. The SRC also deemed the arguments in favour of continuing Hyderabad State, such as its long history and the possibility of the state serving as a carrier of Hindi to the south, as weak. The SRC recommended the disintegration of Hyderabad State so as to help the stability of the other proposed units in south India.

Hyderabad would be split into three parts on the basis of language. The northern Marathi-dominant Marathwada region would be integrated into the proposed bilingual Bombay State and the South-western Kannada-dominant districts would integrate into the proposed Mysore State. However, a question arose over the future of the Telugu-dominant Telangana region in the south and south-east. There was an existing demand from the newly created neighbouring Andhra State (also Telugu-dominant) for the creation of Vishalandhra, which would integrate Andhra State and Telangana. While integration could bring mutual benefits, developmentally and economically, there was the fear that the two regions were unequally placed in relation to each other. Moreover, it was argued that Andhra

---

[9] Report of the States Reorganisation Commission, 1955, p. 101.

State was still in a period of transition, while Telangana could be a stable and viable state by itself.

Hence, the SRC rejected an immediate integration in favour of a wait-and-watch approach. It suggested first spinning Telangana off as a separate state (called the state of Hyderabad) for about five years until 1961. This would give both Andhra and Telangana enough time to stabilize their administrative machinery. Unification could be revisited after the general elections in 1961, at which point the Telangana legislature would have the provision to voluntarily vote themselves into Andhra State by a two-thirds majority. This decision had its supporters and detractors. Even Burgula Ramakrishna Rao, Hyderabad State's first elected chief minister, wasn't entirely in favour of a merger as he felt that the two regions had different cultural formations.[10]

In February 1956, a 'Gentlemen's Agreement' between Telangana and Andhra leaders promised equitable development and representation in Telangana, including a regional council.[11] Hence, when the States Reorganisation Act was passed later that year, the government disregarded the SRC's recommendation and merged Andhra State and Telangana into a single state called Andhra Pradesh. The new State came into being on 1 November 1956. Neelam Sanjiva Reddy of the Indian National Congress (INC) became the chief minister. Kurnool lost its capital city status and Hyderabad became the new capital city.

*

III: Telangana, Part I

The Telangana region had in force long-standing domicile rules known as the 'Mulki Rules'. Instituted in 1919 by the Nizam

---

[10] Rama S. Melkote, E. Revathi, K. Lalitha, K. Sajaya and A. Suneetha, 'The Movement for Telangana: Myth and Reality,' *Economic and Political Weekly*, 45(2) (9–15 Jan. 2010), pp. 8–9.

[11] Ibid., p. 9.

Mir Osman Ali Khan, Telangana's 'Mulki Rules' were meant to protect the locals (Mulkis) in government job appointments. In order to be considered a Mulki, the following conditions had to be met.[12]

a.   one had to be born in Hyderabad State; or
b.   one had to have been a permanent resident for at least fifteen years in Hyderabad State and to have officially abandoned the idea of returning to the place of one's residence by obtaining an affidavit to that effect on a prescribed form attested by a magistrate; or
c.   one's father had to—at the moment of one's birth—have completed fifteen years of employment in Government Service; or
d.   one could, if one were a woman, be married to a Mulki.

In addition, eligible outsiders had to apply for the grant of a Mulki Certificate.

The first Mulki agitation had occurred in Hyderabad State in September 1952 over the large-scale recruitment of non-locals into positions meant for locals in the newly-formed Hyderabad State Government.[13]

In January 1969, students from a number of colleges held demonstrations and burnt effigies of ministers to protest against the violation of the safeguards in the Gentlemen's Agreement.[14] Political leaders of Andhra Pradesh responded swiftly and unanimously, resolving to transfer 'all non-Telangana employees holding posts

---

[12]   Gopal Rao Ekbote, 'Judgement — P. Lakshmana Rao vs State of Andhra Pradesh and Ors on 9 December 1970,' Andhra High Court.
[13]   'Dated September 6, 1952: Hyderabad Incidents,' This Day That Age, *The Hindu*, 6 September 2002.
[14]   'College Students in Telangana Agitation,' *Indian Express*, 16 January 1969, p. 8.

reserved for Telangana domiciles'[15] to the Andhra region, as well as to fully utilize all Telangana surpluses for development of the region during the following five years.[16]

But the issue refused to die down quietly. A political party, the Telangana Praja Samithi (TPS), was founded to campaign for Telangana statehood. Pro-Telangana protests soon became violent, resulting in damaged public property, police firing and injuries.[17] The Mulki Rules were declared void by the Andhra Pradesh High Court but that decision was immediately stayed by a divisional bench of the same high court.[18] The chief minister of Andhra Pradesh, Kasu Brahmananda Reddy, assured both camps that the Mulki Rules would remain in force for another five years with no extensions beyond that.[19]

1 November 1971 marked the fifteenth anniversary of the merging of Telangana and Andhra State to create Andhra Pradesh. This meant that, under Mulki Rules, all the people who had migrated to Hyderabad at the time of the state's creation in 1956 were now eligible to be officially considered as Mulkis. In late 1972, the Supreme Court upheld the Mulki Rules and Parliament passed the Mulki Rules Act in December 1972. This kick-started a counter 'Jai Andhra' movement in the Andhra region demanding an Andhra State separate from Telangana. Ministers resigned from Chief Minister P.V. Narasimha Rao's government in protest. Andhra Pradesh was placed under President's rule in January 1973.

---

[15] 'Accord Reached on Telangana Demands,' *Indian Express,* 20 January 1969, p. 1.
[16] Ibid.
[17] 'Telangana Agitators Fired on: 17 Hurt,' *Indian Express,* 25 January 1969, p. 1.
[18] 'Judgement on Mulki Rules Stayed,' *Indian Express,* 5 February 1969, p. 4.
[19] 'Transfers Challenged in Court by Andhra Employees,' *Indian Express,* 25 January 1969, p. 1.

In September 1973, Prime Minister Indira Gandhi released a six-point formula, which also later became the thirty-second amendment to the Constitution of India. Andhra Pradesh would be divided into six zones. 85 per cent of lower-level government jobs and seats in government colleges and universities were reserved for the local people from that particular zone, while the remaining 15 per cent of non-local jobs and seats were open to people from the remaining five zones.[20] Through this zoning approach, the six-point formula rendered the continuance of the Mulki Rules unnecessary and the Mulki Rules (Repeal) Act was passed in December 1973.

*

IV: Telangana, Part II

The Telangana movement picked up again in April 2001. Kalvakuntla Chandrashekar Rao (KCR) was the Deputy Speaker of the Andhra Pradesh Legislative Assembly and a member of the ruling Telugu Desam Party (TDP). He resigned from his post and the party to establish his own party, the Telangana Rashtra Samithi (TRS). The party's single-point agenda was the creation of a separate state of Telangana with Hyderabad as its capital city.

KCR's individual political fortunes rose and he even earned a Union cabinet post. However, his party didn't fare as well. In the 2009 assembly elections in Andhra Pradesh, TRS won only 8.4 per cent of the seats in the Telangana region. The incumbent chief minister of Andhra Pradesh, Y.S. Rajasekhara Reddy (YSR) of the INC, was re-elected. The Telangana sentiment appeared to have faded, the vote seemed to be against bifurcation.

---

[20] R.J. Rajendra Prasad, 'Bitter Memories,' *Frontline*, Vol. 18 Issue 12 (09–22 Jun. 2001).

On 2 September 2009, however, the situation changed dramatically. Chief Minister YSR's helicopter went missing in the remote Nallamala Forest. The wreckage and the bodies were discovered a day later. In the resulting political turmoil, KCR seized his opportunity.

On 29 November 2009, KCR started a fast-unto-death demanding Telangana State. The fast quickly gathered force with popular support extended by student organizations, employee unions and various other organizations. A mere ten days later, on 9 December, the Union Home Minister, P. Chidambaram, of the Congress-led coalition government at the Centre, announced that Telangana would become a reality.

The actual bifurcation of Andhra Pradesh and Telangana came four-and-a-half years later on 2 June 2014. KCR became the first chief minister. The city of Hyderabad became the permanent capital of Telangana.

* *

TRIPURA

1947–50: A Princely State that Merges with India

At the time of Indian Independence, the princely state of Tripura became 'virtually isolated'[1] from the rest of India due to Partition. Surrounded on three sides by the newly-created East Pakistan (now Bangladesh), Tripura possessed no road or rail connections with neighbouring Assam. The ruler of Tripura, Maharaja Bir Bikram Kishore Manikya Debbarman Bahadur, had died just months before Independence. His son, Prince Kirit, was still a minor and was installed as a nominal ruler. The Maharaja's widow, Maharani Kanchan Prabha Devi, became the Regent, overlooking administration and decision-making.

---

[1]   V.P. Menon, *The Story of the Integration of the Indian States* (United Kingdom: Longmans, Green and Co., 1956), p. 209.

A number of socio-political organizations were created by Bengali professionals, educated tribal youth, communists and liberals in Tripura in the years leading up to Independence, each pursuing a form of responsible government. These included the Jana Mongal Samiti (JMS), Jana Shiskya Samiti (JSS), and Tripura Proja Mondal (TPM). In 1948, the Tripura Rajya Gana Mukti Parishad (TRGMP) was created with the backing of the tribal chiefs; they demanded that democracy replace monarchy, land reform, and an end to the severe police and military oppression. Meanwhile, Partition had led to a severe inflow of Bengali refugees from East Pakistan. An organization named Sengkrak headed by a member of the royal family, Durjoy Kishore Debbarman, led a movement to oust Bengalis and oppose the merging of Tripura with India. In response, the TRGMP launched a massive campaign.[2]

On 9 September 1949, the Regent Maharani signed the Merger Agreement with the Government of India. Tripura became a central commissioner's province from 15 October 1949, administered directly by the Union government. On 26 January 1950, when India adopted its Constitution, Tripura was classified as a Part C state and continued under direct central administration. In September 1951, Parliament passed the Government of Part C States Act which provided for the constitution of a council of advisers to assist the chief commissioner in Tripura. A lieutenant-governor later replaced the chief commissioner.

*

[2] Biswajit Ghosh. 'Ethnicity and Insurgency in Tripura,' *Sociological Bulletin* 52(2) (September 2003), pp. 221–43. https://doi.org/10.1177/0038022920030204

1956–71: A First-class Union Territory that Nearly Wasn't

In December 1953, the Union government set up the States Reorganisation Commission (SRC) which invited memoranda from the public, individually and collectively. One of the proposals put forth a Purbachal State comprising nearly every region around the Assam plains, including Tripura. In its 1955 report, the SRC rejected Purbachal as having neither the resources nor the stability to secure its international border on three sides. Given Tripura's small size, the SRC also declared that the state 'cannot obviously stand by itself'[3]. It recommended merging Tripura into Assam so that the entire eastern section of the international border with East Pakistan could then be brought under the single control of the Assam Government.

When the States Reorganisation Act was passed in August 1956, however, the government rejected any change in Tripura's status. On 1 November 1956, when the Act came into force, all Part C states, including Tripura, were redesignated as union territories that continued to be centrally administered.

As a way to grant some autonomy, Parliament passed the Territorial Councils Act, 1956, which established territorial councils in Manipur, Tripura and Himachal Pradesh. These councils were given the power to oversee local affairs, such as education, public health, roads and animal husbandry. However, these arrangements were not considered adequate and demands for greater autonomy kept growing. So, in 1961, the Centre constituted a committee headed by the Union Law Minister, Ashoke Kumar Sen. In its June 1962 report, the committee recommended that 'the largest possible measure of autonomy should be granted'[4], including the introduction

---

[3]   Report of the States Reorganisation Commission, 1955, p. 192.
[4]   Administrative Reforms Commission. *Report, Study Team on Administration of Union Territories and NEFA*, 1968, pp. 11–13.

of panchayati raj and the transfer of more subjects to the territorial councils. However, the union territories demanded the creation of legislative bodies.

In 1962, once French and Portuguese territories were integrated into India and the State of Nagaland Act was passed, the Union government decided to go above and beyond the recommendations of the Ashoke Sen Committee. It passed the Constitution (Fourteenth Amendment) Act, 1962, and then the Government of Union Territories Act, 1963, which established legislative assemblies and councils of ministers and abolished territorial councils in five union territories, including Tripura, that were considered as being independent standalone entities. These legislative assemblies had powers and responsibilities similar to the state legislative assemblies, including the ability to make laws on subjects in the Union and Concurrent lists. They even had separate consolidated and contingency funds.[5] Tripura got its first chief minister in Sachindra Lal Singh of the Indian National Congress (INC). Statehood now became a possible future for Tripura.

*

1972: Statehood

On 30 December 1971, Parliament passed the North-Eastern Areas (Reorganisation) Act, which brought into existence three new states—Meghalaya, Manipur, and Tripura—and two new union territories—Mizoram and Arunachal Pradesh. On 21 January 1972, the full-fledged state of Tripura was born.

* *

---

[5] Administrative Reforms Commission. *Report, Study Team on Administration of Union Territories and NEFA*, 1968, pp. 11–13.

UTTAR PRADESH

'United Provinces' to 'Uttar Pradesh': 1947–50

The present state of Uttar Pradesh was almost entirely contained in the United Provinces, which had been among the largest provinces of British India until Independence. On 15 August 1947, the United Provinces transferred as it was to the Dominion of India.

The United Provinces was already represented by an Indian— Govind Ballabh Pant. After the end of World War II, the new Labour Government in Britain, in its bid to transfer power to and enable self-governance in India, had ordered fresh elections to its provincial legislatures. The Indian National Congress (INC) won in the United Provinces and G.B. Pant became the Premier (equivalent to today's chief minister) in August 1946. His government continued in power after Independence.

In 1949, three princely states that were within the geographical orbit of the United Provinces were merged into the province. The largest was the Himalayan mountain kingdom of Tehri Garhwal, whose young king, Maharaja Manabendra Shah, had ascended the throne at the age of twenty-five after his father had abdicated his position just a year before Independence. The young Maharaja signed the Merger Agreement on 18 May 1949. On 1 August 1949, Tehri Garhwal joined the other mountain regions of Garhwal and Kumaon as a new district in the north-western corner of the United Provinces.[1]

The smallest was Benaras. The ruler, Maharaja Vibhuti Narayan Singh, was only nineteen years old when India gained independence. On 5 September 1949, as he signed the Merger Agreement, his only ask was that his position with regard to the religious ceremonies at Kashi be protected. On 15 October 1949, Benares became a new district in the south-eastern region of the United Provinces.[2]

The richest of the three princely states was Rampur. The state was renowned for many things aside from its fabulous wealth, including the Rampur–Sahaswan gharana (school) of Hindustani classical music, its hounds and its cuisine. The ruler, Sir Raza Ali Khan Bahadur, requested that the state be placed temporarily under central administration. Hence, a chief commissioner took over the administration on behalf of the Government of India for five months from 1 July 1949. On 1 December 1949, with the agreement of the ruler, Rampur was merged into United Provinces, forming a district in the western section.[3]

The debate to change the name of the state and choose a suitable name started immediately after Independence and went on for over two years. 'United Provinces' (referred to in its abbreviated

---

[1]   Ministry of States, Government of India. *White Paper on Indian States*, 1950, pp. 44–45.
[2]   Ibid.
[3]   Ibid.

form as 'UP') was argued to be a colonial remnant that the local people could not identify with, especially since it was being called by its translated form in Hindi (Samyukta Prant) and Urdu (Mumalik Mutahdda). However, the opposing view held that 'United Provinces' ought to continue as it reflected the unity of two cultures—Hindus and Muslims.[4]

Alternate names suggested by the members of the legislature included 'Oudh', 'Hindustan', 'Hind' and 'Aryavarta'. Once the issue spilled out into the public domain, suggestions flowed in, giving the cabinet a longlist of over twenty names, including 'Brahmadesh', 'Ram Krishna Prant', and 'Uttara Khand'. The paralysis of choice stalled any decision-making on the issue.[5]

In October 1949, the constituent assembly was in the process of finalizing the draft Constitution. This re-energized the name debate in UP since the new Constitution had to feature the names of the provinces in the Union. This deadline helped in arriving at a consensus. An overwhelming majority of the members of the cabinet and the Provincial Congress Committee supported the name 'Aryavarta'. The chief minister, Govind Ballabh Pant, duly conveyed this preference to the constituent assembly on 15 November 1949.[6]

However, there was immediate pushback from not only the central leadership but also from other parts of the country. Rustom K. Sidhwa, a member of the constituent assembly from Central Provinces–Berar, declared that UP was attempting to 'monopolize the name of India' and cast itself as the 'super-most province of India'.[7] This included the other names in the shortlist as well—'Hind' and 'Hindustan'.

---

[4] Gyanesh Kudaisya, *Region, Nation, 'Heartland': Uttar Pradesh in India's Body Politic* (New Delhi: Sage Publications, 2006), pp. 352–56.
[5] Ibid.
[6] Ibid., pp. 356–57.
[7] Ibid., p. 358.

To remove the pressure exerted by the incoming Constitution on the renaming of states, Dr B.R. Ambedkar—the chairman of the drafting committee of the Constitution of India as well as the first minister of law and justice—introduced a bill that empowered the Governor-General to alter the names of provinces. This bill was adopted by the constituent assembly on 25 November 1949.[8]

Meanwhile, back in the United Provinces, another name was quickly agreed upon within the Government—'Uttar Pradesh'. This name had the added advantage of keeping the initials of the State intact—'UP'.

On 24 January 1950, two days before India adopted its Constitution, the official name of the state was changed to Uttar Pradesh. This date is today celebrated as 'UP Diwas' (Uttar Pradesh Day).

*

The (Failed) Moves to Reshape Uttar Pradesh

In the new Republic of India, created from the unification of provinces and princely states, Uttar Pradesh emerged not only as a large state—covering about 9 per cent of India's land area—but also as the most populous state—containing more than one-sixth of India's population. UP had 50 per cent more people than the second-most populous state—its neighbour Bihar.

Two divergent views emerged regarding UP's size. Even the three members of the States Reorganisation Commission (SRC) were unable to agree on what ought to be done with Uttar Pradesh. Two opposing notes were written in their final report in 1955.

K.M. Panikkar held the view that UP was so large and heavily populated in relation to the other states that it upset the balance of a successful federation, to the point where it was 'likely to undermine

---

[8]   Kudaisya, *Region, Nation, 'Heartland'*, pp. 358–59.

the federal structure itself and thereby be a danger to the unity of the country"[9]. UP's outsized influence could be abused to form a powerful political bloc which would allow it to dominate the proceedings of both the Houses of Parliament and cause resentment amongst the other states.

In addition to its external overbearance, it was argued that internally, too, the state had many points against it continuing as a single unbroken unit. There were stark differences between the geography and the people of the rugged Himalayan Garhwal and Kumaon in the north-west to the fertile central plains of the Gangetic Valley to the hilly Bundelkhand in the south. The western half of the central plains was seen as being very different from the eastern half, both economically and agriculturally. Moreover, UP languished near the bottom of various development indices, like literacy, per capita expenditure on social services and education, medical services, road transportation, and maintenance of law and order.

Indicating that the size of the state was probably detracting from UP's ability to govern itself efficiently, K.M. Panikkar proposed to 'reconstitute the overgrown state'[10] by partitioning it. The proposed separate state would largely consist of the divisions of Agra (the city was proposed as the capital), Jhansi, Meerut (minus Dehra Dun district) and Rohilkhand (minus Pilibhit district) and a few districts from the north-western region of today's state of Madhya Pradesh.

A demand for a separate state of Delhi also emerged, which included the Agra, Meerut and Rohilkhand Divisions of Western Uttar Pradesh in full, as well as adjoining regions from today's Punjab, Haryana and Rajasthan.[11]

---

[9]   K.M. Panikkar. 'Note on Uttar Pradesh,' Report of the States Reorganisation Commission, 1955, p. 244.
[10]   Ibid., p. 245.
[11]   Kudaisya, *Region, Nation, 'Heartland'*, pp. 382–83.

Another suggestion was given in 1955 by Dr Ambedkar, then a Rajya Sabha member, as a way to counter the 'consolidation of the north and Balkanisation of the south' as well as 'a safeguard to the minorities'.[12] He advocated the trifurcation of Uttar Pradesh geographically along its western (with its capital at Meerut), central (capital at Kanpur), and eastern (capital at Allahabad) regions.

The counter and, in some ways, the prevailing view overruled all these concerns as 'overstated'.[13] The mere size of Uttar Pradesh should not be the reason for the extreme measure of breaking it up. Arguments were made by members of the state's legislative assembly in favour of the unbreakable cultural and religious integrity of the state that was the heart of India. The demand for a separate state quickly fell apart once Chief Minister G.B. Pant declared his personal support for 'the soul of Aryavarta . . . (whose) culture and language envelop Bharat'[14]. G.B. Pant also became the Union Home Minister in 1955 and oversaw the implementation of the States Reorganisation Act, 1956.

And so, the Hindi heartland of Uttar Pradesh was kept intact.

*

Uttar Pradesh and Uttarakhand, 2000 onwards

The demand for autonomy for the region of Uttarakhand (meaning 'northern region') in the Himalayan mountains was first made in 1937.[15] It consisted largely of the princely state of Tehri Garhwal

---

[12] Dr. Bhimrao R. Ambedkar, *Thoughts on Linguistic States* (Delhi: Author), 1955.
[13] Report of the States Reorganisation Commission, 1955, p. 164.
[14] Kudaisya, *Region, Nation, 'Heartland'*, p. 394.
[15] Shekhar Pathak, 'Beyond an Autonomous State Background and Preliminary Analysis of Uttarakhand Movement,' *Proceedings of the Indian History Congress,* 60 (1999), p. 895.

and the districts of Garhwal and Kumaon, both of which were a part of the United Provinces. This call was based not so much on language but more on identity—that the geography and the people of the mountains were culturally very different from the rest of UP.

Given the hesitation during the 1956 reorganization to create states based on anything other than language, and especially so in the case of Uttar Pradesh, the demand for Uttarakhand went unheeded. In 1960, the UP state government reorganized the mountainous region into two Mandals (administrative areas)—Kumaon (the eastern half) and Uttarakhand (a.k.a. Garhwal, the western half).

The late 1960s and early 1970s saw the growing emergence of regional political parties and social movements in parts of north India and Uttar Pradesh that were built around grassroots issues like social justice and combating economic inequality. This movement helped kick-start a new socio-political conversation, especially in the Uttarakhand mountains, around the management of natural resources, the marginalization of peripheral regions, and the economic rights of local communities.

From 1977–80, the Janata Party became the first non-Congress party to form the government at the Centre. Simultaneously, it also formed the government in Uttar Pradesh for the first time. The Janata Party had been vocal about the need to reorganize state boundaries so as to correct economic imbalances and enable administrative convenience, even calling for a second SRC. One of the states the Janata Party called for was Uttarakhand.[16]

In 1979, a new political party called the Uttarakhand Kranti Dal (UKD) was established; its sole agenda was to campaign for statehood[17], which was also taken up later by the Uttarakhand

---

[16] Louise Tillin, *Remapping India: New States and Their Political Origins* (New Delhi: Oxford University Press, 2013), p. 100.

[17] Ibid.

Sangharsh Vahini (USV). Socio-political activities linked directly to the demand for statehood also increased.

The Bharatiya Janata Party (BJP) leadership—first local, then national—also passed resolutions for the statehood of 'Uttaranchal'. Their reasoning was that they wanted a name that encompassed both parts of the region—the western 'Uttarakhand' and the eastern 'Kumaon' (which came from the word 'Kurmanchal').[18] This was a period of intense political turbulence in the state of Uttar Pradesh when governments changed frequently. The BJP formed its first government in 1991 with Kalyan Singh as chief minister and passed the first resolution in the UP legislative assembly supporting statehood for Uttarakhand/Uttaranchal.

In early 1994, the coalition state government of the Samajwadi Party (SP) and the Bahujan Samaj Party (BSP) appointed the Kaushik Committee to study the grievances of the people in the hills. The committee recommended that the eight mountain districts across Garhwal and Kumaon be made into the state of Uttarakhand. The capital could be the centrally accessible city of Gairsain.[19] Almost parallelly, the government proposed a state-wide affirmative action policy of reserving 27 per cent seats in government jobs and higher education institutions for people from Other Backward Classes (OBCs). Garhwal and Kumaon protested that, since only approximately 2 per cent of their population could be categorized officially as OBC, locals from the mountains would probably be marginalized in universities in the region.

The state government responded aggressively, resulting in the eruption of violence across the region through the second half of 1994. This further consolidated the regional identity and transformed the agitation into a mass-based movement without one clear leadership.

---

[18] Tillin, *Remapping India*, p. 230.
[19] Ibid., p. 157.

Student-led organizations played an active role. Local media helped further the spread of the agitation.

In early 1996, the idea of granting Uttarakhand the status of union territory was floated. In his Republic Day address of January 1997, Prime Minister H.D. Deve Gowda of the United Front coalition promised statehood to Uttarakhand. In December 1998, when the BJP-led National Democratic Alliance (NDA) was in office at the Centre, a bill to create Uttarakhand was tabled in the Lok Sabha. After being reintroduced post-elections in 1999, it received presidential assent in August 2000.

On 9 November 2000, the Uttar Pradesh Reorganisation Act separated the state of Uttaranchal (later renamed as Uttarakhand) from Uttar Pradesh.

**   **

UTTARAKHAND

> **Did You Know?**
>
> *When Uttarakhand was first created on 9 November 2000, it was called Uttaranchal. The name was changed six years later.*

The people of Uttarakhand first demanded autonomy based on identity in 1937.[1] They felt that they were geographically and culturally very different from the plains of the United Provinces. At the time of Independence, the present state of Uttarakhand (meaning 'northern region') existed mainly in three administrative divisions in the Himalayan mountains—the princely state of Tehri Garhwal and the two districts of Garhwal and Kumaon which were already a part of the United Provinces.

Tehri Garhwal had crowned a young king just a year before Indian Independence. The previous king, Maharaja Narendra Shah had abdicated his position and left the princely state under the rule

---

[1] Shekhar Pathak, 'Beyond an Autonomous State Background and Preliminary Analysis of Uttarakhand Movement,' *Proceedings of the Indian History Congress,* 60 (1999), p. 895.

of his twenty-five year-old son Maharaja Manabendra Shah. The young king signed the Merger Agreement with the Union of India on 18 May 1949. On 1 August 1949, Tehri Garhwal became a new district in the north-western corner of the United Provinces along with Garhwal and Kumaon.[2]

The United Provinces, renamed as Uttar Pradesh, emerged as India's largest and most populous state. In its 1955 report, the States Reorganisation Commission (SRC) debated and disagreed on the partition of Uttar Pradesh. One of the Commission's members, K.M. Panikkar, proposed a separate state in the western plains, while the other two members wished to retain Uttar Pradesh undivided. However, none of the three members spoke of creating Uttarakhand and the mountainous region continued as a part of the larger state. In 1960, it was reorganized into two Mandals (administrative areas)— Kumaon (the eastern half) and Uttarakhand (a.k.a. Garhwal, the western half).

Through the late 1960s and early 1970s, grassroots issues like social justice and combating economic inequality gained importance in parts of north India and Uttar Pradesh. Regional political parties and social movements began to emerge in response, which helped kick-start a new socio-political conversation, especially in the Uttarakhand mountains, around the management of natural resources, the marginalization of peripheral regions, and the economic rights of local communities. These gained political significance from 1977–80 when the Janata Party simultaneously formed the government at the centre and the state of Uttar Pradesh, becoming the first non-Congress party to do so. The Janata Party had been vocal about the need to reorganize state boundaries so as to correct economic imbalances and enable administrative convenience, even calling

---

[2]   Ministry of States, Government of India. *White Paper on Indian States*, 1950, pp. 44–45.

for a second SRC. Uttarakhand was one of the states that the Janata Party called for.[3]

The 1970s also witnessed a demand for universities and an Uttarakhand Rajya Sammelan. In 1979, a new political party called the Uttarakhand Kranti Dal (UKD)—whose sole agenda was to campaign for statehood—was established.[4] This was also taken up later by the Uttarakhand Sangharsh Vahini (USV). The 1980s saw an uptick in socio-political activities linked directly to the demand for statehood—strikes, rallies, movements and protests (including against liquor and the new forest regulations passed in 1980). The first results were visible through electoral victories.

In the 1980s, the Bharatiya Janata Party (BJP) took up the cause of statehood for Uttarakhand. Their local leadership first passed resolutions in support, followed by their national council. However, they called the region 'Uttaranchal', a name they felt encompassed both parts of the region—the western 'Uttarakhand' and the eastern 'Kumaon' (which came from the word 'Kurmanchal').[5] The BJP then formed its first state government in Uttar Pradesh in 1991 during a period of intense political turbulence when governments changed frequently. Kalyan Singh became chief minister and passed the first resolution in the UP legislative assembly supporting statehood for Uttarakhand/Uttaranchal.

The flashpoint in the movement for statehood came in 1994. The state government then was a coalition between the Samajwadi Party (SP) and the Bahujan Samaj Party (BSP) led by the chief minister, Mulayam Singh Yadav of the SP. The coalition government appointed the Kaushik Committee in early 1994 to study the grievances of the people in the hills. The committee recommended

---

[3] Louise Tillin, *Remapping India: New States and Their Political Origins* (New Delhi: Oxford University Press, 2013), p. 100.

[4] Ibid.

[5] Ibid., p. 230.

the creation of a new state of Uttarakhand from the eight mountain districts across Garhwal and Kumaon with its capital at the centrally accessible city of Gairsain.[6] At the same time, the government proposed a state-wide affirmative action policy of reserving 27 per cent seats in government jobs and higher education institutions for people from Other Backward Classes (OBCs). However, only approximately 2 per cent of the population of Garhwal and Kumaon could be categorized officially as OBC. Locals from the mountains protested that they would probably be marginalized in universities in their own region.

The state government responded aggressively and violence erupted across the region through the second half of 1994. This further consolidated the regional identity and transformed the agitation into a mass-based movement without one clear leadership. Student-led organizations such as the Uttarakhand Sanyukt Sangarsh Samiti (USSS) and the Uttarakhand Chhatra Sangarsh Samiti (UCSS) played an active role while local media helped further the spread of the agitation by connecting various participants.

The idea to grant union territory status to Uttarakhand was floated in early 1996. Prime Minister H.D. Deve Gowda of the United Front coalition promised statehood to Uttarakhand in his Republic Day address of January 1997. In December 1998, the BJP-led National Democratic Alliance (NDA) at the Centre tabled a bill in the Lok Sabha to create Uttarakhand. After being reintroduced post-elections in 1999, the bill received presidential assent in August 2000.

On 9 November 2000, through the Uttar Pradesh Reorganisation Act, the state of Uttaranchal came into being comprising thirteen districts. This date is today observed as Uttarakhand Divas (Uttarakhand Day). Based on the results of the 1996 Uttar Pradesh

---

[6]   Tillin, *Remapping India*, p. 157.

elections, the BJP formed the first state government in Uttarakhand with Nityanand Swami as the first chief minister.

On 21 December 2006, in response to a long-standing demand on its name, the Uttaranchal (Alteration of Name) Act was passed. From 1 January 2007 onwards, the state was officially known as Uttarakhand.

* *

WEST BENGAL

1947–50: Cleavage of Country and State

At Independence in 1947, Bengal Province was partitioned into west and east by the Radcliffe Line. East Bengal became a part of Pakistan while West Bengal transferred to the Dominion of India. East Bengal was renamed East Pakistan in 1955 and then Bangladesh when it gained independence in 1971. Meanwhile, West Bengal itself was split into two separate parts. The northern districts were separated from the rest of the state by Bihar and the future nation of Bangladesh.

The princely state of Cooch Behar, nestled in the foothills of the Himalayas, sat at a crucial junction of three different administrative areas. To its north and west lay West Bengal, to its east, Assam, and to its south spread out the plains of East Bengal. The ruler, Maharaja

Jagaddipendra Narayan Bhup Bahadur, signed the Merger Agreement with India on 30 August 1949. Given the uncertain border situation at the time and the geographical importance of Cooch Behar, the Government of India took over the administration through a chief commissioner on 12 September.

However, just three months later, Sardar Vallabhbhai Patel, the minister of states, consulted the Premier of West Bengal and decided it was more advantageous to merge Cooch Behar with West Bengal. On 1 January 1950, Cooch Behar became a district in the north-eastern end of West Bengal.[1]

*

1956: Threading West Bengal

The partition of India separated the northern portion of West Bengal from the rest of the state. Bihar and the future nation of Bangladesh stood in between West Bengal and its northern region. For nearly ten years, West Bengal remained the only Part A state that was not a contiguous geographical unit. In 1956, the States Reorganisation Commission (SRC) approached 'one of the most difficult problems'[2] it had faced and rectified it with a slight redrawing of state boundaries.

In addition to existing in two parts, West Bengal had also lost many connectivity options like highways and bridges across rivers. Hence, West Bengal sought large regions of Bihar all the way up to the River Mahananda to not only ensure contiguity but also connectivity. However, after studying census records to understand the language and caste compositions of the disputed districts, the SRC concluded that there wasn't much merit in many of West Bengal's claims.

---

[1]   V.P. Menon, *The Story of the Integration of the Indian States* (United Kingdom: Longmans, Green and Co., 1956), p. 213.

[2]   Report of the States Reorganisation Commission, 1955, p. 182.

Instead, the SRC proposed that two slim but 'essential'[3] tracts of land be transferred from Bihar to West Bengal. These were the portion of Kishanganj sub-division that lay to the east of River Mahananda and a portion of Gopalpur thana (with a special mention that the government of West Bengal retain control of the national highway here). This was done so as to physically integrate West Bengal's northern districts with the rest of the state. Additionally, it gave control of this section of the India–Pakistan border (now India–Bangladesh border) entirely to West Bengal, which was a 'convenient and desirable'[4] administrative advantage.

Where the SRC did see merit was in West Bengal's claim to the district of Purulia further to the south. The SRC cited unmistakable evidence of Bengali influence in the district which had the largest concentration of Bengali-speakers outside West Bengal. Also, the Kangsabati River on which West Bengal was implementing a flood control and irrigation project rose in Purulia, making the district more valuable to West Bengal than Bihar. Hence, Purulia (minus the Chas thana) was transferred to West Bengal, becoming its westernmost district.

*

The 68-Year Exchange of Enclaves

Partition in 1947 created the unique situation of enclaves[5] on the international border of India and the future Bangladesh, unparalleled across the world in 'their complexity, number, political significance

---

[3]   Report of the States Reorganisation Commission, 1955, p. 181.

[4]   Ibid., p. 177.

[5]   Note: An enclave is a portion of one state completely surrounded by the territory of another state. From the point of view of the governing nation, it is an exclave. However, the two terms are used interchangeably and 'enclave' is the more popular one.

and social eccentricity'[6]. A total of 225 enclaves pockmarked both sides of the border. Of these, 130 were Indian and 95 belonged to East Pakistan. Most of the enclaves situated in India lay within the district of Cooch Behar. These enclaves were around 250 years old, having come into existence due to political alliances and battles by landlords of the Cooch Behar kingdom with the Mughals. As a result, estates were fragmented into scattered plots that were detached from the parent estate. Called 'chhit mohol' in Bengali, they paid taxes to one state but were surrounded by the territory of the other state. When the British invaded Cooch Behar in 1772, they simply continued with this system of administration. The Maharaja continued to run Cooch Behar and the British maintained control over the Maharaja.

Neither government knew exactly how to resolve the situation of the enclaves. As a result, the enclave dwellers found themselves marooned and abandoned. They were not legally allowed to sell their own produce (especially jute, paddy and tobacco) or to cultivate land they owned outside the enclave. Only bare essentials were allowed from the mainland into the enclaves, such as oil, sugar, cloth, matches and medicines. They received no infrastructure benefits, such as schools, markets or medical facilities; there was no electricity, police stations or even drinking water. In 1952, when India and East Bengal/Pakistan agreed to introduce passports and visa controls, the enclave dwellers were given no option to legally acquire a passport from their mainland. These complications grew exponentially for enclaves that were situated within other enclaves. There even existed the world's only third-order enclave—a piece of India within a piece of Bangladesh within a piece of India within the nation of Bangladesh.

Discussions to exchange enclaves began around 1950 and the prime ministers of India and Pakistan agreed to the exchange

---

[6]   Willem van Schendel, 'Stateless in South Asia: The Making of the India–Bangladesh Enclaves,' *The Journal of Asian Studies*, 61(1) (2002), p. 117. https://doi.org/10.2307/2700191

in September 1958 with no additional compensation element. However, implementation stalled as debates arose in India about the unconstitutionality of the exchange, with an appeals case going up to the Supreme Court. Two wars with Pakistan followed in 1965 and 1971, the latter leading to the creation of the independent nation of Bangladesh. In 1974, the prime ministers of India and Bangladesh agreed to exchange the enclaves 'as soon as possible'[7]. However, while Bangladesh ratified this agreement, India did not. Over the next forty years, enclave dwellers, their neighbouring nation, and their mainland fashioned compromises and ad hoc workaround solutions that were as varied as the number of enclaves.

A 2011 Protocol was signed that would transfer 'adverse possessions of land' between the two countries. This, too, was not implemented. Finally, in June 2015, a Land Boundary Agreement (LBA), which included the lands of the 2011 Protocol, was agreed upon and ratified by both governments. India transferred 111 enclaves of a total size of 17,160 acres to Bangladesh, and received 51 enclaves adding up to 7,110 acres. This filled most of the holes that had dotted the border maps as the enclaves merged with the surrounding nation. The enclave dwellers were given a one-time choice of citizenship—they could join either country.[8]

* *

---

[7]   van Schendel, 'Stateless in South Asia,' p. 126.
[8]   Sreeparna Bannerjee, Ambalika Guha and Anasua Basu Ray Chaudhury, 'The 2015 India-Bangladesh Land Boundary Agreement: Identifying Constraints and Exploring Possibilities in Cooch Behar,' *ORF Occasional Paper*, 117 (July 2017), p. 2.

UNION TERRITORIES

ANDAMAN AND NICOBAR ISLANDS

> **Did You Know?**
>
> *In 1950, when all the states were classified as Part A, B or C states, Andaman and Nicobar Islands was the only one to be classified as a Part D state.*

Pre-independence, the Andaman and Nicobar Islands were a part of British India but were administered directly by the Governor-General through an appointed chief commissioner. Hence, when India gained independence from the British, the Andaman and Nicobar Islands simply transferred to the Government of India.

When India adopted its Constitution on 26 January 1950, all the other states of India were classified as Part A, B or C, depending on their size, financial viability and the level of direct central government involvement required. The Andaman and Nicobar Islands received their own category of Part D state, representing the highest level of direct central government involvement. They would be administered by the President of India acting through a chief commissioner.

The President had the powers to make regulations for the Islands that had 'the force and effect of an Act of Parliament'[1] and that could 'repeal or amend any law made by Parliament'[2]. The President also nominated the one member who would represent the Islands in the Lok Sabha. From 1965 onwards, however, this member was directly elected by the Islanders.

The States Reorganisation Commission (SRC) constituted in 1953 considered some suggestions regarding the Islands, including hearing the views of the member of Parliament from the Islands. However, since no major change had been proposed, the SRC in its 1955 report decided that there was no need 'for disturbing the status quo'.[3] The SRC report also replaced the previous four-tier classification of states with a new two-tier classification of states and union territories. Andaman and Nicobar Islands became a union territory that was directly administered by the Union government of India.

* *

---

[1] Administrative Reforms Commission. *Report, Study Team on Administration of Union Territories and NEFA*, 1968, p. 8.
[2] Ibid., p. 207.
[3] Report of the States Reorganisation Commission, 1955, p. 203.

CHANDIGARH

Imagining a New Capital City

In 1947, the British partitioned India into two countries. Punjab was one of the states to feel the brunt of that partition as a large-scale migration of refugees began across the border. Lahore, the previous capital and the erstwhile chief administrative and cultural city of Punjab, now lay in Pakistan. Shimla became the temporary capital of East Punjab but it was inadequate to fully accommodate the government machinery.[1] As a result, government offices were scattered across the towns of East Punjab. A new capital had to be found for Punjab.

---

[1]   Ravi Kalia, *Chandigarh: the Making of an Indian City* (India: Oxford University Press, 1998), p. 3.

The existing cities of East Punjab were considered and rejected for a host of reasons. Amritsar and Jalandhar were too close to the international border and had security concerns. Ludhiana was too industrial and already overcrowded, and it had only one bridge across the Sutlej River, which could prove disastrous in case of an emergency. Ambala had a predominantly military character and lacked proper water and electricity facilities. Karnal and Phillaur had similar infrastructure issues. Moreover, the cost implications of adding capital functions—such as essential amenities and adequate infrastructure—to an existing city was comparable to building a new city.[2]

In March 1948, the Union government officially decided to build the entirely new city of Chandigarh as the capital of Punjab. The site chosen had favourable water supply and ground slope and was situated close to sources of building material like sand, cement and stone.

Prime Minister Jawaharlal Nehru considered Chandigarh 'an expression of the nation's faith in the future'[3] and felt that the rehabilitation of East Punjab centred around it. He wanted it to be 'the first large expressions of our creative genius' and 'symbolic of the freedom of India, unfettered by the traditions of the past'.[4] Chandigarh would be 'Indian in spirit'[5] while having the best developments from other countries. As a result, the early development of the city was guided by the Indians P.N. Thapar and P.L. Verma; the planner who drew up the initial plans was the American Albert Mayer; and the planners and architects who finally built the city were the Swiss cousins Charles-Édouard Jeanneret

---

[2] Kalia, *Chandigarh*, pp. 6–7.
[3] Tai Yong Tan and Gyanesh Kudaisya, *The Aftermath of Partition in South Asia* (United Kingdom: Routledge, 2000), p. 190.
[4] Ibid., p. 190.
[5] Annapurna Shaw, 'Town Planning in Postcolonial India, 1947–1965: Chandigarh Re-Examined,' *Urban Geography*, 30(8) (Nov. 2009), p. 859.

(known as 'Le Corbusier') and Pierre Jeanneret, and the English couple Jane Drew and Maxwell Fry.

However, it wasn't entirely smooth sailing for Chandigarh. Almost immediately, the plan was hit by protests by the farmers who would be displaced. The affected villagers formed an Anti-Rajdhani Committee along with the Socialist Party, the Akali Dal, the District Congress Committee of Ambala and the Hind Kisan Panchayat. They demanded that the government revise its policy of building Chandigarh at that location and even consider moving the capital to nearby Ambala, failing which they would start a peaceful and non-violent satyagraha. This protest gained strength with the support of prominent Congress leaders at the provincial and national levels, including the second chief minister of East Punjab, Bhim Sen Sachar, who led the state government for six months starting 13 April 1949. By October 1950, an agreement was reached with the concerned villagers and the agitation subsided.

On 21 September 1953, the capital of Punjab officially moved from Shimla to Chandigarh.[6]

*

Joint Custody

In 1966, following years of violent demands for a separate Sikh homeland, the Union government constituted the Shah Commission to look into the matter of dividing Punjab. Using the 1961 census as its guide to apply the linguistic principle, the Shah Commission recommended the creation of the hill territory of Himachal Pradesh, the Hindi-speaking state of Haryana, and the Punjabi-speaking state of Punjab. Chandigarh was caught on the border, with both Haryana

---

[6]   Meeta Rajivlochan, Kavita Sharma and Chitleen K. Sethi, *Chandigarh Lifescape: Brief Social History of a Planned City* (India: Chandigarh Government Press, 1999), p. 12.

and Punjab demanding the city as their capital. On the basis of a 55 per cent Hindi-speaking population versus a 44 per cent Punjabi-speaking population recorded in Chandigarh in the 1961 census, the Shah Commission awarded the city to Haryana. However, recognizing the possible fallout of such a decision, the Union government overruled the commission's recommendation. Neither state would fully acquire the city. Instead, the Union government would itself administer Chandigarh as a union territory. Moreover, Chandigarh would serve as a joint external capital to both states. Punjab and Haryana would share the city in a ratio of 60:40.

On 18 September 1966, Parliament passed the Punjab Reorganisation Act. Punjab was divided into four parts—two states and two union territories. The Hindi-speaking districts in the South-eastern plains formed the new state of Haryana. The North-eastern hill districts merged with the existing union territory of Himachal Pradesh. The Punjabi-speaking North-western districts formed the new state of Punjab. The city of Chandigarh was reconstituted as a union territory and became the joint capital of Punjab and Haryana housing the common high court for all three territories.[7]

All four new territories came into being from 1 November 1966.

* *

---

[7]   The Punjab Reorganisation Act, 1966.

DADRA AND NAGAR HAVELI AND DAMAN AND DIU

> **Did You Know?**
>
> *An IAS officer was designated the prime minister of Free Dadra and Nagar Haveli for a single day in 1961 so that he could sign the merger agreement with India.*

Not Yet Independent

On 15 August 1947, India gained its independence from the British. However, not all of India had been under British imperialism. Five territories scattered across the western coast of the country continued to be under Portuguese control. These were Goa (the largest territory), Dadra, Nagar Haveli, Daman and Diu. While Diu sat on the southern lip surrounded by the Saurashtra region of present-day Gujarat, the other three enclaves were clustered close to each other on the border of Gujarat and Maharashtra.

India's Prime Minister Jawaharlal Nehru did not plan to let them continue under foreign rule for much longer. At its first session post-Independence held at Jaipur in December 1948, the Indian National Congress (INC) passed a resolution declaring that 'the continued existence of any foreign possessions in India becomes anomalous and opposed to the conception of India's unity and freedom'.[1] Prime Minister Nehru further said in February 1949 that it was natural and proper to unite all foreign possessions in the country with the Union of India and that they would do so 'through friendly discussions with the powers concerned'[2].

In June 1949, India established a diplomatic office in Lisbon, the capital of Portugal, and began to negotiate the withdrawal of Portugal from its colonies in India.[3] Portugal responded that these were not 'colonies' but, in fact, parts of metropolitan Portugal. When Portugal had gained control over these territories in the early 16th century, there was no 'Republic of India', just a number of kingdoms. Hence, the question of transferring them to India simply did not arise. This didn't go down well with India. In June 1953, it withdrew its diplomatic mission from Lisbon[4] and instituted visa restrictions between Portuguese colonies and India.[5]

*

---

[1]   Akhila Yechury, 'Imagining India, Decolonizing "L'Inde Française", c. 1947–1954,' *The Historical Journal,* 58(4) (December 2015), p. 1151.

[2]   Russell H. Fifield, 'The Future of French India,' *Far Eastern Survey,* 19(6) (22 March 1950), p. 62. doi:10.2307/3024284

[3]   Philip Bravo, 'The Case of Goa: History, Rhetoric and Nationalism,' *Past Imperfect,* Vol. 7 (1998), p. 133.

[4]   Sushila Sawant Mendes, 'Jawaharlal Nehru and the Liberation Struggle of Goa,' *Proceedings of the Indian History Congress* 67 (2006-2007), p. 551.

[5]   Brigadier A.S. Cheema, VSM (Retd), 'Operation Vijay: The Liberation of 'Estado da India'—Goa, Daman and Diu,' *Journal of the United Service Institution of India,* Vol. CXLIII, No. 594 (October–December 2013).

Free Dadra and Nagar Haveli

On 21 July 1954, a small party of Goans led by the president and secretary of the United Front of Goans entered Dadra. The Portuguese police opened fire on them but the protestors overpowered them. This agitation now developed into 'an active liberation movement'[6]. Less than two weeks later, on 2 August 1954, members of the Azad Gomantak Dal and Goans People's Party entered Nagar Haveli. This time, the Portuguese administrators had already evacuated the headquarters at Silvassa and Nagar Haveli was liberated without incident.

The people of 'Free Dadra and Nagar Haveli' proclaimed their independence from Portuguese rule and set up their own provisional administration. Dr A. Furtado, a former judge of the administrative court of Panjim, assumed charge as administrator of Free Dadra and Nagar Haveli. The functions of the government were later split between the Varishtha Panchayat (legislative functions), the courts of law (judicial functions) and the administrative council (executive functions).[7]

The liberation of Dadra and Nagar Haveli from Portuguese control inspired similar movements in Goa, Daman and Diu as well. On 15 August 1954, over a thousand satyagrahis attempted to cross into Goa and Daman but were turned back at the border. A year later, on 15 August 1955, three thousand satyagrahis entered Goa, Daman and Diu in a similar attempt. This time, the Portuguese police and military met them with violence, resulting in deaths and injuries.[8]

---

[6]   Administrative Reforms Commission. *Report, Study Team on Administration of Union Territories and NEFA*, 1968, p. 220.

[7]   Ibid.

[8]   Ibid., pp. 172–73.

Prime Minister Nehru immediately broke off diplomatic relations with Portugal.[9] India closed its consulate in Goa and instituted a travel and economic blockade against the three Portuguese territories.[10]

Portugal filed a complaint before the International Court of Justice at the Hague demanding recognition of its sovereignty over Dadra and Nagar Haveli. On 12 April 1960, the International Court of Justice passed a judgement that Portugal did not have sovereign rights and that India had not acted contrary to its obligations[11].

On 12 June 1961, the Varishtha Panchayat of Free Dadra and Nagar Haveli passed a resolution requesting that the territory be integrated with the Indian Union. To enable this, on 11 August 1961—and for that one day only—an Indian Administrative Services (IAS) officer, K.G. Badlani, was designated the prime minister of Free Dadra and Nagar Haveli. As the head of the state, he then signed an agreement with Indian Prime Minister Jawaharlal Nehru to formally merge Dadra and Nagar Haveli with India.[12] The Indian Parliament then passed the Constitution (Tenth Amendment) Act, 1961, and the Dadra and Nagar Haveli Act, 1961, to add the territory to the list of union territories of India as of 11 August 1961 and to extend the President's regulation-making powers over the territory.

*

[9]   Administrative Reforms Commission. *Report, Study Team on Administration of Union Territories and NEFA*, 1968, pp. 172–73.
[10] Archana Subramaniam, 'Goa Comes Home', *The Hindu*, 17 December 2015.
[11] Administrative Reforms Commission. *Report, Study Team on Administration of Union Territories and NEFA*, 1968, pp. 221–22.
[12] Ibid,. p. 222.

Liberating and Integrating Goa, Daman and Diu

In September 1960, India liberalized travel to Goa. In April 1961, it removed the trade ban with Goa, Daman and Diu. Portugal did not reciprocate on both occasions.[13] After fourteen years of attempting to persuade Portugal through patience and non-violence, armed conflict was now a real prospect for India.

Portugal began to reinforce its presence in its Indian territories and even fired unprovoked at an Indian steamer ship from Anjadip, an island they held just south of Goa. On 1 December, India began a surveillance and reconnaissance exercise called Operation Chutney.[14] The Indian Navy mobilized sixteen ships, divided into four task groups. The Indian Air Force (IAF) began reconnaissance flights to lure any Portuguese fighter jets to reveal their positions. The Indian Army stationed troops around the borders of Goa, Daman and Diu. The army would lead Operation Vijay, and the navy and the air force would support it.

Daman had over five hundred soldiers and policemen stationed at the fort, and it was important to take over the airfield. Diu had another six hundred soldiers stationed mainly in the fort who were supported by artillery, mortars, machine guns and a patrol boat.[15]

The operation began at four a.m. in the predawn darkness of 18 December, coordinated across the three territories. In Daman, Indian troops stormed the air control tower but were unable to take the airfield. IAF fighter jets then struck Portuguese mortars and guns in the fort. By the evening, most of Daman was under Indian control, except the airfield and the adjoining town of Damao Pequeno.

---

[13] Administrative Reforms Commission. *Report, Study Team on Administration of Union Territories and NEFA*, 1968, p. 173.
[14] Cmde Srikant B. Kesnur and Lt Cdr Ankush Banerjee, 'How Indian Navy Helped in the Liberation of Goa', *The Daily Guardian*, December 25, 2020.
[15] Brig Cheema (Retd), 'Operation Vijay'.

The IAF launched another round of attacks but the Portuguese still refused to surrender. Finally, the following morning, Indian troops assaulted and overran the airfield. Daman had been liberated.[16]

In Diu, Indian troops faced stiff resistance from Portuguese artillery and mortar fire. Unable to advance, the troops waited for daylight and air and naval support. Air attacks at first light destroyed the air control tower and an ammunition dump, forcing the Portuguese troops to withdraw to the fort. The IAF also sank the patrol boat. Meanwhile, an Indian cruiser ship heavily bombarded the fort, thereby providing support to the under-fire Indian Army and beating down the Portuguese soldiers. By the evening, Diu was liberated.[17]

In Goa, Indian troops marched into the capital city, Panjim, on the morning of 19 December and captured Fort Aguada. That evening, the Governor-General of Portuguese India, Manuel António Vassalo e Silva, offered to surrender.[18]

Operation Vijay had concluded successfully. Goa, Daman and Diu had all been liberated. 451 years of Portuguese rule in India had ended.

*

The Union Territory of Goa, Daman and Diu

On 27 March 1962, Parliament passed the Goa, Daman and Diu (Administration) Act. Applicable retroactively from 20 December 1961, this designated Goa, Daman and Diu as a single union territory (even if they were 1400 km apart from each other) that would be centrally administered by the President of India. On 13 May 1963, the Government of Union Territories Act came into effect in Goa,

---

[16]   Brig Cheema (Retd), 'Operation Vijay'.
[17]   Ibid.
[18]   Ibid.

Daman and Diu. This gave the union territory a legislature consisting of thirty members and a council of ministers.

However, the union territory's existence was threatened almost immediately. Since Goa was economically prosperous, both its neighbouring states—Maharashtra in the north and Mysore State in the east and south—wanted to absorb it. The Maharashtrawadi Gomantak Party (MGP)—led by Dayanand Bandodkar—was founded in 1963 with the objective of 'the integration of Goa into the state of Maharashtra'[19]. In the December 1963 assembly elections, the MGP won sixteen of the thirty seats—an absolute majority. The United Goans Party (UGP), founded by the Christian minority, won twelve. The INC only won the seat in Daman and an independent candidate won the seat in Diu.[20] Chief Minister Dayanand Bandodkar interpreted the resounding electoral victory as a public endorsement of the merger proposal. He passed a resolution in the Goa Assembly demanding the merger of Goa with Maharashtra and Daman and Diu with Gujarat.[21]

Instead, different communities united to form a non-party Council of Direct Action that staged satyagrahas, marches and strikes which began to seriously disrupt daily life.[22] The Union government, led by Indira Gandhi of the INC, was caught in the crossfire and unable to fully support or fully quell either motion. Eventually, in September 1966, it decided to settle the matter through a public vote. The people of Goa, Daman and Diu would decide the fate of Goa, Daman and Diu.

In December 1966, Parliament passed the Goa, Daman and Diu (Opinion Poll) Act to give legal standing to the poll. The Chief

---

[19]   Arthur G. Rubinoff, 'Goa's Attainment of Statehood,' *Asian Survey*, 32(5) (May 1992), pp. 473–74.

[20]   Ram Joshi, 'The General Elections in Goa,' *Asian Survey*, 4(10) (October 1964), p. 1093. doi:10.2307/2642211

[21]   Rubinoff, 'Goa's Attainment of Statehood,' p. 476.

[22]   Ibid.

Election Commissioner would oversee the poll and the results would be published in the official gazette. The Bandodkar government resigned and the territory was placed under President's rule. On 16 January 1967, Goans would have to choose one of two options: 'Merger' (symbolized by a flower) or 'Union Territory' (symbolized by two leaves)[23]. Both the pro-merger and anti-merger factions campaigned vigorously.

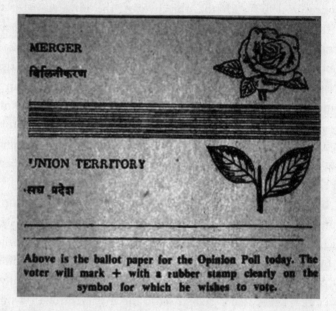

The ballot paper for the 1967 opinion poll in Goa, Daman and Diu[24]

'Union Territory' (two leaves symbol) ultimately won but the voting patterns were very different across the three territories. In Goa, the option received only about 54 per cent of the votes. Voters in Daman

---

[23] Sandesh Prabhudesai, 'The Historic Opinion Poll,' *Goa News*, 20 July 2008.
[24] Aaron Pereira, 'What is Goa's "Opinion Poll Day"?,' *The New Indian Express*, 18 January 2019.

and Diu, however, voted overwhelmingly to retain union territory status; the option received 88 per cent of the votes. The union territory of Goa, Daman and Diu continued to exist in the Union of India as a separate entity. 16 January is observed every year in the three territories as 'Asmitai Dis' (Self-identity Day).[25]

Portugal had refused to recognize India's sovereignty over all five territories all along. In 1974, it underwent a revolution that overthrew the regime and brought about democratic reforms. On 31 December 1974, Portugal and India signed a treaty that recognized that Goa, Daman, Diu, Dadra and Nagar Haveli had 'already become parts of India'[26] and that India had sovereign rights over them from the dates when they each became a part of India.

*

Reorganization

On 23 May 1987, Parliament passed the Goa, Daman and Diu Reorganisation Act to grant statehood to Goa. Daman and Diu was redesignated as its own union territory.

On 9 December 2019, in an effort to improve administrative efficiencies, Parliament passed the Dadra and Nagar Haveli and Daman and Diu (Merger of Union Territories) Act. This merged the two union territories that lay across four unconnected parcels of land and made them one single union territory.

* *

---

[25] Prabhudesai, 'The Historic Opinion Poll.'

[26] Treaty between the Government of India and the Government of the Republic of Portugal on Recognition of India's Sovereignty over Goa, Daman, Diu, Dadra and Nagar Haveli and Related Matters, 1974. http://www.liiofindia.org/in/other/treaties/INTSer/1974/53.html

DELHI

Part C State with a Chief Minister

When India became independent in 1947, Delhi continued as the capital of India. The city was already being administered by a separate chief commissioner ever since it had become the capital of British India in 1912. Independent India continued this system of administration, with the chief commissioner being appointed by the President of India. When India adopted its Constitution on 26 January 1950, Delhi was classified as a centrally administered Part C state.

In 1951, the Government of Part C States Act gave Delhi a council of ministers responsible to the local legislature to aid and advise the chief commissioner.[1] This also gave Delhi its first chief minister,

---

[1] Administrative Reforms Commission. *Report, Study Team on Administration of Union Territories and NEFA*, 1968, p. 27.

thirty-four-year-old Chaudhary Brahm Prakash Yadav of the Indian National Congress (INC). However, the Delhi Assembly's legislative powers were limited. For instance, it had no powers over the police, municipal corporations, or land and buildings in its territory.

*

Union Territory without a Chief Minister

Towards the end of 1953, spurred by the multiple calls for state reorganization across the country, the Union government announced the creation of the States Reorganisation Commission (SRC). There were requests to create a Greater Delhi State as well as to integrate portions of Delhi into surrounding states. The SRC rejected both requests, noting the 'peculiar diarchical structure'[2] of dual control that existed—central control of the national capital along with state-level autonomy. The SRC had already determined that the future for Part C states lay in either merging with a larger state or converting into a centrally administered unit. Since Delhi was both the national capital and a city, it required 'a special dispensation'[3]. Using the examples of the degrees of central control exercised by the governments of France and England over their capital cities of Paris and London, respectively, the SRC believed that national governments needed to be able to exercise effective control over their federal capitals. Even the memorandum submitted by the Delhi government did not dispute this point.[4] On the related issue of demarcating New Delhi as the national capital from Old Delhi and placing both under separate administrations, the SRC deemed it unrealistic, observing that the two Delhis now constituted one integrated unit.[5]

---

[2]   Report of the States Reorganisation Commission, 1955, p. 157.
[3]   Ibid., p. 158.
[4]   Ibid., p. 159.
[5]   Ibid., p. 160.

In terms of the administrative pattern for Delhi, the SRC recommended replacing the popularly-elected state government with a municipal corporation. It considered municipal autonomy as the only solution for Delhi State, since it was 'sound in principle and administratively workable in practice'[6]. This abolished the Delhi legislature and the council of ministers as well as the position of chief minister. Delhi became a centrally administered union territory under the direct responsibility of the President of India. At the end of December 1957, Parliament passed the Delhi Municipal Corporation Act which created the body the following year.[7]

*

In a Class by Itself with a Lieutenant Governor

In August 1962, after French and Portuguese India ceased to exist and their territories were transferred to the Indian Union, Parliament passed the Constitution (Fourteenth Amendment) Act, and then the Government of Union Territories Act, 1963. This created legislatures and councils of ministers in a number of union territories in a sort of throwback to the pre-SRC Government of Part C States Act of 1951. Significantly, it created two classes of union territories, depending on the level of autonomy they were given. Delhi was not included in either class and was considered to be 'in a class by itself'[8]. The Delhi Municipal Corporation passed a resolution protesting against Delhi's exclusion.

In June 1966, the Union government passed the Delhi Administration Act, which came into effect on 7 September 1966. The Act reconstituted the Municipal Corporation as the Metropolitan

---

[6]   Report of the States Reorganisation Commission, 1955, p. 161.

[7]   Government of India. The Delhi Municipal Corporation Act, 1957.

[8]   Administrative Reforms Commission. *Report, Study Team on Administration of Union Territories and NEFA*, 1968, p. 12.

Council, marginally expanded its powers, and made minor tweaks to Delhi's administrative set-up. The centrally appointed administrator was redesignated from chief commissioner to lieutenant governor.[9]

*

National Capital Territory with a Chief Minister

In February 1985, Parliament passed the National Capital Region Planning Board Act. This act imagined the development and evolution of policies for the national capital of Delhi as well as the surrounding districts from the neighbouring states. This cohesive region was designated as the National Capital Region (NCR). The planning board was chaired by the union minister for works and housing; its members included the lieutenant governor of Delhi and the chief ministers of Haryana, Rajasthan and Uttar Pradesh, among others.[10]

The Union government was continually looking into the administrative set-up of Delhi to find ways to resolve underlying issues and streamline the process. In December 1987, the Union government appointed a committee to look into the matter in detail. The committee conducted a detailed inquiry and examination, which included a wide range of discussions, studies of national capital arrangements in other federal countries, and a perusal of debates in the constituent assembly and previous committees. It recommended continuing Delhi as a union territory with the lieutenant governor as administrator but also providing for a popular government in the form of an elected legislative assembly and a council of ministers.

Following the Constitution (Sixty-Ninth Amendment) Act in December 1991 to give the National Capital Territory (NCT) of

9   Government of India. Delhi Administration Act, 1966.
10   Government of India. The National Capital Region Planning Board Act, 1985.

Delhi 'a special status'[11] among the union territories, Parliament passed the Government of National Capital Territory of Delhi Act, 1991. Two years later, the Bharatiya Janata Party (BJP) won a majority in the 1993 legislative assembly elections and Madan Lal Khurana became the chief minister of Delhi. India's NCT had elected a chief minister after thirty-seven years.

* *

---

[11] Government of India. The Constitution (Sixty-Ninth Amendment) Act, 1991.

JAMMU AND KASHMIR

1947: Acceding to the Indian Union

As Indian Independence approached, the ruler of the princely state of Kashmir (also known as Jammu and Kashmir), Maharaja Hari Singh of the Dogra dynasty, was wracked by indecision. He could not decide between the three options that lay before him: accede to India, accede to Pakistan, or declare Kashmir as a separate independent nation. Through the fateful months of June to October 1947, the Hindu Maharaja who ruled over a predominantly Muslim population in one of the largest princely states in British India decided to hope 'for the best, while continuing to do nothing'[1].

---

[1] V.P. Menon, *The Story of the Integration of the Indian States* (United Kingdom: Longmans, Green and Co., 1956), p. 272.

When the Partition of India was decided upon and accepted in early June 1947, Kashmir sat at the crossroads of the future countries of India and Pakistan. In early July, Cyril Radcliffe, a British lawyer, was shipped to India and asked to draw the boundary line between India and Pakistan. He was given five weeks. His boundary line, published in August, cut through Punjab, Rajasthan and Gujarat in the west, and Bengal, Assam and Tripura in the east. Radcliffe did not have to consider the boundaries of Kashmir as its ruler would determine its future.

Except, Maharaja Hari Singh didn't. And then his future was determined for him.

The princely state of Kashmir contained four natural geographic regions: Jammu in the south, Kashmir Valley and the city of Srinagar in the centre, the mountainous Gilgit–Baltistan in the north and north-west, and the plateau of Ladakh in the east. Its religious composition, too, was divided by region. The north and west was predominantly Muslim, the south was more Hindu and Sikh, and the east was largely Buddhist and Muslim. Kashmir also sat gingerly at the confluence of four international regions: Tibet to the east, China to the north-east, Afghanistan to the north and Pakistan to the west.

The political situation within Kashmir in 1947 was volatile, but the Maharaja 'grievously misjudged'[2] it, according to his son (and later member of the Lok Sabha), Karan Singh. A popular movement for representative government was spearheaded by the Jammu and Kashmir National Conference (JKNC, previously known as Jammu and Kashmir Muslim Conference) led by Sheikh Abdullah. However, the movement itself was divided along multiple lines—for instance, between the Hindus, Muslims, Sikhs and Buddhists, or between the Kashmiri Muslims, Jammu Muslims and Punjabi Muslims.

---

[2]   Narayani Basu, *V.P. Menon: The Unsung Architect of Modern India*, (India: S&S India, 2020), p. 359.

Moreover, Sheikh Abdullah and a number of JKNC leaders had been in prison since the autumn of 1946 for demanding the Dogra monarchy to 'Quit Kashmir'.

Kashmir's mountainous geography in its north-west flowed into Pakistan. Its infrastructure at the time, its road and river communications and transportation of forest resources like timber—which constituted a considerable portion of the state's revenue—were almost entirely with Pakistan, while there was just a single road that connected Kashmir to India.[3] Pakistan's Governor-General Muhammad Ali Jinnah even declared that 'Kashmir will fall into our laps like ripe fruit'[4]. On the other hand, Sheikh Abdullah enjoyed a close personal friendship with the Indian Prime Minister Jawaharlal Nehru and even 'appeared to be publicly pro-India'[5]. Maharaja Hari Singh, meanwhile, was neither a friend of Nehru's nor a believer in the idea of an Islamic state; he wanted to protect his own power.

In the third week of June 1947, the Viceroy and Governor-General of India, Louis Mountbatten, went to Kashmir to meet the Maharaja. Over the course of four days and multiple meetings, Mountbatten insisted that accession to either side, and not independence, was the future for Kashmir. Both Pakistan and India were equally viable and available options to the Maharaja—Mountbatten said he had 'firm assurance on this'[6] from States Minister Sardar Vallabhbhai Patel himself—but he would have to choose a side before 15 August to avoid trouble. However, Maharaja Hari Singh evaded making a decision on the matter and even feigned a stomach ailment so he could cancel his last meeting with Mountbatten.

The Maharaja's 'notorious vacillations'[7] irritated Sardar Patel. In a letter to the Maharaja on 3 July 1947, Sardar Patel assured

---

3   Menon, *Integration*, pp. 271–72.
4   Basu, *V.P. Menon*, p. 360.
5   Ibid., p. 366.
6   Menon, *Integration*, p. 271.
7   Basu, *V.P. Menon*, p. 359.

him that the interests of Kashmir lay in 'joining the Indian Union without delay'[8] and that Kashmir's past history and tradition demanded it. 'All India looks up to you and expects you to take this decision,'[9] he wrote.

The Indian Prime Minister Jawaharlal Nehru had an emotional attachment to Kashmir; it 'meant more to him at the time than anything else'[10]. In the weeks leading up to Independence, Nehru considered going to Kashmir himself to take matters into his own hands. This alarmed top Indian government officials, including Viceroy Louis Mountbatten, who felt that a visit to Kashmir then by the prime minister—who was 'under very great strain'—could only produce 'a most explosive situation'.[11] Eventually, Nehru was convinced to stay in Delhi and Mahatma Gandhi went to Kashmir in his stead.

On 12 August 1947, with Independence and Partition at the doorstep, the Maharaja negotiated and signed a Standstill Agreement with Pakistan. India didn't sign a Standstill Agreement, though. According to the secretary of the States Ministry, V.P. Menon, Kashmir had 'its own peculiar problems'[12] and India wanted to examine the implications of signing the agreement. Moreover, India's hands were already full and Menon had simply no time to think of Kashmir. Three days later, three independent nations stood where there had been none—India, Pakistan and Kashmir.

Almost immediately, Pakistan began breaching the Standstill Agreement it had signed with Kashmir in an attempt to force its accession. Pakistan cut off the supply of food, petrol and other essential commodities, and stopped the railway service from Sialkot to Jammu. Travellers could no longer freely move between Pakistan

---

[8]   Basu, *V.P. Menon*, p. 363.
[9]   Ibid.
[10] Ibid., pp. 360–64.
[11] Ibid., p. 364.
[12] Menon, *Integration*, p. 272.

and Kashmir. The 700 km-long border between the two nations saw an increased number of hit-and-run raids, forcing Maharaja Hari Singh to stretch out his troops and thin out his defences. Pakistan applied diplomatic pressure too, sending a representative to Srinagar to gain Kashmir's accession.

In August 1947, the Muslims in the Poonch region of western Jammu started an uprising against the Maharaja. The Poonch Muslims had been living 'under a system of dual oppression'[13] of Maharaja Hari Singh and the Raja of Poonch. The Dogra army retaliated to the uprising violently, and simmering discontent erupted into full-scale revolt. Local leaders organized the Poonch Muslims into the Azad Army with two objectives: to free Poonch from Dogra rule, and to merge Poonch with Pakistan (with which it shared a border).

Towards the end of September 1947, Nehru believed that Pakistan's strategy was to infiltrate Kashmir and 'take some big action'[14] once the onset of winter isolated it. Sheikh Abdullah was released from prison in an effort to arrive at an agreement between him and the Maharaja, but he continued to demand freedom from the Dogra monarchy before accession to either country. India believed that a plebiscite was a logical solution to Kashmir's troubles. However, as everyone was soon to find out, the situation on-ground had advanced much too far.

On 22 October 1947, thousands of tribal raiders from Pakistan's North-west Frontier Province swept into Kashmir in an all-out invasion.[15] This was notoriously difficult terrain to defend; for some eight hundred years, invaders had entered India through this north-western geographical gate. The raiders also came well-equipped with

---

[13] Chitralekha Zutshi, *Oxford India Short Introductions: Kashmir* (India: OUP India, 2019), p. 108.

[14] Basu, *V.P. Menon*, p. 365.

[15] Menon, *Integration*, p. 272.

about three hundred lorries, along with mortars, artillery and Mark V mines. India would later discover that the General Tariq who masterminded the operation and led the raiders was in reality Major-General Akbar Khan of the Pakistan Army.

The north-western and western frontiers of Kashmir were easily breached. The Muslim soldiers in Kashmir's state forces deserted and switched sides; they joined the raiders. Large parts of the border areas of Mirpur and Poonch were already under the control of the pro-Pakistan Azad Army, who then went on to declare the formation of the Provisional Azad Government. The raiding forces rode into Uri on their way to Baramulla and Srinagar. On 24 October, they took over the Mohara Power Station and cut the electricity to Srinagar. The raiders announced that they would celebrate Id on 26 October at the Srinagar mosque.

Maharaja Hari Singh sent a desperate appeal for help—arms, ammunition and troops—to the Indian government, which it received on the evening of 24 October. The Defence Committee of India met on the morning of 25 October and decided they needed more information. The secretary of the States Ministry V.P. Menon flew to Srinagar immediately to study and report on the situation. He landed in a deserted Srinagar where vigilantes patrolled street corners and the state police were entirely absent. At the palace, he found the Maharaja in a helpless panic who pleaded for the Government of India to come to the rescue of Kashmir.[16] Srinagar would not be able to hold out for more than two days.

V.P. Menon made quick decisions and took decisive action. He persuaded the Maharaja that flight was the only recourse available to him at that moment. Late that very night, he put the Maharaja and his family and their valuable possessions on a royal convoy driving south to Jammu and to relative safety. It wasn't a moment too soon, for as Menon returned to the guesthouse and prepared to sleep, he

---

[16] Menon, *Integration*, pp. 273–74.

received a phone call in the predawn darkness. Raiders had infiltrated Srinagar, ran the rumours. He had to leave immediately.

The airfield was crowded this time, with everybody trying to leave the city. At first light on 26 October, V.P. Menon's flight took off and brought him back to Delhi and straight into a Defence Committee meeting. Menon had been unable to collect his thoughts on the flight just a little while earlier but was now clear on his position—India must help the Kashmir government.[17] Pakistan was attempting to repeat history by invading from the north. The invasion posed a grave threat to the integrity of India. 'Srinagar today, Delhi tomorrow,'[18] said Menon. India had to emphasize to the invaders that this could not be permitted.

Viceroy Louis Mountbatten was firm in his opinion that for India to help Kashmir, Kashmir must first become a part of Indian territory. Maharaja Hari Singh would have to sign an Instrument of Accession with India before any military aid could be sent. This could, however, be a provisional accession conditional to a plebiscite being held after the raiders were driven out and law and order was restored.

V.P. Menon flew to Jammu that very day carrying the Instrument of Accession. Maharaja Hari Singh, despondent and believing that he had lost Kashmir, was ready to accede at once.[19] He signed the Instrument of Accession with India—on the same terms as the rulers of every other princely state that had acceded to India—and handed over control to the Indian government over the three subjects mentioned in the document: communications, external affairs and defence. The Maharaja also wrote a letter to Mountbatten to state that he was immediately setting up an interim government headed by Sheikh Abdullah.

[17] Basu, *VP Menon*, p. 371.
[18] Menon, *Integration*, p. 283.
[19] Ibid., pp. 274–75.

On 26 October 1947, the princely state of Jammu and Kashmir acceded to become a part of Indian territory. India's military retaliation against the invasion of Kashmir began the very next day.

*

A Fluid Constitutional Journey

The Instrument of Accession that every ruler signed specified that the document did not 'commit . . . in any way'[20] their princely state to accept any future constitution of India. However, when the Indian Constitution was drawn up, every single ruler accepted it and, in the process, gave up the autonomy of their state in order to fully integrate into India.

Except Maharaja Hari Singh of Jammu and Kashmir. The autonomy of his state was important to him. It was also important to Sheikh Abdullah, who now led the interim government, albeit in a different way.

On the eve of 1948, India formally complained to the United Nations about Pakistan's involvement in Jammu and Kashmir, thereby internationalizing the dispute. On 5 March 1948, the Maharaja issued a proclamation that the state would have its own Constitution drafted by its own constituent assembly. Jammu and Kashmir negotiated the terms of its membership with the Union of India, making it the only state to do so. From May to October 1949, four members of the JKNC, including Sheikh Abdullah, represented Jammu and Kashmir in India's constituent assembly that debated and drafted India's Constitution. Meanwhile, in June 1949, Maharaja Hari Singh handed over the reins of his princely state to his eighteen-year-old son, Karan Singh. India completed drafting

---

[20]   Government of India. Appendix VII, *White Paper on Indian States,* 1950, p. 166.

its Constitution by October 1949 and formally adopted it on 26 January 1950. Jammu and Kashmir was included as a Part B state.

The Constitution of India carried the result of the negotiations in the form of Article 370, which preserved Jammu and Kashmir's autonomy. The state would have its own Constitution drafted by its own constituent assembly, as well as its own flag. This constituent assembly could also decide if the state should accede to India beyond the three subjects in the Instrument of Accession. The President of India, in concurrence with the constituent assembly of Jammu and Kashmir, could alter Article 370. The operational head of the administration—Sheikh Abdullah—was called the prime minister while the nominal constitutional head of the state—Maharaja Karan Singh—was called the Sadar-e-Riyasat.[21]

However, the main opposition party in Jammu and Kashmir, the Praja Parishad, protested and called for complete integration with India with the slogan 'Ek Vidhan, Ek Pradhan, Ek Nishan' (One Constitution, One Head of State, One Flag).[22] Led mostly by officials from the Maharaja's former administration and recently dispossessed Hindu landlords, the Praja Parishad was present mainly in the Hindu-dominated Jammu region and would later merge with the national Bharatiya Jana Sangh party.

In May 1951, Maharaja Karan Singh convened a constituent assembly with sovereign powers for Jammu and Kashmir.[23] All its members were to be elected on the basis of universal adult franchise. Prior to the constituent assembly elections, the nomination papers of nearly half the Praja Parishad candidates were rejected because

---

[21] Zutshi, *Kashmir,* p. 125.

[22] Ramachandra Guha, 'Securing Kashmir—II,' *India After Gandhi: The History of the World's Largest Democracy,* (United Kingdom: Macmillan, 2017).

[23] A.G. Noorani, *Article 370: A Constitutional History of Jammu and Kashmir* (India: OUP India, 2014), p. 143.

of irregularities.[24] Subsequently, the Praja Parishad boycotted the 'completely rigged election'[25] and withdrew all its candidates. The JKNC won all the seats to the body unopposed.

The constituent assembly came into being from October 1951. In his opening speech, Sheikh Abdullah expounded on the advantages and disadvantages of the three options that lay before Jammu and Kashmir: accession to India, accession to Pakistan, or becoming an 'eastern Switzerland',[26] aloof from, but with friendly relations with both countries. In his speech, Sheikh Abdullah went on to reject independence as 'impractical' and accession to Pakistan as 'immoral'.[27] Jammu and Kashmir would join India, but on its own terms.

In May 1952, after India's first general elections, Jammu and Kashmir sent ten appointed representatives to the Indian Houses of Parliament—six to the Lok Sabha and four to the Rajya Sabha.

In June 1952, the Jammu and Kashmir constituent assembly unanimously adopted the interim report of the Basic Principles Committee which recommended that the state be wholly democratic with a head of state (Sadar-e-Riyasat) elected every five years instead of a hereditary or dynastic succession. Indian Prime Minister Jawaharlal Nehru noted that along with this decision to depose the Maharaja—whom the President of India recognized as being equal to the Rajpramukh (Governor) of the State—the constituent assembly must also 'reaffirm'[28] Jammu and Kashmir's accession to India. Nehru then raised wider questions regarding the position of Jammu and Kashmir and its citizens in the Indian Union, and stressed that

[24] Sumantra Bose, *Kashmir: Roots of Conflict, Paths to Peace,* (Cambridge: Harvard University Press, 2005), p. 56.
[25] Ibid., p. 56.
[26] Noorani, *Article 370,* p. 130.
[27] Guha, 'Securing Kashmir—II,' *India After Gandhi.*
[28] Noorani, *Article 370,* p. 148.

Kashmir's relationship with India 'must be fully clarified'[29] before finalizing their Constitution.

Meanwhile, internally, the state was starting to splinter. Hindu-dominant Jammu began to mistrust and resent the dominance of and exclusion by the Muslim-dominant JKNC based in Kashmir. Buddhist- and Muslim-dominant Ladakh regarded the state government as being discriminatory against Ladakhi interests and raised demands for greater autonomy for itself from the state government.[30] Moreover, the JKNC National Conference itself was split into pro-India and pro-independence factions, with Sheikh Abdullah himself courting both options and beginning to favour the latter.

This led to the Delhi Agreement in July 1952 between government officials of India (led by Nehru) and Jammu and Kashmir (led by Sheikh Abdullah). Jammu and Kashmir was a constituent unit like any other.[31] Kashmiris would hold full Indian citizenship. Only 'permanent residents' as defined by an existing state law would be allowed to purchase land and immovable property in Kashmir. The Sadar-e-Riyasat would be recognized by and hold office 'during the pleasure of the President'[32] of India. The President also held emergency powers but only if requested by the state assembly.

On 8 August 1953, as Sheikh Abdullah grew more vocally in favour of independence, the Sadar-e-Riyasat, Karan Singh, cited 'serious differences'[33] in the cabinet and dismissed him and dissolved the council of ministers. Sheikh Abdullah's deputy, Bakshi Ghulam Mohammad, was appointed as the new prime minister of Jammu and Kashmir.

---

[29] Noorani, *Article 370*, p. 153.
[30] Zutshi, *Kashmir,* p. 126.
[31] Noorani, *Article 370*, p. 171.
[32] Ibid., p. 170.
[33] Ibid., p. 273.

On 14 May 1954, Indian President Rajendra Prasad issued a Presidential Order under Article 370 that ratified the modifications agreed upon in the Delhi Agreement. Called the Constitution (Application to Jammu and Kashmir) Order, 1954, it became the basis for the functioning of the relationship between India and Jammu and Kashmir. It extended many parts of the Indian Constitution to the state of Jammu and Kashmir, including fundamental rights and the powers of the Indian Union's legislative, executive and judicial organs, as well as relations on finance, trade and commerce. It also added Article 35A to the Indian Constitution defining the 'permanent residents' of Jammu and Kashmir.[34]

On 17 November 1956, Jammu and Kashmir adopted the State Constitution and the constituent assembly dissolved itself, its work done. The State Constitution, which came into force on 26 January 1957, declared up front that, 'The State of Jammu and Kashmir is and shall be an integral part of the Union of India'[35]. Article 370 became the tunnel—rather than a wall or a mountain—that connected Jammu and Kashmir to India, according to Union Home Minister Gulzari Lal Nanda.[36] Prime Minister Nehru viewed Article 370 as a transitional provisional arrangement rather than a permanent part of the Constitution and felt it was being eroded by later amendments to the State Constitution.[37]

On 10 April 1965, the Jammu and Kashmir state legislature enacted the Constitution of Jammu and Kashmir (Sixth Amendment) Act to rename the positions of Sadar-e-Riyasat and prime minister as Governor and chief minister, respectively. In the 1967 Indian

---

[34] 'From the Archives: The Hindu's Report on the President's Order in J&K, 1954', *The Hindu*, 6 Aug. 2019.
[35] The Constitution of Jammu and Kashmir, 1956.
[36] Noorani, *Article 370*, pp. 344–49.
[37] Ibid.

Lok Sabha elections, Jammu and Kashmir participated directly for the first time, voting for and electing six members of Parliament.

*

2019: Abrogation and Reorganization

On 19 June 2018, the Jammu and Kashmir state government—a coalition between the People's Democratic Party (PDP) and the Bharatiya Janata Party (BJP)—was reduced to a minority after the BJP withdrew its support. Chief Minister Mehbooba Mufti resigned. The following day, the President of India, Ram Nath Kovind, approved the imposition of Governor's rule in Jammu and Kashmir. Accordingly, Governor Narinder Nath Vohra took over the administration of the state. He then retired on 23 August and President Kovind appointed Satya Pal Malik as the new Governor of Jammu and Kashmir. On 21 November, Governor Malik dissolved the legislative assembly 'citing horse-trading and lack of stability to form a government'[38].

According to Article 92 of the State Constitution, Governor's rule would expire after six months. On 19 December, just before his rule expired, Governor Malik recommended the imposition of President's rule in the state, which President Kovind gave his assent to.

In the May 2019 Lok Sabha elections in India, the BJP won an absolute majority and returned to form the Union government.

On 5 August 2019, President Kovind passed a Presidential Order with the concurrence of the government of the state of Jammu and Kashmir.[39] Called the Constitution (Application to Jammu and Kashmir) Order, 2019 and effective immediately, it

[38] 'After Governor's Rule, President's Rule Comes into Force in Jammu and Kashmir,' *The Economic Times,* 20 Dec. 2018.
[39] The Constitution (Application to Jammu and Kashmir) Order, 2019.

'superseded'[40] the Presidential Order of 14 May 1954. This order applied all the provisions of the Indian Constitution to Jammu and Kashmir, thereby rendering the State Constitution of November 1956 inoperative.[41] It effectively integrated the state of Jammu and Kashmir fully with India and brought it on an equal footing with the other units of the Indian Union. A further Presidential notification then removed the tunnel of Article 370 and abrogated Article 35A. The 'permanent residents' were later redefined as the 'domiciles' of Jammu and Kashmir.

The Union government immediately followed this Presidential Order with the Jammu and Kashmir Reorganisation Bill, 2019. The bill proposed to reorganize the state of Jammu and Kashmir into two union territories—Jammu and Kashmir, and Ladakh. The Governor of the state would now become the lieutenant governor for both the union territories. Jammu and Kashmir would have a legislative assembly; the provisions of Article 239A that applied to Puducherry would apply to Jammu and Kashmir as well. Ladakh would not have a legislative assembly and would be administered directly by the President acting through the lieutenant governor.[42]

Both the Houses of Parliament passed the bill with a majority vote in two days and President Kovind gave his assent to the Act on 9 August. The Jammu and Kashmir Reorganisation Act came into effect on 31 October 2019 and resulted in two new union territories in the place of one state.

* *

---

[40]   The Constitution (Application to Jammu and Kashmir) Order, 2019.
[41]   Ibid.
[42]   The Jammu and Kashmir Reorganisation Act, 2019.

LADAKH

Early Demands for Autonomy

Modern political demands for Ladakhi autonomy and separation of Ladakh from Jammu and Kashmir began around the same time as Indian Independence and Kashmir's accession to India. In 1947, the Ladakh Buddhist Association (LBA) made three proposals to Maharaja Hari Singh, the ruler of Jammu and Kashmir, for the future of Ladakh:

- The Maharaja rules Ladakh directly; or
- Ladakh merges with the Hindu majority parts of Jammu and forms a separate province; or
- Ladakh merges with East Punjab.

In May 1949, prior to Prime Minister Jawaharlal Nehru's visit to Ladakh, the LBA made its first official demand for regional autonomy and for Ladakh's right to self-determination. In its memorandum to the prime minister, the LBA declared Ladakh as 'a separate nation by all the tests—race, language, religion, culture'[1] and reiterated its previous three proposals. It also specified that it had presented the first two proposals as a formality, and what it really wanted for Ladakh was a separation from Kashmir and a 'direct merger with India'[2]. The LBA's definition of Ladakh was Buddhist and differentiated along religious lines from 'the people of Baltistan including Skardu and parts of Kargil tehsils predominantly populated by Muslims . . . nor by the people of Gilgit'[3]. Although Nehru was sympathetic, he refused to make any specific arrangement for Ladakh, given the situation at the time in Jammu and Kashmir.

A second delegation also made a pitch to Nehru in May 1949. This delegation was led by the 19th Kushok Bakula Rinpoche, Thupstan Chognor, who was the head of the Gelugpa branch of Tibetan Buddhism in Ladakh. It protested the Kashmir-dominated administration of Ladakh and argued that, with Indian Independence and the Lapse of Paramountcy, 'Ladakh was free to choose its own destiny'[4]. It demanded a direct merger with India, failing which it hinted at a possible reunification with Tibet.

When Nehru did visit Ladakh in July 1949 along with Jammu and Kashmir Prime Minister Sheikh Abdullah, they appointed Kushok Bakula Rinpoche as the district president of the Jammu and Kashmir National Conference (JKNC), of which Sheikh Abdullah was the president. However, in 1953, during a budget session,

---

[1]   Martijn van Beek, 'True Patriots: Justifying Autonomy for Ladakh', *Himalaya, The Journal of the Association for Nepal and Himalayan Studies, Himalayan Research Bulletin,* 18(1) (1998), p. 38.

[2]   Ibid., p. 38.

[3]   Ibid., pp. 38–39.

[4]   Ibid., p. 39.

Bakula Rinpoche attacked and condemned the Jammu and Kashmir state government, demanding that the Centre protect Ladakh since 'Ladakh is not communal, but the state is'[5]. While his speech received widespread national media coverage, it failed to secure any discernible action from the Union government, whose hands were tied by the larger issue of the disputed status of Jammu and Kashmir.

*

Jammu and Kashmir's Constitutional Journey

From May to October 1949, four members, including Sheikh Abdullah of the JKNC, which led the interim government in Jammu and Kashmir, represented the state in India's constituent assembly that debated and drafted India's Constitution. In June 1949, Maharaja Hari Singh handed over the reins of his princely state to his eighteen-year-old son, Karan Singh. India completed drafting its Constitution by October 1949 and formally adopted it on 26 January 1950. Jammu and Kashmir was included as a Part B state.

Article 370 was included in the Constitution of India as a way to preserve Jammu and Kashmir's autonomy. The President of India, in concurrence with the constituent assembly of Jammu and Kashmir, could alter Article 370. The constituent assembly would draft the state Constitution and also decide if the state should accede to India beyond the three subjects in the Instrument of Accession. The operational head of the administration—Sheikh Abdullah—was called the prime minister while the nominal constitutional head of the state—Maharaja Karan Singh—was called the Sadar-e-Riyasat.[6]

In July 1952, government officials of India (led by Nehru) and Jammu and Kashmir (led by Sheikh Abdullah) announced the

---

[5]   van Beek, 'True Patriots', p. 39.
[6]   Chitralekha Zutshi, *Oxford India Short Introductions: Kashmir* (India: OUP India, 2019), p. 125.

Delhi Agreement. Jammu and Kashmir was a constituent unit like any other.[7] Kashmiris would hold full Indian citizenship. Only 'permanent residents' as defined by an existing state law would be allowed to purchase land and immovable property in Kashmir. The Sadar-e-Riyasat would be recognized by and hold office 'during the pleasure of the President'[8] of India. The President also held emergency powers but only if requested by the state assembly.

On 14 May 1954, the Indian President Rajendra Prasad issued a Presidential Order under Article 370 that ratified the modifications agreed upon in the Delhi Agreement. Called the Constitution (Application to Jammu and Kashmir) Order, 1954, it became the basis for the functioning of the relationship between India and Jammu and Kashmir. It extended many parts of the Indian Constitution to the state of Jammu and Kashmir, including fundamental rights and the powers of the Indian Union's legislative, executive and judicial organs, as well as relations on finance, trade and commerce. It also added Article 35A to the Indian Constitution defining the 'permanent residents' of Jammu and Kashmir.[9]

On 17 November 1956, Jammu and Kashmir adopted the State Constitution, which came into force on 26 January 1957. It declared up front that, 'The State of Jammu and Kashmir is and shall be an integral part of the Union of India'[10]. Article 370 became the tunnel—rather than a wall or a mountain—that connected Jammu and Kashmir to India, according to Union Home Minister Gulzari Lal Nanda.[11] Prime Minister Nehru viewed Article 370 as a transitional provisional arrangement rather than a permanent part of

---

[7]   A.G. Noorani, *Article 370: A Constitutional History of Jammu and Kashmir* (India: OUP India, 2014), p. 171.

[8]   Ibid., p. 170.

[9]   'From the Archives: The Hindu's Report on the President's Order in J&K, 1954', *The Hindu*, 6 Aug. 2019.

[10]   The Constitution of Jammu and Kashmir, 1956.

[11]   Noorani, *Article 370*, pp. 344–49.

the Constitution and felt it was being eroded by later amendments to the State Constitution.[12]

*

Ladakhi Autonomy

In the 1960s, a younger, more radical movement for Ladakhi autonomy began to emerge. This culminated in a communal agitation in mid-1969 with a number of political demands, including Scheduled Tribes status for Ladakhis and union territory status for Ladakh to protect its identity.[13] However, except for minor concessions like giving a cabinet post to Sonam Wangyal, a close colleague of Bakula Rinpoche, these larger demands remained unmet.

In July 1979, Ladakh was split into two districts—Kargil and Leh. Kargil was a Muslim-majority district, while Leh became a Buddhist-majority district.[14]

In July 1989, following a clash between Muslims and Buddhists, the LBA alleged that Ladakh had always been treated as a colony and Ladakhis were being neglected—socially, politically and economically—as 'third-rate citizens of J&K State'[15]. It launched a movement called the Ladakh People's Movement for Union Territory Status (LPMUTS). The violent insurgency that exploded in the neighbouring Kashmir Valley in 1989 allowed the LBA to

---

[12] Noorani, *Article 370*, pp. 344–49.

[13] Martijn van Beek and Kristoffer Brix Bertelsen, 'No Present Without Past: the 1989 Agitation in Ladakh,' in *Recent Research on Ladakh 7: Proceedings of the Seventh Colloquium of the International Association for Ladakh Studies*, eds. Thierry Dodin and Heinz Räther (Ulm: Universität Ulm, 1997), pp. 43–65.

[14] Directorate of Census Operations, Jammu and Kashmir. District Census Handbook: Kargil (2011).

[15] van Beek, 'True Patriots', p. 40.

position itself as patriotic and non-communal while simultaneously imposing a 'social boycott' of Muslims, banning all Buddhists from interacting with Muslims.[16]

The Union government finally began to make concessions. On 8 October 1989, nearly the entire population of Ladakh was declared as members of eight Scheduled Tribes. Three weeks later, on 29 October, the LBA, the Ladakh Muslim Association (LMA), the Jammu and Kashmir state government, and the Union government met regarding the issue of Ladakhi autonomy. Union territory status was not possible just yet due to the fear that it could further fuel the insurrection in the Kashmir Valley. Instead, the parties agreed to constitute an Autonomous Hill Development Council (AHDC) in Leh and Kargil as an interim measure.

Three years passed and no council was established. The LBA lifted its social boycott of Muslims and joined forces with the LMA to form a coordination committee, consisting of Sunni, Shia, Christian and Buddhist representatives. On 8 September 1992, the coordination committee delivered an ultimatum to the government to establish the AHDC within five weeks, failing which agitations would resume.

A year later, in October 1993, the Union government met with LBA and LMA representatives and resolved the details of the AHDC Act, short of 'a few minor issues, such as the name for the council'[17]. However, in January 1994, rumours swirled that the draft bill had dropped the word 'autonomous'. In June 1994, the coordination committee threatened to relaunch the agitation but was pacified by Rajesh Pilot, the minister of state for internal security. The AHDC was rumoured to be imminent through the rest of the year.

Finally, fearing that the Union government might shelve the AHDC plan permanently, the coordination committee relaunched

---

[16]　van Beek, 'True Patriots', p. 41.

[17]　Ibid., p. 43.

the agitation with a 'ferocity of public sentiment'[18] in early March 1995. This finally galvanized the Union government into action. Two months later, on 8 May 1995, the Ladakh Autonomous Hill Development Councils Bill was passed and the Act came into effect on 1 June. Leh got its first AHDC in early September 1995. Kargil blocked the creation of the council in its district and only allowed it in July 2003.

Leh viewed the AHDC as an interim measure rather than a final solution.[19] In 2002, all the political parties in Leh unanimously dissolved themselves and joined together to form the Ladakh Union Territory Front (LUTF) to continue to press for union territory status.

*

2019: Abrogation and Reorganization

On 19 June 2018, the chief minister of Jammu and Kashmir, Mehbooba Mufti of the People's Democratic Party (PDP), resigned. The Bharatiya Janata Party (BJP) had withdrawn its support from the coalition government, reducing it to a minority. The following day, the President of India, Ram Nath Kovind, approved the imposition of Governor's rule in the state and Governor Narinder Nath Vohra took over the administration.

Governor Vohra then retired on 23 August and President Kovind appointed Satya Pal Malik as the new Governor of Jammu and Kashmir. On 21 November, Governor Malik dissolved the legislative assembly 'citing horse-trading and lack of stability to form a government'[20].

---

[18] van Beek, 'True Patriots', p. 43.
[19] Martijn van Beek, 'Ladakh: Independence is Not Enough,' *Himal* (March/April 1995).
[20] 'After Governor's Rule, President's Rule Comes into Force in Jammu and Kashmir,' *The Economic Times*, 20 Dec. 2018.

As per Article 92 of the State Constitution, Governor's rule could be in force for only six months. On 19 December, just before his rule expired, Governor Malik recommended the imposition of President's rule in the state, which President Kovind gave his assent to.

In the May 2019 Lok Sabha elections in India, the BJP won an absolute majority and returned to form the Union government.

On 5 August 2019, President Kovind passed a Presidential Order with the concurrence of the government of the state of Jammu and Kashmir.[21] Called the Constitution (Application to Jammu and Kashmir) Order, 2019 and effective immediately, it 'superseded'[22] the Presidential Order of 14 May 1954. This order applied all the provisions of the Indian Constitution to Jammu and Kashmir, thereby rendering the State Constitution of November 1956 inoperative.[23] It effectively integrated the state of Jammu and Kashmir fully with India and brought it on an equal footing with the other units of the Indian Union. A further Presidential notification then removed the tunnel of Article 370 and abrogated Article 35A. The 'permanent residents' were later redefined as the 'domiciles' of Jammu and Kashmir.

The Union government immediately followed this Presidential Order with the Jammu and Kashmir Reorganisation Bill, 2019. The bill proposed to reorganize the state of Jammu and Kashmir into two union territories—Jammu and Kashmir, and Ladakh. The Governor of the state would now become the lieutenant governor for both the union territories. Jammu and Kashmir would have a legislative assembly; the provisions of Article 239A that applied to Puducherry would apply to Jammu and Kashmir as well. Ladakh would not have a legislative assembly and would

---

[21]　The Constitution (Application to Jammu and Kashmir) Order, 2019.
[22]　Ibid.
[23]　Ibid.

be administered directly by the President acting through the lieutenant governor.[24]

Both the Houses of Parliament passed the Bill with a majority vote in two days and President Kovind gave his assent to the Act on 9 August. The Jammu and Kashmir Reorganisation Act came into effect on 31 October 2019 and resulted in two new union territories in place of one state.

* *

---

[24] The Jammu and Kashmir Reorganisation Act, 2019.

LAKSHADWEEP

Multiple Islands, Two Administrative Arrangements

The Lakshadweep Islands consist of thirty-six islands (of which only ten are inhabited) grouped into three subgroups: Aminidivi (northernmost, also referred to as Amindivi, with five inhabited islands), Laccadive (central, with four inhabited islands), and Minicoy (southernmost, a single inhabited atoll). However, under British rule, the three subgroups were not administered as one unit. The northern Amindivi subgroup was handled out of South Canara, while Laccadive and Minicoy were handled out of Malabar.

When India gained independence from the British, the Islands as well as the separated administrative arrangement transferred to India. As both South Canara and Malabar formed a part of Madras

Province (renamed to Madras State after 26 January 1950), this was not an issue administratively.

*

1956: India's Smallest Union Territory

The Union government constituted the States Reorganisation Commission (SRC) in 1953 to look into the matter of redrawing state boundaries. In its 1955 report, the SRC recommended integrating South Canara district with Mysore State and Malabar district with Kerala. The SRC considered the administrative fallout for the Islands as well and recommended that the Amindivi subgroup be brought under the administrative care of Kerala, which already handled Laccadive and Minicoy.[1]

However, on considerations of security and development, the Union government decided to place the Islands under the direct care of the President of India who would act through an administrator. Hence, when the States Reorganisation Act came into effect from 1 November 1956, the union territory of Laccadive, Minicoy and Amindivi Islands also came into being. It is India's smallest union territory in terms of land area and population. The jurisdiction of the Kerala High Court extended to the union territory.

*

1973: Renaming

In order to foster the 'feeling of oneness'[2] that had been growing among the islanders, given the considerable improvement in the

---

[1]   Report of the States Reorganisation Commission, 1955, p. 86.
[2]   The Laccadive, Minicoy and Amindivi Islands (Alteration of Name) Act, 1973.

inter-island communication facilities, the Administrator's Advisory Council—which consists of representatives of the local people— suggested that the Islands be collectively named as Lakshadweep. The Home Minister's Advisory Committee endorsed this suggestion. On 26 August 1973, Parliament passed the Laccadive, Minicoy and Amindivi Islands (Alteration of Name) Act. From 1 November 1973 onwards, the Islands were collectively known as Lakshadweep.

* *

PUDUCHERRY

> **Did You Know?**
>
> *Puducherry is the only union territory to have beaches on both the Arabian Sea and the Bay of Bengal.*

Not Yet Independent

On 15 August 1947, India gained its independence from the British. However, not all of India had been under British imperialism. Five tiny enclaves scattered across the country were under French control. These were:

- Pondicherry (now Puducherry): the capital, on the eastern coast, about 150 km south of Madras (now Chennai);
- Karikal (now Karaikal): on the eastern coast, about 130 km further south of Pondicherry;
- Yanaon (now Yanam): on the eastern coast, over 800 km north of Pondicherry;

- Chandernagore (now Chandannagar): on the outskirts of Calcutta (now Kolkata), nearly 2000 km north of Pondicherry;
- Mahé: on the western coast, over 600 km west of Pondicherry.

*

Referendums, Postponed

When India freed itself from the British, these five territories continued under French control, though there were a number of demonstrations within the territories demanding a merger with India. India's Prime Minister Jawaharlal Nehru did not plan to let them continue under French control for much longer. At its first session post-Independence held at Jaipur in December 1948, the ruling Indian National Congress (INC) passed a resolution declaring that 'the continued existence of any foreign possessions in India becomes anomalous and opposed to the conception of India's unity and freedom'.[1] Prime Minister Nehru further said in February 1949 that it was natural and proper to unite all foreign possessions in the country with the Union of India and that they would do so 'through friendly discussions with the powers concerned'[2].

Even though India and France had issued a joint declaration on 28 August 1947 to resolve the matter in an amicable and friendly manner, France was deeply concerned about the possible repercussions the decisions regarding its Indian territories might have on the future of the rest of its colonial holdings around the world. Hence, France was anxious to prolong negotiations and postpone actual decolonization for as long as it could.

---

[1]   Akhila Yechury, 'Imagining India, Decolonizing "L'Inde Française", c. 1947–1954,' *The Historical Journal,* 58(4) (December 2015), p. 1151.
[2]   Russell H. Fifield, 'The Future of French India,' *Far Eastern Survey,* 19(6) (22 March 1950), p. 62. doi:10.2307/3024284

In June 1948, the French and Indian governments agreed to hold separate referendums in each of the five territories to allow the local population to determine their future. In September and October 1948, elections were held to the governing municipal councils in the five territories. France refused to let India send observers to the elections.[3] Only Chandernagore elected a strongly pro-Indian government while pro-French candidates won majorities in the other four territories. From here on, Chandernagore's path diverged from the other four territories.

In March 1949, the municipal councils of the four territories of Pondicherry, Karaikal, Yanam and Mahé decided that the referendums would be held on 11 December of that year. However, the municipal assembly of Chandernagore declared a referendum unnecessary and attempted to merge with India. The French rejected this decision and attempted to postpone the referendum to December. Eventually, the referendum was held on 19 June 1949. The people of Chandernagore voted almost unanimously to merge with India. France transferred the administration of Chandernagore to India on 2 May 1950 and legally ceded the territory by signing a treaty on 2 February 1951. In 1954, Chandannagar was merged into the state of West Bengal.[4]

Meanwhile, in the remaining four territories of French India, both the French and Indian governments raised charges and counter-charges of external and economic pressure to influence the results of the referendums. France attempted to make the issue a purely domestic matter for France and offered Pondicherry the status of an associated state having free autonomy in the French Union. India enforced restrictions around French India, including ones like

---

[3] Administrative Reforms Commission. *Report, Study Team on Administration of Union Territories and NEFA*, 1968, pp. 178–79.
[4] Ibid.

customs duties and residents needing passports to travel through Indian territory.[5]

Eventually, both sides arrived at a compromise and relaxed many of their restrictions and demands. The desire for an immediate referendum had cooled on both sides and it was postponed from 11 December 1949 to 15 February 1950 and then indefinitely. The debates over a merger with India did not lessen, however. Over the next four years, many pro-French members of the territories' municipal councils also began to support the calls for a merger, while many residents of French India opposed a merger as they feared the loss of identity and economic prosperity.

*

A Delayed Integration, Suddenly

Even as French India was divided on the question of a merger, the trigger came unexpectedly from an international event. After suffering heavy defeats in battles in South-east Asia, France signed the Geneva Accords on 20 July 1954 and agreed to remove all its troops from Vietnam. Suddenly, France had no use for its Indian territories, which had been a transit point and supply line to South-east Asia. As a result, when India and France met in New Delhi in September 1954 for what would be the final round of talks, France agreed to drop the idea of a referendum. Instead, the elected representatives of French India would decide the fate of the territories.[6]

On 8 October 1954, the elected representatives of French India met at Kizhoor and voted almost unanimously in favour of a merger with India. France signed an agreement to the same effect less than

---

[5]   Administrative Reforms Commission. *Report, Study Team on Administration of Union Territories and NEFA*, 1968, pp. 178–79.

[6]   Yechury, 'Imagining India,' pp. 1163–64.

two weeks later and the formal transfer of power from France to India occurred on 1 November 1954. Pondicherry (which also included Karaikal, Yanam and Mahé) was brought under central administration. Although a formal treaty of cession of the territory was signed by both the Indian and French Governments on 28 May 1956, only India ratified the treaty immediately. France delayed its ratification for six years until 16 August 1962, at which point Pondicherry (inclusive of the three other territories) was designated as a union territory.

The year after French ratification, the Indian Parliament passed the Government of Union Territories Act, 1963, which established legislative assemblies and councils of ministers in five union territories—Manipur, Tripura, Himachal Pradesh, Goa and Pondicherry. This was significant because it created two classes of union territories. The first class, consisting of these five union territories, was considered to be at a more advanced stage and seen as being independent standalone entities. Their legislative assemblies had powers and responsibilities similar to the state legislative assemblies, including the ability to make laws on subjects in the Union and Concurrent lists. They even had separate consolidated and contingency funds.[7] Édouard Goubert, who was one of the pro-French elected representatives who had later turned pro-merger, became the first chief minister of Pondicherry as a member of the Indian National Congress (INC).

*

Pondi to Pudu

Pondicherry was a westernized take on the original Tamil name of Puducherry, which meant 'new village'. On 13 September 2006,

[7] Administrative Reforms Commission. *Report, Study Team on Administration of Union Territories and NEFA*, 1968. pp. 11–13.

the Pondicherry (Alteration of Name) Act was passed, and Pondicherry's name returned to its original Tamil name of Puducherry.[8]

**

[8]   Government of India. The Pondicherry (Alteration of Name) Act, 2006.

BIBLIOGRAPHY

'Accord Reached on Telangana Demands'. *Indian Express*. 20 January 1969.

'After Governor's Rule, President's Rule Comes into Force in Jammu and Kashmir'. *The Economic Times*, 20 Dec., 2018.

Ahluwalia, Manjit Singh. *Social, Cultural, and Economic History of Himachal Pradesh*. India: Indus Publishing Company, 1998.

Ambedkar, Dr Bhimrao R. *Thoughts on Linguistic States*. Delhi: Author, 1955.

Bal, S.S. 'Punjab After Independence (1947–1956)'. *Proceedings of the Indian History Congress*, 46 (1985): 416–430.

Banerjee, S.K. 'Manipur State Constitution Act, 1947'. *The Indian Journal of Political Science*, 19(1) (Jan.–Mar. 1958): 35–38.

Bannerjee, Sreeparna, Ambalika Guha and Anasua Basu Ray Chaudhury. 'The 2015 India–Bangladesh Land Boundary Agreement: Identifying Constraints and Exploring Possibilities in Cooch Behar'. *ORF Occasional Paper*, 117 (July 2017).

Bareh, Hamlet. *Encyclopaedia of North-East India: Mizoram*, India: Mittal Publications, 2001.

Basu, Narayani. *V.P. Menon: The Unsung Architect of Modern India*. India: Simon & Schuster India, 2020.

Bose, Sumantra. *Kashmir: Roots of Conflict, Paths to Peace.* Cambridge: Harvard University Press, 2005.

Brass, Paul R. *Language, Religion and Politics in North India.* United States: iUniverse, 2005.

Bravo, Philip. 'The Case of Goa: History, Rhetoric and Nationalism'. *Past Imperfect,* Vol. 7 (1998): 125–154. https://doi.org/10.21971/P72P4B

Brigadier A.S. Cheema, VSM (Retd). 'Operation Vijay: The Liberation of "Estado da India"—Goa, Daman and Diu'. *Journal of the United Service Institution of India,* Vol. CXLIII, No. 594 (October–December 2013).

Chatterjee, Suhas. *Mizo Chiefs and the Chiefdom.* India: M.D. Publications, 1995.

Chaube, S.K. *Hill Politics in Northeast India.* India: Orient Blackswan, 2012.

Cmde Srikant B. Kesnur and Lt Cdr Ankush Banerjee. 'How Indian Navy Helped in the Liberation of Goa'. *The Daily Guardian.* 25 December 2020.

'College Students in Telangana Agitation'. *Indian Express.* 16 January 1969.

Copland, Ian. 'The Master and the Maharajas: The Sikh Princes and the East Punjab Massacres of 1947'. *Modern Asian Studies,* 36(3) (July 2002): 657–704.

Devi, Bandita. *Some Aspects of British Administration in Orissa, 1912-1936.* India: Academic Foundation, 1992.

Dhillon, Gurdarshan Singh. 'Evolution of the Demand for a Sikh Homeland'. *The Indian Journal of Political Science,* 35(4) (October–December 1974): 362–373.

Doad, Karnail Singh. 'Punjabi Suba Movement'. In *The Encyclopaedia of Sikhism, Volume III M–R,* edited by Harbans Singh, 392–94. India: Punjabi University, Patiala, 1997.

Fifield, Russell H. 'The Future of French India'. *Far Eastern Survey,* 19(6) (March 22, 1950): 62–64. doi:10.2307/3024284

Fifield, Russell H. 'The Future of Portuguese India'. *Far Eastern Survey,* 19(7) (5 April 1950): 71. doi:10.2307/3024038

'From the Archives: The Hindu's Report on the President's Order in J&K, 1954'. *The Hindu,* 6 Aug. 2019.

Gangte, Priyadarshni M. 'Political Climate of Manipur during the Transitionary Period, 1946–52: Some Reflections'. *Proceedings of the Indian History Congress,* 74 (2013): 667–674.

Ghosh, Biswajit. 'Ethnicity and Insurgency in Tripura'. *Sociological Bulletin,* 52(2) (September 2003), 221–243. https://doi.org/10.1177/0038022920030204

Guha, Ramachandra. *India After Gandhi: The History of the World's Largest Democracy.* United Kingdom: Macmillan, 2017.

Gupta, Ranjan. 'Sikkim: The Merger with India'. *Asian Survey,* 15(9) (September 1975): 786–798. doi:10.2307/2643174

Gyati, Aruna. 'Panchayat Raj Institutions in Arunachal Pradesh: A Historical Perspective'. *The Indian Journal of Political Science,* 72(4) (Oct.–Dec. 2011): 1019–1030.

Haokip, Thongkholal. 'Political Integration of Northeast India: A Historical Analysis'. *Strategic Analysis,* 36(2) (March 2012): 304–314. https://doi.org/10.1080/09700161.2012.646508

'India: Intolerable Goa'. *Time.* 22 December 1961.

Indrakumar, Konthoujam. 'Colonialism and Movement for Democracy in Manipur'. In *Colonialism and Resistance: Society and State in Manipur,* edited by Arambam Noni and Kangujam Sanatomba, 56–71. New York: Routledge, 2016.

Jha, S.N. 'Historical Roots of Regional Variations in the Performance of Local Institutions of Development'. In *Public Governance and Decentralisation: Essays in Honour of T.N. Chaturvedi, Volume 1,* edited by S.N. Mishra, Anil Dutta Mishra and Sweta Mishra, 563–586. India: Mittal Publications, 2003.

Joshi, Ram. 'The General Elections in Goa'. *Asian Survey,* 4(10) (October 1964): 1093–1101. doi:10.2307/2642211

'Judgement on Mulki Rules Stayed'. *Indian Express.* 5 February 1969.

Kalia, Ravi. *Chandigarh: the Making of an Indian City.* India: Oxford University Press, 1998.

Krishna, Balraj. *India's Bismarck, Sardar Vallabhbhai Patel.* India: Indus Source Books, 2007.

Kudaisya, Gyanesh. *Region, Nation, 'Heartland': Uttar Pradesh in India's Body Politic.* New Delhi: Sage Publications, 2006.

Kumar, Ajit. 'Statehood for Vidarbha'. *Economic and Political Weekly,* 36(50) (December 15–21, 2001): 4614–17.

Kumar, B.B. *Reorganization of North-East India: Facts and Documents.* India: Concept, 2017.

Mehta, Usha. 'The Second General Elections in Greater Bombay'. *The Indian Journal of Political Science,* 19(2) (April–June 1958): 151–60.

Melkote, Rama S., E. Revathi, K. Lalitha, K. Sajaya and A. Suneetha. 'The Movement for Telangana: Myth and Reality'. *Economic and Political Weekly,* 45(2) (9–15 January 2010): 8–11.

Mendes, Sushila Sawant. 'Jawaharlal Nehru and the Liberation Struggle of Goa'. *Proceedings of the Indian History Congress,* 67 (2006–2007): 549–55.

Menon, V.P. *The Story of the Integration of the Indian States.* United Kingdom: Longmans, Green and Co., 1956.

Monirul, Hussain. 'Tribal Movement for Autonomous State in Assam', *Economic and Political Weekly,* 22(32) (8 August 1987): 1329–1332.

Mukerjee, Dilip. 'Assam Reorganization'. *Asian Survey,* 9(4) (April 1969): 297–311. doi:10.2307/2642547

'Mysore, an Indian State, is Renamed as Karnataka', *The New York Times,* 30 July 1972. https://www.nytimes.com/1972/07/30/archives/mysore-an-indian-state-is-renamed-as-karnataka.html

Nag, Sajal. 'Bamboo, Rats and Famines: Famine Relief and Perceptions of British Paternalism in the Mizo Hills (India)'. *Environment and History,* 5(2) (June 1999): 245–252.

Nayar, Baldev Raj. 'Punjab'. In *State Politics in India*, edited by Myron Weiner, 435–502. United States of America: Princeton University Press, 1968.

Negi, Jaideep. 'The Begar System in the Shimla Hill States during the British Period'. *Proceedings of the Indian History Congress,* 55 (1994): 693–697.

Nehru, Jawaharlal. 'Tryst With Destiny'. Speech delivered to the Indian Constituent Assembly, 15 August 1947.

Noorani, A.G. *Article 370: A Constitutional History of Jammu and Kashmir.* India: OUP India, 2014.

Pathak, Shekhar. 'Beyond an Autonomous State Background and Preliminary Analysis of Uttarakhand Movement'. *Proceedings of the Indian History Congress,* 60 (1999): 893–907.

Pereira, Aaron. 'What is Goa's "Opinion Poll Day"?' *The New Indian Express.* 18 January 2019.

Pingle, Gautam. 'The Historical Context of Andhra and Telangana, 1949–56'. *Economic and Political Weekly,* 45(8) (20–26 February 2010): 57–65.

Prabhudesai, Sandesh. 'The Historic Opinion Poll'. *Goa News.* 20 July 2008.

Prasad, R.J. Rajendra. 'Bitter Memories'. *Frontline,* Vol. 18 Issue 12. June 09–22, 2001.

Rajivlochan, Meeta, Kavita Sharma and Chitleen K. Sethi. *Chandigarh Lifescape: Brief Social History of a Planned City.* India: Chandigarh Government Press, 1999.

Reddy, G. Samba Siva. 'Making of Micro-Regional Identities in the Colonial Context: Studying the Rayalaseema Maha Sabha, 1934–1956'. *Proceedings of the Indian History Congress,* 67 (2006–2007): 500–513.

Rose, Leo E. 'India and Sikkim: Redefining the Relationship'. *Pacific Affairs,* 42(1) (Spring 1969): 32–46. doi:10.2307/2754861

Rotter, Andrew J. *Comrades at Odds: The United States and India, 1947–1964.* United Kingdom: Cornell University Press, 2000.

Rubinoff, Arthur G. 'Goa's Attainment of Statehood'. *Asian Survey*, 32(5) (May 1992): 471–487. doi:10.2307/2644978

Sarangi, Asha and Sudha Pai. 'Introduction: Contextualising Reorganisation'. In *Interrogating Reorganisation of States: Culture, Identity and Politics in India*, edited by Asha Sarangi, 1–25. India: Routledge, 2020.

Sarmah, Bhupen. 'India's Northeast and the Enigma of the Nation-state'. *Alternatives: Global, Local, Political, Vol.* 42, No. 3 (August 2017): 166–78.

Seshadri, K. 'The Telangana Agitation and the Politics of Andhra Pradesh'. *The Indian Journal of Political Science*, 31(1) (January–March 1970): 60–81.

Sharma, Sadhna. *States Politics in India*. India: Mittal Publications, 1995.

Shaw, Annapurna. 'Town Planning in Postcolonial India, 1947–1965: Chandigarh Re-Examined'. *Urban Geography*, 30(8) (Nov. 2009): 857–878. https://doi.org/10.2747/0272-3638.30.8.857

Sidhu, G.B.S. *Sikkim: Dawn of Democracy*. India: Penguin Random House India Private Limited, 2018.

Singh, Chandrika. 'Nagaland: From a District to a State: Culmination of Democratic Political Process'. *The Indian Journal of Political Science*, 41(4) (Dec. 1980): 815–832.

Singh, Haorongbam Sudhirkumar. 'Socio-religious and Political Movements in Modern Manipur (1934–51)'. *Doctoral Thesis submitted to Jawaharlal Nehru University* (2011).

Singh, Manju. 'Arunachal Pradesh: Wonderland with Explosive Frontier'. *The Indian Journal of Political Science*, 72(1) (Jan.–Mar. 2011): 205–220.

Singh, R. K. Jhalajit. *A Short History of Manipur*. India: O.K. Store, 1992.

Singhal, D.P. 'Goa—End of an Epoch'. *The Australian Quarterly*, Vol. 34, No. 1 (March 1962): 77–89.

Sinha, Nirmal Chandra. 'The Sikkim Agreement 1973'. *India Quarterly,* 29(2) (April–June 1973): 155–158.

Sitlhou, Makepeace. 'Accord'. *Fifty-Two* (27 Nov. 2020), https://fiftytwo.in/story/accord/

Subramaniam, Archana. 'Goa Comes Home'. *The Hindu.* 17 December 2015.

Sundar, Nandini. 'Interning Insurgent Populations: The Buried Histories of Indian Democracy'. *Economic and Political Weekly,* 46(6) (5–11 Feb. 2011): 47–57.

Swain, Pratap Chandra. *Panchayati Raj: The Grassroots Dynamics in Arunachal Pradesh.* India: APH Publishing Corporation, 2008.

Tan, Tai Yong and Gyanesh Kudaisya. *The Aftermath of Partition in South Asia.* United Kingdom: Routledge, 2000.

'Telangana Agitators Fired on: 17 Hurt'. *Indian Express.* 25 January 1969.

Tillin, Louise. *Remapping India: New States and Their Political Origins.* New Delhi: Oxford University Press, 2013.

'Transfers Challenged in Court by Andhra Employees'. *Indian Express.* 25 January 1969.

van Beek, Martijn and Kristoffer Brix Bertelsen. 'No Present Without Past: the 1989 Agitation in Ladakh'. In *Recent Research on Ladakh 7: Proceedings of the Seventh Colloquium of the International Association for Ladakh Studies,* edited by Thierry Dodin and Heinz Räther: 43–65. Ulm: Universität Ulm, 1997.

van Beek, Martijn. 'Ladakh: Independence is Not Enough'. *Himal* (March/April 1995).

van Beek, Martijn. 'True Patriots: Justifying Autonomy for Ladakh'. *Himalaya, The Journal of the Association for Nepal and Himalayan Studies, Himalayan Research Bulletin,* 18(1) (1998): 35–45.

van Schendel, W. 'Stateless in South Asia: The Making of the India–Bangladesh Enclaves'. *The Journal of Asian Studies,* 61(1) (2002): 115–147. https://doi.org/10.2307/2700191

Weinraub, Bernard. 'Indian State Sets New Course'. *The New York Times*, 2 Nov. 1973. https://www.nytimes.com/1973/11/02/archives/indian-state-sets-new-course-pride-and-sentiment-area-has-rich-past.html

Yechury, Akhila. 'Imagining India, Decolonizing "L'Inde Française", c. 1947–1954'. *The Historical Journal*, 58(4) (December 2015): 1141–1165.

Yediyurappa, B.S. 'Kalyana Karnataka: Harking Back to a Humanist History'. *The Hindu*, 17 September 2019. https://www.thehindu.com/news/national/karnataka/kalyana-karnataka-harking-back-to-a-humanist-history/article29433502.ece

Zutshi, Chitralekha. *Oxford India Short Introductions: Kashmir*. India: OUP India, 2019.

GOVERNMENT OF INDIA DOCUMENTS

Administrative Reforms Commission. *Report, Study Team on Administration of Union Territories and NEFA*, 1968.

Ambedkar, Dr B.R. Constituent Assembly Speech, 4 November 1948.

Delhi Administration Act, 1966.

Directorate of Census Operations, Jammu and Kashmir. District Census Handbook: Kargil (2011).

Ekbote, Gopal Rao. "Judgement–P. Lakshmana Rao vs State of Andhra Pradesh and Ors. on 9 December, 1970." Andhra High Court. https://indiankanoon.org/doc/1378936/?type=print

Final Report, Annexure VII, Appendix D. *Constituent Assembly Debates Official Report*. New Delhi: Lok Sabha Secretariat, 2014.

Government of India, Census India, Karnataka Administrative Divisions, 1872-2001.

Government of India, Ministry of Law and Justice. The Constitution (Fifty-sixth Amendment) Act, 1987.

Manipur Merger Agreement, 1949.

Memorandum of Settlement (Mizoram Accord), 1986.

Ministry of Information & Broadcasting, Films Division. *MNF: The Mizo Uprising*, 2014.

Ministry of States, Government of India. *White Paper on Indian States*, 1950.

Report of the Commission on the Hill Areas of Assam, 1965-66.

Report of the States Reorganisation Commission, 1955.

Statistical Report On General Election, 1951 To The Legislative Assembly Of Bihar Election Commission Of India.

The Andhra Pradesh Decentralisation and Inclusive Development of All Regions Act, 2020.

The Andhra State Act, 1953.

The Andhra State Act, 1953.

The Assam Lushai Hills District (Acquisition of Chiefs' Rights) Act, 1954.

The Assam Reorganisation (Meghalaya) Act, 1969.

The Bihar Reorganisation Act, 2000.

The Census of India, 1951.

The Constitution (Application to Jammu and Kashmir) Order, 2019.

The Constitution (Sixty Ninth Amendment) Act, 1991.

The Constitution (Thirteenth Amendment) Act, 1962.

The Constitution (Thirty-Fifth Amendment) Act, 1974.

The Constitution (Thirty-Sixth Amendment) Act, 1975.

The Constitution of India, 1949.

The Constitution of Jammu and Kashmir (Sixth Amendment) Act, 1965.

The Constitution of Jammu and Kashmir, 1956.

The Dadra and Nagar Haveli Act, 1961.

The Dadra and Nagar Haveli and Daman and Diu (Merger of Union Territories) Act, 2019.

The Delhi Municipal Corporation Act, 1957.

The Goa, Daman and Diu (Administration) Act, 1962.

The Goa, Daman and Diu (Opinion Poll) Act, 1966.

The Goa, Daman and Diu Reorganisation Act, 1987.

The Government of National Capital Territory of Delhi Act, 1991.

The Government of Union Territories Act, 1963.

The Himachal Pradesh and Bilaspur (New State) Act, 1954.

The Jammu and Kashmir Reorganisation Act, 2019.

The Laccadive, Minicoy, and Amindivi Islands (Alteration of Name) Act, 1973.

The Madhya Pradesh Reorganisation Act, 2000.

The Madras State (Alteration of Name) Act, 1968.

The Mulki Rules (Repeal) Act, 1973.

The Mulki Rules Act, 1972.

The Naga Hills-Tuensang Area Act, 1957.

The National Capital Region Planning Board Act, 1985.

The North-Eastern Areas (Reorganisation) Act, 1971.

The Orissa (Alteration of Name) Act, 2011.

The Pondicherry (Alteration of Name) Act, 2006.

The Punjab Reorganisation Act, 1966.

The State of Himachal Pradesh Act, 1970.

The State of Mizoram Act, 1986.

The State of Nagaland Act, 1962.

The States Reorganisation Act, 1956.

The Uttar Pradesh Reorganisation Act, 2000.

The Uttaranchal (Alteration Of Name) Act, 2006.